Monseigneur Besson, Mary E Herbert

Frederick Francis Xavier De Mérode, Minister and Almoner to Pius IX., Archbishop of Melitinensis

His Life and his Works

Monseigneur Besson, Mary E Herbert

Frederick Francis Xavier De Mérode, Minister and Almoner to Pius IX., Archbishop of Melitinensis
His Life and his Works

ISBN/EAN: 9783742814685

Manufactured in Europe, USA, Canada, Australia, Japa

Cover: Foto ©Thomas Meinert / pixelio.de

Manufactured and distributed by brebook publishing software
(www.brebook.com)

Monseigneur Besson, Mary E Herbert

Frederick Francis Xavier De Mérode, Minister and Almoner to Pius IX., Archbishop of Melitinensis

FREDERICK FRANCIS XAVIER DE MÉRODE,

MINISTER OF PIUS IX. AND ARCHBISHOP OF MELITINENSIS.

FREDERICK FRANCIS XAVIER DE MÉRODE,

MINISTER AND ALMONER TO PIUS IX., ARCHBISHOP OF MELITINENSIS.

HIS LIFE AND HIS WORKS.

BY

MONSEIGNEUR BESSON,
BISHOP OF NÎMES, UZÈS AND ALAIS.

TRANSLATED INTO ENGLISH

BY

LADY HERBERT.

LONDON:

W. H. ALLEN & CO., 13, WATERLOO PLACE, PALL MALL, S.W.

—

1887.

PREFACE OF THE AUTHOR.

—o—

The Author of this book, having been admitted on the
20th January, 1883, to a private audience of Pope
Leo XIII., asked leave of His Holiness to write the
Life of Mgr. de Mérode. Not only did the Pope
deign to answer that he was pleased with the idea,
but he told him many little traits relating to the life
of this Prelate, whom he had known while he was
Nuncio at Brussels, and whose father was one of his
best friends. He added, "How terribly we miss
Mgr. de Mérode in these days ! "

Encouraged by this high patronage, the Author had
little difficulty in collecting materials for this biography.
The name of Mgr. de Mérode belongs to the history
of the nineteenth century and of the States of the
Church, during the period which preceded the triumph
of the Revolution in Rome and throughout Italy. His
glory is allied to that of Pius IX., whom he served
with such faithful devotion ; and with the heroic
defence organized by himself and Lamoricière to

ensure the independence of the Temporal Power. The travellers and writers who frequented Rome from 1850 to 1874 studied this great Prelate in the theatre of his zeal, and have all recorded their admiration for his noble and original character, for his courage and devotedness, for his extraordinary generosity and charity, and for the boldness of his undertakings. Their testimony is precious; but, to complete it, his family, his intimate friends, his servants, the Religious Communities whom he had so greatly benefited—all had to be questioned. His letters, which have been communicated to us by all his people with a kindness for which we cannot thank them enough, add greatly to the interest of these Memoirs. Such are the elements of our work. We have not done much more than put them together and arrange them in pages—only too happy to be edified by the study of so beautiful a life; and still more happy and thankful if we should be enabled, in our turn, to edify the public by the recital of such virtues as this biography brings before them.

The hero of this life will, we venture to hope, not be displeasing to politicians, to whom success is not the measure of their esteem; nor to religious-minded men, who honour a virtue so entirely without pretension or affectation, and whose straightforward uprightness bowed to none but God. Mgr. de

Mérode has a grand and glorious place among the servants of the Church and of the Papacy. It is useful in these days, when the question of the temporal power again agitates men's minds, to bring forward in strong relief what he thought of a cause for which he would gladly have sacrificed his fortune and his life. We shall see how beautiful that cause is; what moral grandeur it gives to those who labour for its triumph; and how, by their fidelity and magnanimity, they ensure the admiration both of beholders and posterity.

CONTENTS.

— o —

CHAPTER I.

From 1820 to 1832.

CHAPTER II.

From 1832 to 1841.

CHAPTER III.

FROM 1841 TO 1847.

CHAPTER IV.

FROM 1847 TO 1851.

CHAPTER V.

FROM 1850 TO 1859.

CHAPTER VIII.

FROM 1865 TO 1870.

CHAPTER IX.

FROM 1870 TO 1874.

CHAPTER X.

CHAPTER XI.

CHAPTER XII.

1874.

EULOGIUM.

LIFE

OF

MONSEIGNEUR DE MÉRODE.

CHAPTER I.

From 1820 to 1832.

The Birth of Xavier—His Paternal and Maternal Family—The History of the de Mérodes, their Warlike Exploits, their Patriotism and their Piety—The Grammonts and the Noailles—The Marquise de Grammont—The Residence of Count Felix de Mérode at the Château of Villersexel—The Belgian Revolution—Xavier's First Education at his Grandmother's House—He makes his Apprenticeship in the Practical Exercise of Charity.

FREDERICK FRANCIS XAVIER GHISLAIN DE MÉRODE was born at Brussels on the 20th of March, 1820, and was baptized the next day in the Church of the Minims. He was the seventh son of Count Felix de Mérode and of Rosalie de Grammont. The blood which flowed through his veins had been mingled for centuries with that of saints and heroes. To understand the noble *rôle* which God reserved for him we will say a few words on the eminent services rendered by his ancestors. His character,

B

the chivalrous generosity of which was allied to the highest nobility, is, as it were, a Summary of the History of his House.

The first who bore the name of de Mérode was Raymond Bérenger, son of the Count of Barcelona, and a descendant of the ancient kings of Arragon. After having received at Vézelay the Cross from the hands of St. Bernard, he established himself in the Rhenish Provinces and married, in 1147, Aleyde, daughter of Hugo, Baron de Rode. He changed his name to that of de Mérode, and from that time the château of Mérode became the principal residence of his posterity. Burgraves of Cologne and Counts of the Holy Empire, with a seat in the Diet on the benches of the Counts of Westphalia, Knights of the Golden Fleece, Field Marshals, Spanish Grandees, allied to the Sovereign Houses of Oldenbourg, Holstein, Nassau, and Hohenzollern, related also to the kings of Hungary, every possible title and dignity was the portion of the de Mérodes. But they loved best to trace their descent from St. Elizabeth of Hungary; and prodigies of charity and self-devotion are recorded in their history side by side with the most brilliant feats of arms.

A hundred years after the death of St. Elizabeth, Werner de Mérode, to whom St. Matthias had appeared in a dream, as well as to his wife and chaplain, founded, by the desire of the Apostle, the Monastery of the Order of the Holy Cross, commonly called the Monastery of Schwartzenbroch. He cut down the thick forest where he had seen the apparition, built a monastery there, endowed it with annual revenues, and assigned land to the monks, who lived under the rule of St. Augustine. This monastery existed until the time of the Revolution: the tradition of the country, the hymns and prayers composed in honour of the Apostle and the sermons preached on his Feast, all confirm the popular belief in the apparition.

A generous temerity is hereditary in the de Mérodes. Without dwelling on their feats of arms in the Crusades or in the most dangerous tournaments, they took an important part in all the wars of modern times. In the sixteenth century the Archduke Ferdinand of Austria pleaded for the hand of Marguerite de Mérode for his son, Prince Charles, and five letters regarding this proposed alliance have been preserved in the archives of Simancas, the first dated the 28th April, 1577, the last on the 10th of June. But Philip the Second of Spain and Don Juan of Austria opposed this marriage from political reasons. The seventeenth century still further raised the military reputation of the de Mérodes. One of the heroes of the Thirty Years' War was John Baron de Mérode, who was created a general by Wallenstein. He was killed at the battle of Oldendorp in 1633, and was considered the best officer in the Imperial Cavalry. After him, Field Marshal Count de Mérode Westerloo distinguished himself in all the campaigns of the eighteenth century. At sixteen he was a Knight of the Golden Fleece, and fought like Marlborough and Prince Eugène. He wrote also some very stirring "Memoirs," restored and enlarged the château of Mérode, and died in 1732, with the reputation of being one of the most valiant captains of his time. We must also mention Alexander de Mérode, killed at the battle of Senef; Louis, killed at the siege of Maëstricht; John, killed in the battle of Hanseln; and Albert, killed at the siege of Landrecies. During the war in Flanders between Louis XV and Marie Thérèse, John, Comte de Mérode and 'Marquis de

Deynse defended the town of Berg-op-Zoom against
the French; and having had the four fingers of his
right hand cut off by a sabre, he took the reins of
his horse in his teeth and continued the fight with his
left hand. This hero died in 1774. In fact, the blood
of the de Mérodes has flowed on all sides, and everywhere their motto has been gloriously justified :
" *Plus d'honneur que d'honneurs.*"

The nineteenth century reserved another glory for
the de Mérodes. They were no longer distinguished
solely as great soldiers, but as wise politicians, and
as taking a leading part in the most delicate affairs of
European diplomacy. Their very name is associated
with the resistance to the despotism of the Emperors,
the freedom obtained by Belgium, and the elevation
of that little State to the rank of European monarchies.

It was the Comte de Mérode, Prince of Rubempré,
one of the grandees of Spain, and who was also minister plenipotentiary to Joseph II. at the Hague, who
had the courage to resist that sovereign when his arbitrary measures placed the Belgians in the painful
alternative of having to choose between their oath to
the Emperor, and the equally sacred one to the constitution of their country. Driven out of his property by
the French Revolution, he took refuge in Brunswick,
where the Duke of that name gave an asylum to so
many exiles. Under the first Napoleon he became a
French Senator, Mayor of Brussels, and Grand Marshal
at the Court of the Low Countries. He took an
important part in the Commission of the Senate
appointed to consider the question of the union of
the Roman States—declaring that if the votes were
in favour of a measure tending to the spoliation of

the Church, he should protest loudly against it in the Chambers.

Such was the paternal grandfather of our Prelate. His four sons increased the reputation of fidelity and devotion to the Church which his brave stand for her interests had already won. The second, Comte Felix de Mérode, was born at Maëstricht in 1791, and during his childhood lived under French dominion. The property of Trélon, situated in that part of Hainault which had been conquered by Louis XIV., gave him intimate and agreeable relations with France, which was strengthened by his marriage in Franche-Comté with one of the Grammonts. This illustrious family counted among its ancestors M. Theodore, Bishop of Sion, one of the chaplains of Charlemagne. Protectors of the Abbey of Lieucroissant, they had mounted guard over the relics of the Magi Kings when they rested in this abbey on their way to their final interment in the Cathedral of Cologne. The abbey took then the name of " *The Three Kings*," and the Grammonts adopted for their motto, " *Dieu aide au gardien des Rois !* " Faithful to this recollection, they showed themselves always as pious as they were brave. They gave three archbishops to the diocese of Besançon, of whom one deserved to be termed the " Borromeo " of this vast diocese. They were looked upon by the whole country as the most popular and beloved among the old nobility. The Marquis de Grammont, on the fatal 10th of August, was among the grenadiers at the Tuilleries who endeavoured in vain to save the Royal victims of the Revolution. During the Reign of Terror he was obliged to hide : but his château of Villersexel was respected by the Revolution, being dear to the people as a centre of charity and virtue. The inde-

pendence he maintained during the Empire ensured
him at the Restoration the post of deputy, and after
the July Revolution he was steadily re-elected until
his death.

His political principles were as staunch and true as
his religious convictions were strong and deep.. His
Christian practices, of which he made neither parade
nor mystery, were less a tradition of hereditary honour
than the fruit of an honest conviction, courageously
carried out under every political system.   In the wife
he had chosen, he found a woman of admirable virtue
and goodness, and likewise one of the most accomplished persons of her age, so that she was looked
upon as one of the marvels of Franche-Comté.

She was the youngest of the five daughters of the
Duc d'Ayen.   Her eldest sister died on the scaffold
with their mother, the Duchesse d'Ayen, and her
grandmother, Mde. de Noailles, on the 27th of June,
1793, absolved and blessed on their way to the scaffold
by the Abbé Carichon, who, amidst a frightful storm
of thunder and lightning and torrents of rain, suddenly
showed himself among the soldiers of the escort and
made himself known to them.   The three noble victims had naught but words of pity and pardon for
their executioners ; and the priest who had assisted
them went home praising God, like the first Christians
when they returned from the gates of a town red with
the blood of the martyrs.

The three remaining sisters survived the horrors of
the Revolution, though separated by the sad events of
that period.   Mde. de Lafayette, after having been
made prisoner in France, had gone to Olmutz, where
her husband was in prison also, and where she had
obtained leave to share his cell.   Mde. de Montagu

fled to England, and afterwards to Belgium and Switzerland, always striving to find her sister, Mde. de Grammont, whose fate was unknown. But a pedlar discovered her in the château of Villersexel, which she had scarcely left, although her husband had been proscribed by the Terror.

The three sisters, united for a moment in 1799 at Vianen, devoted their time, thoughts and prayers to the attainment of greater perfection under the protection of those whom they looked upon as their martyred saints, and in whose honour they composed a Litany, which they recited every day at the sorrowful hour when the guillotine had fallen on their mother and sister. This Litany ended with the following words:—

"Let us strive to enter into the feelings of these dear victims when preparing for their martyrdom, and so full of holy resignation and ardent charity. Let us pray for their enemies, and, as they wrote in the last lines of their will, not only forgive them but ask of God to fill them with His grace and extend His mercy towards them."

M. and Mde. de Grammont remained at Villersexel, where Mde. de Montagu often came to visit them. She called her sister's house " a little kingdom of virtue and charity, and the capital of peace." She described all the blessings which she found there : " Simplicity, harmony, ease, hours well-regulated, love of duty, burning charity, and an earnest desire after the highest good."

It was in a home of this kind that Comte Felix de Mérode came to seek for his wife. His faith and piety gained the esteem and confidence of the whole house, and his marriage with Mlle. Rosalie de Grammont was soon settled. He had found not only a wife after his own heart, but a home at Villersexel which fully realized his ideal of what a Christian and Catholic home should be. Popular, like his father-in-law, pious, like his mother-in-law, no one could see him without being filled with admiration both for the nobility of his character and the grand simplicity of his manner.

In the mountains of le Doub a sister of the Marquis de Grammont lived, the Marquise de Maiche, who was the providence of the whole country. A widow and without children, she shared everything with the poor, and divided between them and her relations all the affection of her loving heart. Comte de Mérode never missed a year without paying her a visit and enjoying the shade and fresh air in the pine woods of La Maiche. He used to bring his children there also from their earliest years, and they became warmly attached to a place, which was a perfect model of purity, of faith and morals, and of inviolable fidelity to the principles of social order.

Comte Felix de Mérode's marriage with Rosalie de Grammont was visibly blessed by God, Who gave them seven children, of whom only three died as babies. The two remaining sons and daughters were educated partly at Brussels and Trélon, but more often at Villersexel. The two daughters married Frenchmen of noble birth, of whom one became Comtesse de Montalembert and the other Marquise de Wignacourt. The eldest of the sons, being born in France, profited by this circumstance to claim the exercise of his civil rights, deserve the suffrages of his fellow-citizens and a seat in the Chambers. This is the present Count Werner de Mérode. The youngest was Xavier, perhaps the dearest of all to his mother, who loved him as one loves one's youngest child, and who had given him the name of the Apostle of the Indies, in the hopes that he would be one day a priest. But Xavier was not long to enjoy this tender love, his mother dying when he was only three years old. This was the most terrible trial to the Marquise de Grammont, who had been nine times a mother, and from whom death had carried off eight times the fruit of her womb. But in her perfect Christian resignation she only said with Job: "The Lord has given, and the Lord has taken away, blessed be the name of the Lord."

Count Felix de Mérode felt that he must, after a time, replace, if it were only for his children's sake, the terrible loss he had sustained. He would not seek in any other home such a second treasure of love and devotion, and so married Philippine de Grammont, who became the tenderest mother of the little ones to whom she had been the most devoted aunt. One little girl, Albertine, was the fruit of this second marriage, and added to the closeness of the ties which bound together all the members of this family.

Xavier, however, remained chiefly with his grandmother, the Marquise de Grammont, who had, in spite of her age, a wonderful skill in bringing up children according to the old traditions of French education, and with that firm and vigorous tenderness of which the secret now seems lost. She was short, and rather stiff in manner, with very marked features, and none of the softness or graces of women of her birth, unless it were her extraordinary goodness. This was indeed inexhaustible, but shown more in deeds than in words. The loving caresses of the child would have been her natural reward, if nature had still asserted its rights in this chosen soul. But for a long time she had only obeyed the voice of duty, in spite of her love for her belongings and her wish to do them good. The little Xavier, whom she had adopted when he was only three years old, had a special share in her maternal and spiritual care. As the thought of winning eternal salvation was her dominant feeling, she strove to initiate the same sentiment into the heart of the boy. There was no over-anxiety, nor bitter zeal in her maternal solicitude; and Xavier followed her lead insensibly, without dreaming of opposing her will. As he was always with her, we may say that he was thus early trained on the straight road to Paradise.

It was in his grandmother's favourite books that he first learned to read. These books were neither very varied nor very deep. When we have mentioned the "Imitation," the "Introduction to a Devout Life," "The Lives of the Saints," the "Annals of the Propagation of the Faith," and one or two more of the same kind, we shall have exhausted Mde. de Grammont's little library. She never could see that, to revive one's devotion, it was necessary to read a heap of new books or invent novel practices of piety. The same prayers and the same pious reading satisfied her, for, as she justly said, the object which a Christian strove to attain was always the same. When fortune smiled upon her she appeared as insensible to it as she had been to the misery which attended the Revolution. She certainly had reason to rejoice in her old age. Her husband and son were universally esteemed and beloved. Her son-in-law, after having laid the foundations of the Belgian monarchy, remained in that country, the arbiter of all important public affairs. Montalembert, who had married one of her granddaughters, returned annually to her home with the fresh laurels which his noble eloquence had won, and which religion had inspired and blessed. Her grandson, Werner de Mérode, was early elected as deputy to the Chambers, and has ever since secured the like honours and popularity.

Certainly the Marquise de Grammont had great compensations for great sorrows. But she let all pass, without surprise and without illusions. She never seemed to grow any older. Her style remained as firm as her thoughts; her handwriting was an index of this brave soul up to the hour of her death.

In 1848, one of her grandchildren was speaking of the anarchy which seemed inevitable, but could not rouse her attention. At last she said: "But, grandmamma, if you were to see the guillotine reestablished in the public squares as in the Days of the Terror!"

"My poor dear child!" she answered, "that is not the question. Must not one die some day? The great thing we have to do is to be always ready. As for the kind of death, that is only a matter of detail."

We alluded just now to the Revolution in Belgium. If ever a revolution were justifiable it was in this case, for in 1815 all Belgian interests had been sacrificed to those of the Dutch; and under the name of the "Low Countries" two nations had been united who had neither origin, nor religion, nor language, nor character, nor commercial interests in common. All parties were united to resist this unnatural alliance, and when the French Revolution of 1830 broke out, the insurrection burst forth, the Dutch army was driven out of Brussels, a Provisional Government was established; and by the 1st of October Belgium had forced herself from the Dutch yoke.

Comte Felix de Mérode was at the head of this great movement. His three brothers had embraced the same cause, and one of them, Count Frederick, while leading the Volunteers, who were driving the Dutch from the Belgian territory, fell mortally wounded, at only thirty-eight years of age, thus giving his blood and his life for the cause of Faith and Liberty. His fellow-citizens then offered the crown to Count Felix. The new Government needed a head, and no one was so likely to conciliate the votes of the majority. The towns were unanimously in his favour; the country people admired his charity and generosity; the clergy his faith and piety. His probity and uprightness, his great simplicity of manners, and his winning reception of every one, would have made him a most popular king. But he gave, himself, the most striking example of self-abnegation. He had at once felt, and made his colleagues understand, that, to establish a new kingdom on the narrow soil of Belgium, and in a country without natural frontiers, foreign alliances capable of protecting it were absolutely necessary. His whole energy was therefore directed to this end; and he went backwards and forwards from the Hague to London, thinking only of the interests of his country and nothing of himself.

When Prince Leopold was finally decided upon, the new king had no firmer supporter. Later on, when any ministerial crisis came about, the king invariably sent for Count Felix de Mérode. These appeals used often to arrive when he was at his château of Trélon. One of the king's couriers would bring him a despatch. The Count would spring into his carriage, go back with him to Brussels, have a long consultation with the king, and then take charge of public business till a new ministry was formed in accordance with the spirit of the Constitution.*

The revolutions in France and Belgium did not make any change in the Christian habits of the two families. The château of Villersexel remained, like that of Trélon, a centre of peace, virtue and charity. Xavier de Mérode learned, from his father's self-abnegation, to despise fortune and dignities for himself, and to use them only for the good of others. If any feelings of pride ever arose in his heart, his grandmother promptly repressed them. She only spoke to him of the world to take away the idea that he was to play an important figure in it. She watched his growing tastes and inclinations with a jealous eye, and tried to inspire him with the fear of God and the taste for piety and charity. It was a special grace that he was thus formed by one whom all looked upon as a saint in the great school of Christianity. It is true that the boy did not always listen, that he only partially understood her recommendations, and that he showed now and then some natural impatience at her warnings and preachings, but the lesson was none the less useful and durable. One day all would come back to his mind, and Xavier would remember what he had not cared for at the time. Twenty years later, when he had given himself up entirely to the service of God and His Church, he blessed the grandmother who had first taught him to love and serve his Divine Master.

We will quote a letter from M. de Montalembert to M. Rio to show our readers all the charms of Villersexel, the home of which the little Xavier was the spoiled child :

* See "*Le Roi Léopold et la Reine Victoria*," par Saint Réné Taittandier, I. 314.

"I have been for more than four months at Viller-sexel, and never, at any moment of my life, has time passed so pleasantly and rapidly. I should say I was only too happy, for nothing ever comes to trouble my enjoyment; and I feel that such happiness inspires a certain softness and laziness of which you used to complain also, when speaking to me of your delightful stay at Florence. But what a happy revolution in my life, after such agitations and so much solitude!

"You cannot fancy a more delightful family gathering than we have here. We are often fifteen at dinner, all full of love and affection towards one another, full of gaiety and freedom; above all, full of sympathy on all religious and political questions, which, when discussed, are interesting to the last degree, yet without a shade of bitterness.

"This large family party is presided over by the Marquis de Grammont, who is seventy years of age, and who has preserved all the exquisite grace and courtesy of the old school, while faithful to the ideas of 1789, which makes him a worthy brother-in-law to General de Lafayette. Then there is his wife, *née* de Noailles, of the same age as himself, all of whose moments are consecrated to the relief and education of the poor in the neighbourhood, and to the care of her own home. Both are the most amiable heads of a family one ever saw, and the least exacting, not choosing to be either cared for or accompanied, leaving everybody free to do as they like, and only living for the happiness of others. Afterwards comes the eldest son of the house, married to Mlle. de Crillon: then M. de Mérode, my father-in-law, the most honest man I ever met with, whose every thought, word, and deed, has but one object—the good of the Church and of his neighbour. He is perfectly adored in this country, where he always lived till the Belgian Revolution. Last of all is my mother-in-law, the faithful inheritor of her mother's virtues, and also her almoner. One and all follow in the same steps and are equally beloved. You can fancy how delicious it is for me to enjoy the love of my wife, not only *tête-à-tête*, but in the bosom of a family where everything responds to the feelings in our two hearts. I must confess that, until now, I never guessed what could be the noble and salutary influence of a family so profoundly Christian as this one in a country like ours, and especially in these days. The House of Grammont has given three successive archbishops to the diocese of Besançon, and these prelates founded the seminary, the principal hospitals, the schools, and in fact all the pious establishments in the diocese, so that the people look upon the Grammonts as the heads and benefactors of all the religion and charity in the province. The Marquis de Grammont has amply fulfilled his mission in that respect; and at the same time he has had the happiness of always possessing the political confidence of the county, which he has represented for twenty years, by his moderate yet firmly liberal opinions.

"In this magnificent old château, though there is much comfort, there is no luxury or ostentation; all is kept for the poor, who are constantly about the place. Close by is a beautiful hospital, built and endowed by the de Grammonts. A little further on is a great convent, where eighty young girls are educated, partly by alms, but mostly by the tender care of the family. I have seen here with my own eyes marvels of charity, such as I have related in my life of St. Elizabeth of Hungary. I have seen Mde.

de Grammont herself helping to make the soup, so that it might be more abundant, for the sick poor. I have seen her taking in her own carriage scrofulous patients, disgusting in appearance, for more than twenty leagues, either to show them to some famous doctor or to leave them at some waters."*

Xavier de Mérode is not mentioned in this letter; but it was because he had just gone back to college. His name was, however, on every tongue, and his childhood has left ineffaceable recollections in the minds of every one at Villersexel. His good grandmother had employed him from his earliest years in various ministrations of charity, both that he might acquire the habit and be inspired with a real love of the poor. She used to speak to him of the eminent dignity of poverty, showing him Jesus Christ under the rays of misery, and familiarizing him with hideous wounds, which she said should be sacred to us, for that they recalled those of Our Lord's Passion. The boy listened and asked questions which revealed a real compassion for the suffering members of Jesus Christ. She made it a reward to be allowed to visit the poor and to give them alms; and whenever she was very much pleased with him she took him with her on her charitable rounds, and interested him in the fate of the most destitute cases. Very soon he went to visit them on his own account, using his little hands to cultivate vegetables in his garden for their use, and collecting all the old wood he could find in the park for their fires. Having got together his little store of fuel and provisions, he would load his donkey with them and knock joyfully at the doors of the most neglected old men and women, who were his special

* Letter dated from Villersexel, the 26th October, 1837.

favourites. The little Xavier was always received with joy, and his bright and merry jokes doubled the value of his charity. He chattered away without fear, asked many questions, and rather disconcerted the dull peasants sometimes by his witty remarks. Full of fun, rejoicing in having something to give away, with a horror of lying or dissimulation, incapable of holding his tongue, or of keeping a penny in his pocket, the people would cry out, "He is a true Mérode! and a true Grammont!" which two names were synonymous in their minds for honour and charity. Such he appeared in his childhood; and such he remained all through his life until the hour of his death, with that practical charity which was the great passion of his life, and that extreme frankness which was the admiration of those who loved him, but which brought upon him not a few enemies.

The beautiful château of Villersexel is now, alas! only a memory. The Germans occupied it in 1871, and when they were driven out of it by the French, they set it on fire before their evacuation, and made its owners pay dearly for the only victory which consoled France for the losses in that miserable campaign, in which the whole army was annihilated. But the family of the de Grammonts survives in all its honour, piety, and popularity. The memory of the saintly Marquise is still held in veneration throughout the country; and those who used to watch the little Xavier de Mérode accompanying his grandmother in her charitable visits, often say that they had foreseen the day when he would become a great Prelate and an Almoner of the Vicar of Christ, a worthy successor and great-nephew of Antoine Pierre de Grammont, who was one of Besançon's noblest archbishops.

C

CHAPTER II.

From 1832 to 1841.

How Xavier had learned at Villersexel to hear and serve
Mass—His First Communion at St. Thomas d'Aquin—His
Education begun by Professors—He is placed with the
Jesuits at Namur—He leaves Namur for Juilly—His
Studies and his Practical Jokes—His Conduct at a *Table
d'Hôte*—His Journeys during his Holidays—His Intimacy
with his Brother-in-law, the Count de Montalembert—His
Hesitation as to his Career—The Advice of the Papal
Nunzio at Brussels, Mgr. Joachim Pecci—Xavier enters
the Military College—His Religious Conduct, his Character,
and his Relations with his Companions.

THE day which often decides the fate of a young man
is the day of his first Communion.   One may be
faithless to grace after having received it worthily ; but
it is rare for any one to repent after having done so
great an act badly ; or that one can repair so grave a
fault, with all the consequences it entails.   Xavier de
Mérode had been prepared from his earliest years for
this great mystery by watching the venerable Rector
of the parish church at Villersexel during the celebra-
tion of the Holy Sacrifice.   This man was the Abbé
Tramus, one of the many priests who had confessed
the faith in exile with the greatest courage, and who
preached it the most efficaciously by his example.   He
was the first Catechist and Confessor of the young
Xavier.   With a somewhat stern and austere manner,

he had the most loving heart, an ardent charity, and an incomparable dignity : it was said that he was favoured with extraordinary spiritual graces. The profound impression which he felt while celebrating the Holy Sacrifice communicated itself to all around him and filled his hearers with awe and recollection. Xavier, in spite of his youth, had been immensely struck by it. Hence, while assisting or serving at his Mass, he conceived the deepest respect and reverence for the Blessed Sacrament of the Altar. Thus the early years he spent at Villersexel were like a special preparation for his first Communion. He carried with him to Paris the remembrance and example of the venerable Curé, who was a perfect model of the clergy in Franche-Comté, and who had disposed him all the better for the great action which was to decide his life.

It was in 1833, in the church of St. Thomas d'Aquin, that he received his God for the first time. He had just entered his thirteenth year. His family retain a vivid recollection of the punctuality and fervour with which he followed the Catechisms of the Abbé Hamelin, and of the immense pains this eminent priest took about his soul. M. Hamelin, like a wise director, found out how to soften his character without breaking his spirit, and gained his entire confidence during his instructions. He became a prodigy of faith and piety among the other children of his age. His general confession occupied him for fifteen days. He questioned his stepmother and his sisters about his faults, was enlightened by their decisions, and submitted them to his confessor as a last resource. The day he received absolution was one of joy to the whole house. He came home, his face beaming with

delight, and exclaimed: "I never thought to be so
happy! Now I am quite white, just as I was after
my baptism!" This radiant emotion was shared by
all his belongings, for they all knew that he never
said what he did not feel. The next day, which was
that of his first Communion, redoubled their joy.
Xavier seemed positively transformed. One saw him,
ever after, at Holy Communion as he was later at the
altar. Grave, recollected, full of a deep and holy
joy, no one could recognize his former capricious and
hasty temper; the child seemed to have disappeared,
he was like an angel who veils his face with his wings
respectfully at the approach of his God.

To these recollections of his faith and piety we
must add, however, occasional outbursts of idleness
and mischief, as if to show all that grace effected
later in this ardent nature. His father first tried to
bring him up at home with a tutor, in accordance with
the advice of the Abbé Busson, who was then Chaplain
to Charles the Tenth, and Secretary to the Minister of
Ecclesiastical Affairs. He was the director of the
Mérodes, the Grammonts, the Montalemberts—in
fact, of all that Parisian aristocracy who wished to live
in the world while following the precepts of the law of
God. Later on, he followed Charles the Tenth to
Holyrood, and prepared Mademoiselle, daughter of the
Duc de Berry, for her first Communion. After having
several times refused the Episcopate after the Restoration, he equally declined the offer of the Curé of Notre
Dame made to him by the July Government, and
quietly retired to Besançon, where he died amidst
universal veneration. His authority and wisdom in
matters of education and spiritual direction were
recognized by all, and he thought that the fine character

of Xavier de Mérode would be ruined with the discipline of a college, while a good tutor, by combining gentleness with firmness, would influence in the best manner this clever but hasty and over-excitable nature. The advice was wise, but the execution of it was difficult. A good tutor is extremely rare, and the more one seeks for perfection the less likely one is to find it. Xavier used up two or three, without benefiting in any way, either in character or studies. The first, M. Pelier de la Croix, was a man of note in the Church; but he was no longer young, and the painful events in which he had been mixed up had moved him too much to admit of his giving his mind to looking after the education of a boy. Having been chaplain to the Prince de Condé at the château of St. Leu, he had undertaken, after the tragic death of his master, to redeem his memory from the charge of suicide, which had been attributed to him. This Mémoir occupied him so fully that he forgot his pupil. He had also such a dread of the emissaries of the Baronne de Feuchères that he never slept without a loaded pistol by his bedside. Xavier used laughingly to say to his parents: "It is at the risk of my life that I go into the Abbé's room during the night; all day he does nothing but "*feuchériser*" (write against Madame de Feuchères); "so that is why I learn neither Greek nor Latin." The Abbé called his pupil "Gilotin," on account of his love of mischief, and the boy, in return, overwhelmed him with epigrams.

The other tutors were not more fortunate. Xavier defeated them all, either by a passive and invincible resistance, or else by replies which, however witty and original, did not fail to be extremely impertinent.

The last succeeded the worst of all, and resorted to blows and brute force, which caused his speedy dismissal. Finally it was decided that Xavier should go to the Jesuit College at Namur; but that it might appear that they parted on good terms, the tutor insisted on accompanying him there. Either on purpose or by accident, while crossing the street leading to the College, Xavier put his foot into a puddle and splashed the tutor from head to foot. The tutor, furious at his toilet being thus spoiled, gave him a violent blow. Xavier cried with rage, and came into the College with very red eyes. "You have been crying, my boy," said the Superior to him kindly. "Are you sorry, then, to come to us?" "Oh, no!" quickly replied the tutor, "it is because he is so grieved to part with me!"

Xavier only spent one year at Namur. His stepmother, having come to live in Paris, moved him to the College of Juilly, to have him nearer to her. The Abbé de Salinis, who was Superior of this House, was the intimate friend of his father, and the system pleased him, because of the freedom and liberty given to the boys, and their frank and simple ways. Xavier here was more respectful to the heads of the College, and only played tricks on the professors. But his character did not change. One of the masters was one day giving them a meditation on the ingratitude of men towards God, and expressed himself as follows:

"I give a bone to a dog—he is grateful, and loves me. God gives us His Blood, and we are indifferent to Him—ungrateful creatures that we are! Learn our duty from a beast."

"Yes, yes! that's just it," exclaimed Xavier, and all the boys repeated it in chorus. The Prefect of Studies was changed; his successor, who was a very simple-minded man, easily fell into the trap laid for him by Xavier. "Sir," he exclaimed after the first day's lesson, "you do not yet know our customs. It is our business to put you in the way of them. The Abbé de Salinis, who is always so kind to us, wishes us to celebrate your arrival by a little extra treat, so he grants to all the students leave to gather the artichokes in the kitchen garden."

The master, never doubting the fact, carried off the merry troup into the garden. In a moment the whole bed of artichokes, which had been reserved for illustrious guests, was cleared. M. de Salinis, who had watched the "razzia" from his windows, called to the master to ask him what on earth it all meant.

"It was M. de Mérode who told me," he replied in excuse.

"De Mérode! you ought to have known him better. He will play you plenty more tricks."

It all ended by a good laugh. The master was warned, and Xavier, satisfied with his exploit, belied M. de Salinis' words by behaving ever after with the utmost respect to the new master.

These practical jokes, however, did not lead to very brilliant studies. But a great taste for certain sciences awoke in this adventurous spirit; and Xavier excelled in mathematics, and carried off the prize for algebra, though he took care to say nothing about it. When reproached by his family for his silence, he answered, "That nothing was more natural, for he had heard his brother Werner say, that those who carried off prizes at College were generally the greatest fools in after life!"

Xavier's brilliant, biting wit did not spare the free-thinkers who came in his way. In spite of his joyous humour, he never forgot the laws of the Church; and even if he could get nothing but dry bread, he rigorously observed all days of abstinence, even at a *table d'hôte.* One Friday he found himself in front of a commercial traveller, who began outrageously praising his goods, which were of cast iron. Xavier, who had asked for something *maigre* and found none, was contenting himself with some potatoes. The commercial traveller began to laugh at him. " Well, young gentleman, is it papa or mamma who has forbidden you to eat meat? Come, come; eat this wing of a chicken—it will do you no harm."

"Come, come," replied Xavier in the same tone, " stick to your cast iron, and leave me alone." Everyone at the table burst out laughing, and the traveller, ashamed and silenced, paid dearly for his incredulity and bad taste.

This story came to the ears of his masters at Juilly, and raised Xavier very much in their esteem. His large and generous heart, his lively faith, and his frank and joyous ways, made him extremely popular in the College, and highly considered by the masters. The Abbé de Salinis was too wise to take offence at his practical jokes.

Towards the end of his stay at Juilly, Xavier heard that a negotiation had been set on foot for M. de Salinis to give up the College to the Abbé Bautain. He went straight to M. de Salinis and said brusquely: "You have no right to dispose of your scholars in that way, and I give you warning that I won't be sold." Instead of being angry, M. de Salinis only laughed and replied: " My dear Xavier, I shall not sell you, for no one would have you at any price; but I shall throw you into the bargain!"

This answer enchanted Xavier, who, M. de Ségur says, laughed heartily twenty-five years after while telling him the story.[*]

The boyish tricks of the student were, in fact, quickly forgotten; while M. de Salinis always reckoned Xavier de Mérode among the young men who did the greatest honour to the College. The future justified his prevision, and on the annual feasts at Juilly the name of the great Prelate is placed next to that of Berryer, among the glories of the House.

If he did not bring back many laurels when he returned for his holidays to Trélon or Villersexel, he was, as ever, the delight of the whole family, from his frank, joyous, loving ways, his caustic wit and brilliant intelligence. His brother-in-law, Charles de Montalembert, was devoted to him, and in writing to his wife of a little journey in the mountains which they took together, speaks of him with unmixed admiration, adding at the end: "Xavier is more amusing and more witty than ever." At that time Xavier had left Juilly. He was in his nineteenth year, and hesitating as to his future career. Montalembert, already so illustrious from his writings and his speeches, was his oracle. Xavier admired him as much as he was himself beloved by him, and confided to him all his thoughts and feelings. He told him of the advice that a certain Religious had given him, which was to marry as soon as possible, representing this as a necessary check to his growing passions. This good man had altogether mistaken his character. Montalembert rejected the idea with indignation, and did his utmost to dissuade him from an early marriage. "You are too young and, as yet, too inexperienced," he

[*] "*Un Hiver à Rome,*" p. 129, by the Marquis de Ségur.

exclaimed, "to be the founder of a house. Is it
necessary to indulge one's senses to that extent? At
your age, a Mérode should be a soldier and not a
husband. Go and exhaust in active service the
impetuosity of your nature, and learn to live under a
sterner rule than that of a schoolmaster. You will
see much that is evil, perhaps; but you will avoid it
yourself, for it will disgust you. Impiety will strive to
keep you from your duties, but you have strength and
faith enough to resist bad examples, and the good one
you will give will bear rich fruit. After having served
for five or six years, your character will have acquired a
certain firmness; you will then be able to decide on
your future career: and, whatever you may do, you will
justify your motto—"*Plus d'honneur que d'honneurs.*"

Comte Felix de Mérode had, however, some hesitation on the military vocation of his son. He went to
consult the Nunzio at Brussels, who was his neighbour
and his friend. He was a young prelate, who was just
starting in his diplomatic career, but whose wise
counsels were already held in great esteem by the
family. The Nunzio's name was Joachim Pecci—no
other than he who now sits on the Papal Throne as
Leo XIII. He shared Montalembert's opinion and
reassured the anxious father. "You belong," he said,
"to the great nobility of the country. Your name is
associated with the whole military history of Flanders
and the Low Countries. Allow your son to follow his
natural inclination for the army. Who knows if he will
not, like his ancestors, attain to the highest military
honours? He is pious and chaste. God will keep
him; and his virtue will only be strengthened by
trials."

Reassured by this advice, Comte de Mérode presented

his son at the Military College at Brussels. He entered
as a simple soldier in 1839 and was promoted to the
post of officer in 1841. The interest which he had inspired in the Nunzio made him take as deep an interest in
the development of his character as his military chiefs
did in his education. He passed through all his examinations with the greatest credit ; while his private
conduct was worthy of his name and his faith. At
night he would say his prayers kneeling at the foot of
his bed ; he assisted at High Mass on Sundays at the
Church of St. Gudule ; and in the evening he went to
the house of the Nunzio, or to talk with his auditor or
secretary. Mgr. Pecci rejoiced in his perseverance in
well-doing, and congratulated himself on the advice he
had given.

The companions of the young soldier were very
curious to see how, with his name and his pious ways,
he would bear the *régime* of the College and the rail-
leries of the irreligious amongst them. He soon showed
them that he was firm in his faith, but without infring-
ing the liberty of the rest, and respecting in others
what he demanded for himself. The very first night
he was put to the proof. One of his companions remarked that he said his prayers kneeling by the side
of his bed before lying down. It was only for a few
minutes, but it was enough to aggravate his impious
neighbour, who exclaimed out loud : " I say my prayers
to Venus and think small things of your Paternosters."
Xavier turned round and said, dryly but firmly, " Say
your prayers to whom you please, but don't tread on
my toes." Another went further. During a drawing
class, he turned what he called " bigots " into ridicule,
pointing to Xavier in a scornful way. Xavier asked
him " if it were to him that he was addressing these

remarks ?" "Yes," replied the other. "Very well.
I will give you your answer when the lesson is over."
An hour later they all defiled out of the room, and
Xavier, going up to his insulter, said, "Is it true you
meant to provoke me ?" "Yes ; because I know that
saints like you will not fight a duel and are too much
afraid of their skins to risk a cut of a sword."
Xavier replied, "It is true that my principles do not
allow me to fight a duel or to kill a man for his insolent
speeches ; but as you insist on an explanation I will
give it you in a way which will make you remember
me. You see my two fists, which are big and strong,
and very much at your service. With them I shall
call to order those who choose to insult me. But I
would rather tend them to you in good fellowship."
This speech was loudly cheered by the rest, and the
offender was shamed into silence. In this way Xavier
defended his religion boldly during his military training, and while forcing his companions to respect him
yet determined at any price to avoid a duel. He had
promised this to God the day he entered the College,
and he kept his word. Yet, in the sight of men, and
knowing the natural impetuosity of his character, no
one could have been more easily excused. But what is
impossible to nature is possible to grace ; and of this
Xavier de Mérode gave a striking proof. We shall see
on the battle-field (the sole field where such things are
lawful) how bravely he fought and how nobly he won his
spurs. True, no one could foresee in him at that time
the patient soul of a priest. But St. Peter, before
suffering for Jesus Christ, showed his zeal by cutting
off the ear of Malchus !

CHAPTER III.

From 1841 to 1847.

Xavier is appointed Sub-Lieutenant in the Belgian Army—His Life in Garrison—His Military Spirit—His Piety and Mortification—Three Months' Leave—Voyage to Madeira—His Service in the French Army—His Sojourn in Algeria—His Brave Conduct noticed by Marshal Bugeaud and by the whole Army—His Return to Belgium—He begins to think of the Ecclesiastical State.

XAVIER, who had left the Military College in 1841, was at once enrolled as Sub-Lieutenant in the second Infantry Regiment in garrison at Mons. He had to look out for a lodging with one of his companions, and having seen one which seemed clean and comfortable, he inquired the price. The proprietor rudely replied that he did not let his apartments to private soldiers. The two young men went away laughing; but a few minutes after, the lodginghouse-keeper having found out his mistake, and that he had refused a Mérode, ran after him and implored him, with many excuses, to return to his house. Xavier replied that as he was a private, he would not lodge where he was not welcome. This little incident delighted the regiment, not only for the lesson given to the lodginghouse-keeper, but also because Xavier was content with the accommodation they had themselves. His excellent character, his gaiety, and his high spirits, won for him the sympathy and affection of every one around him.

The superior officer to whom we owe these little details, tells another story of Xavier which shows all his warmth of heart and yet all his imprudence. Having gone on some duty to Liège, he found in the middle of the street a little boy of four or five years old whom the parents had abandoned, and of whom the neighbours took no heed. It was the month of November; the cold was intense, and the poor little fellow had only a little shirt on, and shivered in a way which went to one's heart. Xavier took him to an hotel, got some clothes for him, and asked the landlord to make every possible inquiry about the child's family. Everything, however, was in vain; the child could not speak, and there was no way of finding out the unworthy parents. What did Xavier do? He told the landlord to send him to his regiment, and a day or two later the poor little waif arrived at his bachelor's lodgings. But very soon he was ordered to Liège, where he was to go through a new kind of drill. He carried off the baby with him, attending to the child as if he were its nurse, day and night—awkwardly enough, it is true, but with a zeal and a gaiety which made his very awkwardness the more amusing. In the mean time, he got a few days' holiday and brought his little boy with him to Brussels, where he had to undergo a very sharp scolding from his grandmother, who represented to him to what misrepresentations he was exposing himself. Finally, she persuaded him to place the child in a charitable institution, where Xavier paid his pension for ten or twelve years. But he was rewarded for his charity. The child grew up a good and strong man, and got an excellent situation in a great German house. But he never forgot his benefactor or omitted any opportunity of expressing his gratitude.

The young Belgian Sub-Lieutenant, who was so tender with the destitute and unfortunate, treated his own ease and comfort with supreme disdain. In spite of his epaulettes, he was the most austere of Christians, practising already that contempt of material wants which made him as ready for the priesthood as it disposed him to be brave and self-denying under arms. It was represented to him that all Bishops dispensed soldiers from abstinence during Lent. He replied, " That is very true ; but I don't see that they have dispensed us from fasting. The fast, then, should be rigorously observed." They used to go to practice at nine o'clock, and it was not over till three ; but Mérode would eat nothing till then. The miserable food which they brought him in an earthenware pot, and which had all become dried up while waiting for him, would not have tempted a beggar. But he made such fun over it, and met the observations made to him on the subject with such a hearty laugh, that people ended by letting him alone. This spirit of mortification made many of his friends foresee that sooner or later he would leave the world, the luxuries and superfluities of which so greatly alarmed his delicate conscience. One might also foresee the bent of his mind from his passion for Liturgic chaunts and Church music. But it must be owned that this passion was rather trying to other people's ears. He used to go to Compline at the cathedral and come back quite full of the chaunts, which he reproduced at the top of his voice all through the house, to the dismay of his neighbours. The books of Don Guéranger used to lie on his table pellmell with books of history and military tactics. The Polish General Schrensky, who had come to Belgium at the invitation of King Leopold, went to pay a visit

to Mérode in his humble rooms. He found him absorbed in a book of Don Guéranger's and asked him
with some surprise, " If it were thus that he was
studying military theories ?"

Xavier had then quitted Liège to join a regiment of
Grenadiers quartered in Brussels.   His tall command-
ing figure, his great name, and his relations with all
the aristocracy of the capital, pointed him out as the
most remarkable among the young officers in the
regiment.   But he had at heart the fulfilment of every
barrack duty, and that with the greatest exactitude,
so that no one might fancy he had joined the army
merely as an amateur, or that he reckoned on his
position to obtain more privileges than his brother
officers.   He had taken up the study of history,
going over all his old class books and learning all
that, as he pretended, his masters had never taught
him.   He did not remember their lessons, for the
simple reason that he had never listened to them !
It cost him a good deal to tear himself away from
some interesting book or animated conversation to
fulfil some vulgar barrack duty.   But his comrades
say that they never remember his having failed a
single time in his duty.   Only, he would arrive at the
very last moment, out of breath, with a smile on his
face and a ready joke, which would disarm the severe
look on the captain's face.   In fact, he was immensely
beloved, both by officers and men.   The entire absence
of haughtiness or timidity which characterized him
had won the respect of the latter and the affection of
the former.   If any one, to provoke him, risked a bad
joke on serious matters, or on his religious practices,
the answer he received turned the laugh on Xavier's
side, without offending the perpetrator of the unfortunate remark.

In 1844 the young sub-lieutenant obtained three months' leave of absence to go and see his sister in Madeira, Mde. de Montalembert, who had been ordered there by the doctors. Her husband had accompanied her, leaving with regret the French Chambers, where he had recently fought with such success the battle for liberty in education, and who had by his magnificent speeches attracted the attention of all Europe. But he was one of those men who thought nothing a sacrifice which was done for others. They stayed in Madeira for eighteen months. Xavier de Mérode shortened the weariness of this exile for three months during the winter of 1844.

There his tastes for both military and ecclesiastical affairs showed themselves in still stronger relief. He took the same interest in tactics as in plain chaunt, sharing in all his brother-in-law's interest in the religious affairs of France; and by mixing and conversing with the inhabitants of the island, gathered up all those touching popular traditions and traits of deep faith and piety which still characterised this people. From time to time he had fits of sadness and depression, as of one aspiring to a more perfect life; but he did not yet realize all that God would one day require of him.

His spirit of enterprise and love of investigation tempted him to make an excursion to the Peak of Teneriffe. He started for the Canary Islands in a wretchedly small and badly-found sailing-boat, where he had to share his meals with the sailors. When he arrived at Teneriffe he joined a party of Englishmen to make the ascent of the Peak. Halfway up, his companions, seeing that sunset was at hand, and dreading to pass the whole night in the open air, determined to go back to the town. But Xavier would not hear of this, and alone, without a guide, and without a cloak, he continued the ascent of the mountain. Towards nightfall he reached the summit, but found no shelter, and was obliged finally to hide himself as well as he could in the trunk of a tree, where the heavy dews fell less directly upon him. There he remained till morning, trembling with cold, dying of hunger and with a sharp attack of fever. He could only find a path down the mountain when the sun rose, and followed it as well as he could in his exhausted state. His companions, who thought he must be dead, hastened up the mountain as soon as it was light, and met him halfway down. They had brought a litter and a mattrass, besides food and other remedies in case he was still alive. They were beyond anything astonished when they saw him walking, but his face showed plainly how much he needed help. They brought him back to Teneriffe, where he had to spend several days in bed until the fever had diminished. This adventure made quite a sensation in the place. Everyone asked who was this stranger who had exposed himself to so great a danger? They all wanted to see and speak to him. Xavier de Mérode was only too glad to escape from the curiosity of one set of people and the admiration of others, and returned as quickly as he could to his sister. He left Madeira during Lent, stopping at Seville on his way home, where he was immensely edified at the ceremonies of Holy Week in the Cathedral, and said he should only be too glad if some day he might himself celebrate them at the altar. It was under this strong religious impression that he returned to Belgium. His ecclesiastical vocation had made a step in advance, but time was needed to ripen it.

A life in garrison at Brussels could not long satisfy
Xavier de Mérode. He wanted to see active service,
and to take part in the dangers and fatigues of a
campaign. There was peace in Europe; but in
Algeria there was a camp and daily fighting. There
Bugeaud was about to undertake an expedition against
the Emperor of Morocco, and the Kabyles thought to
profit by this diversion to reconquer their independence.
It was under these circumstances that, under the
advice of Charles de Montalembert, Xavier asked permission of the King of the Belgians to take part in
the operations of the French Army in Algeria. The
leave was granted, and he was put on the staff of
Marshal Bugeaud. Having arrived at Algiers in the
middle of September, just after the battle of Ilsly, he
at once joined the expedition set on foot by the
Marshal to punish the revolt of the Kabyles.

"He had more courage than any of us!" exclaimed
one of his comrades on meeting a friend of his a few
years later under the walls of Rome. And on the
friend expressing his surprise at the statement
the officer continued: "Yes, he had more courage
than us, for he did what we had not the strength to
do. A few days after he had joined the French army
he was provoked to fight a duel. The moral courage
with which he declined it astonished everybody; but
some chose to doubt his bravery. Eight days later
that was put to the proof. We saw the way he with-
stood the charge of a whole host of Arabs, the balls
whistling all round him; and it ended by no officer
being more esteemed and loved than he was."

The expeditionary force which he had joined was
composed of three battalions of infantry and two field
batteries, under the command of General Comman and

D 2

Colonel St. Arnaud. The general had carried the out-
posts of the enemy; but the Kabyles had intrenched
themselves behind the wood and rocks which crowned
the village of Abizzar. There they were completely
sheltered from the balls of the French, having also
thrown up redoubts of mud and stone, which were the
more impregnable from the accidents of the ground.
Bugeaud determined to storm this position, being
persuaded that the least hesitation would make them
believe that the French were afraid of them. He
accordingly ordered the assault, and both officers and
soldiers, sword and bayonet in hand, precipitated
themselves upon the enemy, escalading the crest of the
mountain in spite of its steepness, and dislodging the
Kabyles along the whole line. The spirit and energy
of the attack was not slackened for a moment. The
Kabyles had more than three thousand men, of whom
many hundred remained on the field, while the others
only escaped from the nature of the ground, and by fling-
ing themselves into the wooded ravines below. The
Marshal in his report of the fight said that there were
so many single-handed combats, and such prodigies of
bravery among both officers and men, that he could fill
four pages with the names of those who deserved
honourable mention. But he signalled out a certain
number, and among them was Xavier de Mérode. He
had, in fact, in this his first battle, shown a courage
which astonished and delighted the whole expeditionary
force. He was following St. Arnaud on horseback when
he came upon a man badly wounded. To spring off
his horse, put the wounded man on it, and escort him
out of reach of danger was the work of a few moments.
Then, returning rapidly to the front, he seized a gun,
dashed forward, gained the ridge of the hill among the

foremost, and went on fighting till the end of the day, chasing the Kabyles from rock to rock, and from bush to bush, till they finally disappeared, after firing a last volley at their pursuer. All the newspapers signalized this exploit as a marvel of bravery, and Marshal Bugeaud was as proud of Xavier as if he had been his own son. He wrote a beautiful letter to his father, Count Felix de Mérode, to congratulate him; and obtained from the king, Louis Philippe, the Cross of the Legion of Honour for the young Belgian lieutenant who had made so brilliant a *début*. " Mérode has fought admirably : I am very pleased with him," he wrote in his first letter. Mde. de Mérode was congratulated on all sides, while his two sisters, Mde. de Montalembert and Mde. de Wignacourt, could not contain their joy, and Montalembert, remembering the advice he had given to his young brother-in-law, thanked God for the happy inspiration.

Let us see how Xavier himself received all these congratulations. His faith, his modesty, and his good sense are all revealed in the following letter :—

" It is impossible for me to express, my dear and much-loved brother, how your letter of the 4th of November, written on your feast day, has touched me ; and yet it is difficult for me to answer it. It is not with you, who have, as you say, bowels of brotherly and almost paternal love for me, that I wish to pretend to ' *do the modest* ' in this circumstance. My whole heart flowed out in tenderness and affection towards those whom I love the best on earth for all the kindness they have shown me. But in spite of the pleasure their letters have given me, I own I am embarrassed at accepting, even tacitly, such exaggerated praises. They were rather too Spanish, to use your own phrase. In

reality, I did no more than the immense majority of men
who were there; no more than those poor soldiers who
in a few months will go back to their ploughs, or those
infantry officers destined to live and die in obscurity
when they go back to their garrisons, and who have
been here for eight, ten, twelve, or fourteen years!
Thus, even for the satisfaction of my own self-love, I
cannot accept more of your praises than what fairly
belongs to me. The truth is that, as the men said,
being my first fight, '*I was as good as an old hand;*'
but, after all, according to the proverb, '*bon chien doit
chasser de race.*' That is the compliment Marshal
Bugeaud made me! If, in the midst of some special
danger, I had rescued a wounded man on the point of
being massacred by the enemy, well and good! But
when one is able to walk, to put a man with a broken
thigh on your horse is no such glorious action as my
dear Anna* makes out! You must allow that nothing
shows a degenerate race so much as to be proud of
doing what hundreds of others have done before you.
During the retreat, which was carried out with some
difficulty, I seized a gun from a dying man and joined
the sharpshooters—but very often we were short of
cartridges. So grave an affair as it turned out to be
was so little foreseen that, instead of having sixty or
eighty cartridges, which is the ordinary soldier's charge,
we had but forty. We were obliged, therefore, to fall
back on our bayonets; but each time that we made a step
or two forward a Kabyle sprang up from behind every
rock, or shrub, or hollow in the ground and fled,
wrapped in his white burnous, after having discharged
his gun in our faces, without our ever being able to
reach one of them. I feel more than ever the need of

* Mde. de Montalembert.

your advice and exhortations, only one must have the strength to follow them. Anna's letter filled me with joy; I could only cry and thank God and our Lady. I could not help kneeling down and thanking our Lord when I read your letter, to have been able to give such pleasure to you all. But I entreat of you, if another brush with the enemy comes off, do not put my modesty to such a trial, for you do not know how afraid I am of being made ridiculous, even to myself, by your exaggerated compliments. It is like my drum-major, who compared my Uncle Frederick to Napoleon!"

A soldier who thus set aside any idea of glory with the one feeling of having simply done his duty, thought of many other things on the battle-field. He wrote to his sister, Mde. Montalembert, as follows:—

"I thought of you so much during the battle of the 17th, seeing the number of dead and wounded, who were subsequently buried without the shadow of a religious rite, for alas! there isn't a single priest attached to this expeditionary force. I said to myself, I wonder what my poor Anna would invent to give some help to these poor fellows? Anyhow I made up my mind I would write to you and ask you to have some Masses and prayers said for them. But I entreat you, above all, to say nothing about it to any one, for otherwise people would repeat it everywhere, which would annoy me extremely."

Xavier de Mérode's success did too much honour to the Belgian army not to ensure his promotion. The King declared he would not sign any nomination before that of the young hero of Dellys, and for ten successive days he put every paper in his box without choosing to read them. Yielding to his persistence, the War Minister at last brought him the Commission to sign.

Every one was delighted, and the oldest among the sub-lieutenants were ready to acknowledge that his promotion over their heads was well deserved.

It is interesting to follow Xavier throughout the campaign, and to hear how he speaks of war and its horrors. He was furious when the Arabs had their cave set fire to in which they had taken refuge. But in the midst of the excitements of the battle-field he did not forget home interests. He writes enthusiastically of the magnificent speeches of his brother-in-law in the Senate on liberty of teaching, adding gaily, " I am living now on the glories of my *brother-in-law-ship* with singular advantage to myself." He congratulates Montalembert with his whole heart on having despised the miserable quarrels for place and power in order to think only of the glorious interests of religion and the Church; and prophesies for him a noble future.

When sent to the Province of Oran he describes the habits of the different tribes, and paints in glowing colours the courage of a race which will only yield to superior force, and which persists in refusing its heart to France.

But the French had among them chiefs of rare bravery; soldiers of a truly noble and Christian stamp, who were the astonishment of the desert. Let us quote another of his letters, which, in addition to military details, gives also some curious descriptions of the habits of the country.

" ORAN, 10*th March*, 1845.

" I can imagine your astonishment at having no news of me for forty days. But I cannot reproach myself with idleness, as you will see. As I told you, I started for Mascara and Tiaret on the 30th January.

My suite was composed of my servant, mounted on my second horse, an orderly, and two mules, which General de Lamoricière, who is always so kind to me, had placed at my disposal. I had also an Arab guide. The first day we slept close to the River Sig, where they are building a magnificent wear or dam, so as to retain the water during the summer. Thanks to this work, an immense plain of 40,000 hectares will be irrigated at all times, and in consequence will rival in fertility the Huerta of Valence. The next day I reached Mascara, the country of Abdel-Kader, which becomes every day more of a French town. New buildings are springing up in all directions, for during the war it was pillaged and sacked several times. It was only in 1841 that it was occupied by the French troops. The day after my arrival at Mascara the weather became abominable, but towards mid-day the sky lightened a little. The Commandant prophesied fine weather, and trusting in his knowledge of the climate, I set off for Tiaret, which is at a four days' distance from Mascara, and which General de Lamoricière had sent me to visit.

"Hardly had I left the town, however, than the rain came down in torrents, and then changed into heavy snow, which soon filled up all the tracks, so that towards evening there was no possibility of finding one's road. The guide made us turn and twist in every direction till ten o'clock at night, without having evidently the smallest idea of where we were. We had to resign ourselves to pitch our tent on soaking ground, which had besides ten inches of snow. Happily the lions did not pay us a visit, which often happens in this country in bad weather. The next morning at break of day we started off to resume our journey, as

the weather seemed a little more favourable. I went
to sleep at Fortasia, a Marabout's hut situated on the
borders of the Oued-el-Abt. The snow had begun
again, together with a driving wind, which made the
cold almost intolerable. The horses sunk in up to
their hocks, and in spite of all they had told me about
snow not lasting more than two days together, I
saw no prospect of its abating.

"I was hospitably received in an Arab tent; but it
was impossible to conceive anything more dirty. It
was really a sink of filth, in which sheep, goats,
donkeys and calves sunk in the mud up to their bellies.
In the middle was a little oasis of dry earth, on which
the fire was lit. Each person on coming in took a
fagot of brushwood from a heap at the door of the tent,
to make a seat for himself, so that he might not sink
into the mud like the sheep and the calves. Add
to this a blinding smoke and the braying and lowing
of the animals, and you will have a correct idea of the
Arab establishment where I passed the night. The
wretched women wallowed in the filth with the beasts,
and worked like niggers. All the most laborious em-
ployments are for them; while the men, comfortably
squatted round the fire, smoked, talked, and said
their prayers. The next day I started as early as
I could, and after five or six hours' march I stopped
to breakfast at Sidi-Djelali-ben-Amour, a French
redoubt now unoccupied, but guarded by an Arab. I
installed myself there with joy, after the pleasant experience I had had of an Arab tent. I was obliged,
however, to push on in the afternoon and sleep at
Souama, on the banks of the Oued Souama, where I
found exactly the same hospitality as at Fortasia. The
next day was finer, the sun shone brightly and there

was no wind; in fact, the sort of day we have in
Belgium in the month of February when there is a
thaw. But the snow was still deep, and it was very
heavy work for the horses. After having marched for
some hours, I came to Tagdempt, a town founded by
Abdel-Kader in 1837 on some Roman remains, but
which was ruined by the war. In 1840 it contained twenty thousand souls. Now it is completely
deserted. After having threaded these silent streets
and ruined buildings almost hidden by snow, for
some time we followed a very steep road cut in the rock
till we reached the Fort of Tiaret.

"This establishment, founded two or three years ago
by General de Lamoricière, is situated on a ruin which
is both important and curious. It is that which bounds
the Tell to the south. This 'Tell' is a tract of fertile
land stretching the whole length of Algeria along the
sea shores, and is about forty leagues broad. Where
it ceases, the land can no longer be cultivated, but
serves as pasture to the flocks. It is impossible to
imagine a more abrupt transition. The 'Tell' stops
at the foot of a wall of rocks, which in some places is
quite vertical, and more than twelve hundred feet high;
these rocks are called Kefs. There are only a few of
which the summit can be reached. When you get to
the top you find a totally different country, and quite a
different vegetation. It is a region of high latitudes,
the country of the Hanyades. Turning round, you see
beneath you the whole Tell, with its richly cultivated
plains; while on the other side you see around you, on
this high level, grassy plains undulating like the waves
of the sea, in the midst of which rise, like islands, the
mountains of Serson and Djebel-Amour. On and above
these Kefs live the pastoral Arabs with their innumer-

able flocks and herds, up to the great desert of Sahara ; but a great deal of this region is still completely unknown.

"To come back to Tiaret. It is situated at the entrance of the gorge of Gertoufa. This position is one of extreme importance, because it commands the principal highway of the pastoral Arabs, who go down to sell their beasts in the ' Tell ' and to buy there the grain which they need. The occupation of this position, therefore, is a guarantee for their submission. The fort is in command of a first-rate officer, M. de Pontevés, brother of the Marquis de Sabran, a most excellent man in every way. He received me in the kindest manner, and wanted to induce me to stay even longer than my forced residence with him, which was upwards of a month. The garrison generally consists of two or three hundred men, but a column of upwards of a thousand, commanded by M. Charras, an old pupil of the Polytechnic College which played so important a part in the July Revolution, were also there, having been forced to take shelter from the cold and the snow, which are so terrible in these high regions. We were then extremely crowded. M. de Pontevés had put three officers in his dining-room, a company of grenadiers in his drawing-room, and had taken the Commandant Charras and myself into his own bed-room, where we all three eat, lived, and slept. Heavy snow having come on the day after my arrival, I was forced to remain there a whole month, not being able to leave till the 26th. The cold was so intense that many of the Arabs were frozen round the camp. A courtier, bringing letters from Djebel-Amour, had his feet frozen, and died of tetanus two days later.

"On the 22nd M. Charras received tidings from

Mostaganem that three '*Douars*,' of the tribe of the Flittas, who had not yet submitted to the French, and who had been fruitlessly pursued for two years, had come and encamped within five or six leagues of Tiaret. Amongst them was an important chief, Mustapha-ben-Snoussi, noted for the murder of several officers and soldiers.

"As soon as he had received this intelligence the Commandant Charras sent a spy to obtain exact information as to the position and strength of these *Douars*. When he returned and was questioned several times as to the accuracy of his report, and whether his word were to be relied upon, he answered : 'You may trust me. I am an honest man, and devoted to you. Say to me, "Go and bring me the head of your father," and in an hour I will bring it to you in my saddle-bags!' I quote his words, which were spoken with all the warmth of injured innocence, to give you a specimen of Arab character.

"All necessary information having been obtained, a small force of a hundred cavalry and five hundred infantry started at midnight for the *Douars*. The weather was fine, and we marched by a beautiful moonlight in the deepest silence. We went down the Gorge of Gertroufa, seeing in the distance the snow-covered top of the 'Ouamseris' mountain ('Eye of the World'), which I had seen for the first time from Medeah, and which seemed like a great phantom. At daybreak we were on the banks of the Oued-Temda, and heard, at a few hundred steps beyond us, the barking of the dogs in the encampment which we were about to storm. The cavalry galloped forward. In less than a quarter of an hour the whole camp was surrounded while the inhabitants of the tents were still

fast asleep. There were only one or two shots fired at
those who tried to escape, but there was no resistance.
The surprise was complete. You cannot imagine what
it was to hear the cries of distress of these poor people,
who knew well what to expect. They were all turned out
of their tents, men, women, children and flocks ; and all
carefully guarded. Then the soldiers, going in, took
whatever they pleased, the neighbouring Arabs joining
in the pillage, for they all do this sort of thing to one
another. Very soon a few broken pots and some
barley scattered on the ground were all that remained
of what, a few minutes before, were the riches of more
than a hundred families. Nothing can be sadder than
such a sight. The lowing of the flocks and herds, the
cry of the camels, the jests of the soldiers at each fresh
discovery of hidden treasure, the indifferent attitude
assumed by the prisoners, who seemed accustomed to
this kind of operation—which every Arab goes through
once or twice in his life—all made upon me a most
painful impression.

"At last, when there was nothing more to take, not
even the tents, which the neighbouring Arabs hastened
to appropriate, we resumed our march homewards,
driving before us three thousand sheep, a hundred
camels, three or four hundred bullocks, cows and
calves, forty horses and as many mules, and two
hundred and odd prisoners, from whom even the
greater portion of their clothing had been taken, in
spite of the efforts of the officers to prevent it.
Nothing could be more miserable than to see the
women carrying their children on their backs, most of
whom were at the breast, while the men never
attempted to help them in any one way. Towards
two or three o'clock in the morning we were back at

Tiaret. In a few days all but the chiefs of these poor people will be sent away to the country where they laboured in the autumn. They tell me that they are sure to have some money concealed in a safe hiding-place. But with the sufferings they will have to endure in the meanwhile only the strongest children will survive. And unhappily it is only by proceedings of this rigorous nature that the French can act upon the Arabs and compel their submission. . . .

" I took the same road to return from Tiaret to Oran ; but this time the weather was fine, and I had no trouble or accident."

"ALGIERS, *20th March,* 1845.

" . . . I came back here on the 17th, at six o'clock in the morning, after a delicious navigation of thirty-six hours on a sea as smooth as glass, and by a glorious moonlight. We followed the coast almost all the way at only a quarter of a league distance. One saw all the sinuosities of the ground and of the mountains, as if one had been on a river. The ship which had been announced at Oran not having made its appearance, I gave up my plan of passing the Holy Week at Carthagena, in spite of the attraction of the magnificent ceremonies still in use in Spain, where Catholic worship is seen in all its splendour. The Cathedral here is very well kept, and this evening I assisted at the 'Tenebræ,' which were very well chaunted.

" Before leaving Oran General de Lamoricière made me breakfast with the famous Trumpeter, Escoffier, who allowed himself to be taken prisoner by Abdel-Kader himself, by giving his horse to his captain, whose own animal had just been killed under him. 'You are more useful than I to the squadron,' he exclaimed. 'Take my horse, and save yourself.

There is no harm in my being taken.' To be taken
prisoner by the Arabs, one must remember, was, in
general, equivalent to a horrible death.   This brave
fellow was dragged about for eighteen months, through
all the Empire of Morocco.   He told us the most
interesting things about his captivity.   One day a
Morocco officer, belonging to the army which was
afterwards defeated at Isly, came to pay a visit to
Abdel-Kader, and hearing that he had a French
prisoner in his tent asked to see him.   Escoffier had
his trumpet with him, and was asked to play it.   He
instantly sounded a charge.   The officer asked what
that meant ?   Escoffier replied through the interpreter,
' Tell him that when he hears that music the best
thing he can do will be to turn his horse and fly.'
The officer, furious at this answer, wanted to have
him bastinadoed, but Abdel-Kader would not allow it,
and added, to his still greater displeasure, that the
Morocco troops would not fail to fly at the sound of the
French trumpet ! Another day Abdel-Kader proposed to
give him a horse and three wives, and to make him an
officer of regulars, and various other advantages, if he
would only become a Mussulman.   'I will betray
neither my God nor my country !'   replied Escoffier.
' You had better cut off my head at once.'   ' Be at
peace,' replied the Emir; 'I have no intention of
cutting off your head, and I would much rather hear
you speak like that than if you had accepted my proposals, and the next day deserted with the horse I had
given you !'   Escoffier always speaks of the Emir in
terms of the greatest respect.   One feels that he is a
man of immense influence over all those who come
near him.   Escoffier assured us that if he had not had
a letter bearing his seal they would have murdered

him a hundred times in the Rif, in spite of the escort
he had from the Emperor of Morocco.

" I think of remaining on here till the return of the
Marshal, and then make some expeditions."

*   *   *   *   *

On his return to Algiers Xavier frequented all the
Holy Week services at the Cathedral, comparing them
with those in Spain, which he had so much enjoyed
the year before. Each excursion that he made gave
him some opportunity for exercising his faith and
charity. One day he found a dying Arab child on
the borders of the desert. He took it up on his horse,
and baptized it at the first spring he came across. On
another occasion he found an Arab abandoned by his
tribe, and dying of thirst. He took care of him, as the
good Samaritan did to the wounded man on the road to
Jericho. His provisions on the road were always
shared with his soldiers, or with any whom he found
in need on the way. Very often he left himself
scarcely enough to keep body and soul together.

Each engagement with the enemy added to his reputation for bravery and coolness. In 1845 he formed
part of the expedition to Aurés with General Bedeau.
One of the most brilliant battles was that of d'Aydoussa,
under General Comman. At the hottest moment of
the fight M. de Mérode rushed to the front, and for
more than four hours held a difficult and dangerous
post in spite of the Arab fire. The greater part of
the men with him were either killed or wounded, but
he seemed to bear a charmed life, and was almost the
only man who escaped. Though not wounded his
clothes were simply riddled with shot, and two balls
passed through his sleeve and his epaulet. After this

E

feat (which was on the 20th of May, 1845), he was
sent to the garrison at Tlemcen, where he passed
several months with General Cavaignac and Colonels
Charras and Forest.

But his family were becoming impatient for his
return to Brussels. He was just twenty-five, and
many electoral bodies thought of him for their repre-
sentative. The Queen of the Belgians was constant
in her inquiries after him, declaring that after this
last expedition to Kabylia it was his duty to leave
Africa, and not expose so precious a life to the intense
heat of summer. His step-mother, while giving him
all these details, added, "I do not know when we
shall have you back as a member of Parliament, but I
should like that career for you, as I think it would
give you some things in which you are still wanting.
Moderation and deference are two qualities indispensable to youth : by them one gains a great deal,
and one becomes acceptable to every one. Such
Christian courtesy is indispensable also in a de
Mérode." . . . She ends her letter with these words :
"Like your Father, I pray to God every day that He
may guard you from all harm, and I implore of you
to deserve it."

Xavier returned to Belgium towards the end of
1845, and resumed his garrison life. But he dreamed
of other things, and his vague ambition was not satisfied.
Charles de Montalembert wanted him to volunteer for
the war in the Sonderbund, as we see by the following
answer to his proposal :—

"BRUSSELS, 26*th December*, 1845.

"I have thought seriously over what you say about
Switzerland ; but you have not touched upon the

great difficulty. How could I obtain leave from the Government to take part in such a war, after all the laws which forbid one to serve in a foreign country without the consent of the king; and especially in a war which will make such a stir throughout Europe? As to other obstacles, I need not speak of them; for as to the effect it would produce on the foolish and idle members of society, I am supremely indifferent. Thank God! I feel myself now above what such people choose to think or say; but what does really stop me is my military duty. Tell me how you would look upon it from that point of view; for I agree with you that I do not see any cause on this earth for which one would sacrifice one's life with greater pleasure.

"I don't know if you have read in the *Revue de Bruxelles*, of December, an article written *Aux Abonnés*, which I gave to the editor, whom I found sadly discouraged, and ready to give up this publication, which is falling off day by day. I will send you also the new prospectus which I have tried to draw up, as soon as it is printed. I think that with a choice of articles, which one can get from various sources, it would be possible to make a most interesting Review. It would fight against the popular literature of the day, which is only fitted to destroy all spirit of nationality and religion in the country, and to falsify all right ideas."

Montalembert's proposal had no result; but Xavier went on confiding to his brother-in-law all his tastes for higher and religious subjects, not without mingling with them some thoughts of an ecclesiastical vocation.

" LACKEN, 25*th March*, 1846.

" MY DEAREST CHARLES—

"I have seen with delight your admirable
speech upon Poland. What a gift you have of being able
to *move human souls !* Mine was simply transported
while reading your inspired words, doing justice as they
did both to her patriots and her martyrs. Each time
that I read what you have said, and especially this
time, I feel myself another man, and you might do
with me what you would. I have just been reading a
pamphlet of M. Nisard's on 'Parisian plain Chaunt,'
which interested me very much. I recommend to
you, if you have not already read it, the note on page
twenty on the singing at St. Sulpice, which I think
is very ill-used ! I am going to try and get it inserted
in the *Revue de Bruxelles.* Adieu, my dearest brother
and guide, adieu !"

A few months later his correspondence with M. de
Montalembert takes a still more religious tone. One
feels that this grand and noble soul is detaching itself
more and more from earthly things.

" BRUSSELS, 14*th December*, 1846.

" . . . . You ask me what I am doing. I am
waiting patiently till God points out to me what I should
do. In the meantime, I go on quietly with my military
duties. It is possible that I may be elected a member
of Parliament at the June elections. They are going to
augment the number of representatives in proportion to
the population, and it is very possible that I shall be
one of those elected. Until then, it is only at a fire
that one can be of any use ! (He had just saved a
number of people in a great fire in Brussels.) An

insurance company has just sent me a silver medal, and I am told I am to have another in silver gilt from the Government. Such are, since my return from Algeria, the only distinctions which I have been able to win!

" Good-bye, my dear and excellent brother. I love you very deeply, and I cannot help groaning when I see you sometimes misunderstood and badly supported. Yes, you are the man whom I love the most in the world, and with whom I can say that one day is worth a thousand elsewhere. *Dies una super millia !* And when I see to what annoyances, troubles, and deceptions men like you are exposed, I cannot express how great is my discouragement, or all the disgust I feel for the world. I seem to realize more and more that it is *God* ALONE that one must love. GOD ALONE that one must have in view in this Valley of Tears! Also, every day I feel more drawn to a thought of which, if you remember, we talked one day between Gibraltar and Ceuta. It is of that idea I should have liked to have talked to you, if I could have seen you soon, as I wished. You desired me to go and make war in Algeria. You would do much better to decide me to make it against the enemies of Jesus Christ and His Church!"

CHAPTER IV.

From 1847 to 1851.

Death of the Comtesse Felix de Mérode—Xavier's Departure
for Rome—His Ecclesiastical Vocation—His Studies—
His Feelings—The Roman Revolution—Xavier Receives
the Diaconate—He Posts up the Bull of Excommunication
—His Noble Conduct during the Siege of Rome—His
Captivity—His Deliverance—The Entry of the French—
The Mission of M. de Corcelles—Xavier's Zeal in seconding
his Views—He is ordained Priest, and becomes a Military
Chaplain—Pius IX. attaches him to his Person as
Cameriere Segreto—Correspondence with Montalembert on
the Law of 1850.

ONE sees by Xavier's last letter to what end his thoughts
were turned—a cruel loss hastened his determination.

In the month of March, 1847, Count Felix de Mérode
lost his second wife, who had only given him one
daughter, but who had been the most loving, devoted,
and wise mother to her four step-children, and especially
to Xavier. Her death was worthy of her life. She
left this world with so much resignation, fervour, and
piety, that she left behind her more consolation than
sorrow. No one felt it more deeply than the brilliant
young officer, whose military glories had so flattered
her maternal pride, but whom she loved even more for
his piety than for his courage. The death-bed of this
loving mother still further helped to detach him from
the vanities of earth, and the first grace she obtained

for him was a resolution to embrace the Ecclesiastical State.

Charles de Montalembert approved highly of this decision, and just as he had congratulated him on his military successes in Africa, so now he encouraged him in every way to go to Rome and study for the priesthood.

This departure took place in October, 1847. Two of his fellow-countrymen, Mgr. Aerts and F. Janssens, welcomed him with the interest which his pious vocation inspired, and with all the deference due to his merits and his great name. He consulted Abbé Gerbet and F. Ventura, hesitated for a short time between the Religious life and that of the Secular Clergy, and finally decided on the latter. As soon as he had made his decision, he wrote to his father in the following terms:—

"Rome, 30*th November*, 1847.

"At the moment when I am about to enter on a new career I come to implore you, my good and dear father, to grant me your blessing. I ask your pardon very humbly for all the trouble I have given you, and for all the faults of which I have been guilty towards you.

"You have too often made me see the vanity of all things in this miserable world for me to fear that my present resolution will cause you too keen a sorrow. I understand what you will feel to be painful in our separation for some years, especially after the cruel trial which God has so lately sent you; but I hope that my stay in Rome may attract you to the Eternal City.

"Adieu! my good Father. I enclose in this letter my resignation of my lieutenancy, begging you to be

kind enough to give it to the Colonel of my regiment." . . . .

Xavier would have liked to begin by the study of
St. Thomas's "Summa." But F. Janssens dissuaded him, and made him follow the course of theology in the Roman College. The more he advanced
in science and piety, the more his vocation was
strengthened and developed. He wrote all the details
of his new life to his family with his usual frankness,
congratulating himself on having listened to Montalembert, who had saved him from marriage, to make
him follow a higher life. But in writing to the great
Catholic orator himself he would not make him responsible for his vocation, though he had indirectly
helped it on.

" MY VERY DEAR CHARLES,—

"I hasten to reassure you as to your responsibility regarding my present resolution. Even if it had
been in consequence of your advice I should never have
reproached you with it, any more than if anything had
happened to me in Algeria. When one follows a counsel
voluntarily, one only does what one wishes. I hasten,
then, to relieve your mind on this subject ; but at the
same time I must add that the way you made me feel
the greatness of the cause and the grandeur of the Church,
with the necessity for devoting one's life to something
better than eating, drinking and sleeping (which few
people seem to understand in these days), very much contributed to my present determination. As for the rest,
I hope God Himself has inspired my vocation, for now I
feel perfectly happy and satisfied."

The good resolution which Xavier had taken to

devote himself entirely to theology could not be altogether carried out in the actual state of Rome, which
was already saddened by revolutionary demonstrations.
The defeat of the Sonderbund, the capitulation of Fri-
bourg and the taking of Lucerne were celebrated as
triumphs even by those who still cheered the Pope.
They went to congratulate the Swiss Consul, and
Xavier, in writing to his father asks, if that were
what Père Lacordaire expected when he said, " That
God wished to give men the spectacle of a Christian
revolution !" He adds—

" For the last few days they insult the Jesuits as
they pass through the streets, wishing them ' accidents,' that is, attacks of apoplexy. The mob cried
out in their ears—' *Viva Gioberti !* the *Christian Philosopher !* " The enthusiasm for this Gioberti goes on
increasing. They sell portraits in the streets which,
seen obliquely, represent on one side, the Pope, and
on the other, the ' *great Philosopher.*' The Radical
party is evidently gaining ground. The Pope is
in a terrible position, between those who see no
safety but in Austria, and those who only make use of
the cry ' *Viva Pio Nono !* ' to cover their evil designs.
Until now, no one dares to think of upsetting the
Pope. The worst among them feel that he gives
Rome an importance which nothing could replace.
But they want to make him a Constitutional King,
which would end by placing him at the mercy of any
Frère-Orban who might present himself."

The year 1848 hastened Xavier's ecclesiastical
noviciate. The triumphs of Pius IX. were changing
into trials, and the Revolution of February, which
had its rebound throughout Europe, was specially
felt at Rome. Xavier followed all the vicissitudes

of public affairs with intense anxiety, encouraged
the good papers and took an active part in the efforts
made by the Pope to defend himself from the Revolutionists.   The Jesuits, as usual, were the first
victims. Xavier defended them in his cassock as he
had done in his uniform in Belgium, and wrote on the
24th of April to his brother-in-law :—

" I thank you for your kind letter, in spite of the
exaggerated view you take of what I did for those poor
Jesuits. I own that the strongest feeling I had at the
moment of their departure was shame to find myself
a tranquil spectator of such an iniquity. It was like
the feeling of a troop watching a battle, and yet unable
to take part against the enemy."

The Comte de Montalembert, who had been turned
out of the House of Lords by the February Revolution,
was elected, that same day, member for the Doubs in
the National Assembly, which had proclaimed the
Republic and tried to maintain it.   Having made
neither advances nor compliments to the new Government, he kept his proud independence, and spoke words
at the Tribune, the eloquence and truth of which the
melancholy days of June only confirmed.   His speech
delighted Xavier, who wrote to him on the 6th of July,
1848, as follows :—

" My Dearest Charles,—

" I have hardly the courage to congratulate you
on your magnificent speech, which must prove to you
that one must never despair, and that you have still
a great work to do, both for God and men. I think
we ought to thank Providence to have let us be born
in a time where there are so many occasions of devoting one's self, and of performing actions, which to

generous souls are easier than little practices of ordinary virtue."

After receiving Montalembert's account of those
terrible days he writes again :—

"I have just received your most interesting letter
of the 28th of June, which helped to enlighten me as
to the terrible gravity of the events which happened
under your very eyes. What I admire in the midst
of all this is, as you say, that religion seems to be the
only thing which survives the overturn of all other
institutions, which will stop God only knows when!
How eternally strong is this so-called weakness of the
Church! She has neither money nor power, nor
diplomatic ability. Yet alone she rises amidst the
anarchy which swallows up all that was most powerful
here below. I own that I tremble at thinking of you
in this cauldron; but I do not pity you. One is too
happy when God gives one a clear duty to fulfil—a
duty which demands the entire devotion and sacrifice
of one's own person. It is a fight in which one is
sure to win, provided one always marches forward."

On the 17th of September, 1848, Xavier received
the tonsure, and on the 23rd of the same month the
first two minor orders. He wore his ecclesiastical
habit with all the more fidelity as this dress became
the object of suspicion and hostility to the Revolutionary party, who were beginning to triumph in
Rome. But under his cassock the African soldier felt
his heart burn within him. Until the end of the fatal
16th of November he could contain himself. On that
day he hears that the Prime Minister Rossi has been
assassinated at the foot of the staircase of the Quirinal,

and that the Vicar of Jesus Christ, abandoned by all
those who were bound to defend him, had only eighty
soldiers around him of his faithful Swiss Guard.
Xavier, only thinking of his faith and courage, throws
aside his cassock, takes other clothes, and with two
pistols concealed in his vest flies with a friend to the
Quirinal.   Sterbini and his emissaries are there, and
are spreading terror in every quarter of the town.
When he gets to the square of Monte Cavallo Xavier
finds it deserted up to the Obelisk.   But there barri-
cades had been thrown up, defended by armed men.
M. de Mérode feigns not to see them, and without
hastening or slackening his pace he reaches the gate
of the Palace.   There a hundred guns are pointed at
him.   He strives in vain to open the door, and only
yields before the sheer impossiblity of getting into the
Quirinal.   It was only by the sheer mercy of Providence that he escaped ; for Mgr. Palma, Chamberlain
of his Holiness, had just been assassinated in the
Palace.

The assassination of de Rossi, the flight of Pius IX.
to Gäeta, and the triumph of the Mazzinians in the
Eternal City, might have dissuaded a less noble soul
than Xavier's from remaining in Rome to pursue his
ecclesiastical studies.   But he was not shaken for one
moment in his resolution, and only sought how he
could make himself more worthy of receiving the last
steps which lead to the priesthood.   The day when he
received the last of the minor orders (23rd December,
1848), he wrote to his grandmother, the Marquise de
Grammont, sending her at the same time his good
wishes for the New Year :—

" I could not close this day (so full to me of precious impressions) without sending you my heartiest

wishes for 1849—the year on which you will have
entered by the time this reaches you. This morning
I received the two last minor orders, and have nothing
now between me and the day when I shall take the
most irrevocable and indissoluble of vows.

"I only wish I could translate for you the magnificent words which the Church places for this ceremony
in the mouth of her Bishop. The further I advance
on this road, of which the exterior is so sad, the more
deeply do I feel the treasures of mercy and the abundance of consolations which God has reserved for those
that fear Him. I prayed as well as I could for you,
dear grandmamma! You who have been, to us all, the
instrument which God made use of so that we might
know and love Him. I could not tell you how many
things I now recall, which had made little impression
upon me at the time you said them, but which now
have returned to me in their full force, and have greatly
helped me."

The more the Revolutionary party committed sacri-
leges in Rome, the more Xavier felt himself strengthened
in his vocation ; and his stay in Rome became dearer
to him from the very fact of the dangers he had to
brave. Ordained sub-Deacon on the 3rd of March,
1849, he wrote the following answer to Mde. de
Montalembert, who has entreated him to return to
Belgium to complete his ecclesiastical studies in greater
peace, and to follow the common way :—

"ROME, *8th of March*, 1849.

"I have the conviction that God speaks to us
clearly in such matters, if we will only listen to the voice
of conscience. All that I have seen since I came here
has made me understand more and more the utility,

even in a temporal point of view, of submission and obedience, and has shown me why the Church has such a horror of innovators. This has inspired me with an absolute confidence in traditions which so many fools have thought they could lightly set aside. I am, therefore, very far from fancying that life in a seminary is useless; but I think also that there are cases in which it is less necessary than in others, and that is why the Church has not made this course a *sine quâ non* condition for the reception of holy Orders. There are many other regulations which were fixed by the Council of Trent, and which are not observed, because the Church has found grave reasons for not applying them. I have, therefore, no anxiety whatever about following a usage universally received and adopted at Rome, and which may most legitimately be followed by those who, desiring to receive holy Orders, are older than ordinary candidates. Adieu! my dearest sister. I have given you a long homily. But, believe me, I do not wish to act under any illusion. Even if I could persuade the whole world, what would that serve me before Him who will judge us all, and more severely than others those who are called to serve Him in the ecclesiastical state? I try, therefore, to do my poor best, as conscientiously as I can; and no one knows more than I how very poor that best is! But at least my soul is in peace, which is more necessary than anything else, and which I am doing my best to preserve. Oh! my God! I feel that I ought to lead a far more perfect life; but I have confidence that God will lead me further on if He wills, as He has already brought me, bit by bit, to where I now am. Be thoroughly persuaded that I have no other wish, on my return to Belgium, than to place myself in the hands of my Archbishop, who will do with me whatever he finds me capable of doing. I feel that an active life is necessary for me; but I have not the smallest intention of throwing myself into any extraordinary enterprise. If it please God, I shall ever show as much respect, and as hearty an obedience, to my ecclesiastical superiors as I have shown towards my military chiefs."

A month later (the 7th April, 1849,) he received Deacon's Orders. He had already expressed a hope of this to his sister in terms which fully reveal his faith and courage, which events in Rome were daily to strengthen and confirm.

"ROME, 24*th March*, 1848.

"I hope to receive Deacon's Orders on Holy Saturday, although I am not yet quite sure. I fancy you will say I am going too quickly! At other times I should have waited till Trinity; but in these days one is so little sure of what may happen. What a grace to be made a deacon in St. John Lateran's, in this great Basilica where so many saints have been ordained, in this city where St. Lawrence exercised his ministry! It is there that I am going to receive the order of the first of martyrs, and this consideration has decided me."

Hardly had he received the Diaconate than he gave a striking proof of his fidelity and devotion to the Church. The dethronement of the Pope had been decided upon and declared by the Revolutionary Government, and the Pope had replied to this insult by a sentence of excommunication. The Abbé de Mérode seized the Bull, gave a pot of paste to a workman who

followed him, and in the middle of the day posted up
the excommunication on the doors of the Basilicas and
of all the public buildings of Rome.

The siege of Rome placed his courage and charity in
a still stronger light. The Convent of the Ladies of
the Sacred Heart at the Trinità dei Monti had been
invaded by the Mazzinians, who had established themselves there ; and the poor nuns, who had fled to a
little house in the lower part of Rome, had had no time
to carry away anything with them. Xavier determined
at least to save the sacred vessels. He went to the
Convent, and profiting by a moment when the guards
were playing at cards, he got into the enclosure. A
soldier met him, and asked him what he was doing
there. He promptly replied, " What you are doing
yourself. I am taking a walk." His confident tone
and cool manner reassured the soldier, who let him
pass, and himself walked away. But Xavier, taking
advantage of these few moments of liberty, flew into the
church and the sacristy, opened the cupboards and the
tabernacle, crammed all the chalices and ciboriums into
his pockets, and tied the rest in a pocket-handkerchief,
which he concealed under his great cloak. He managed
to get out as quickly as he had got in, and ran with all
possible speed by the Pincio to the poor ladies of the
Sacred Heart. Unfortunately his packet was badly
tied. As he arrived at the Piazza del Popolo, in the
midst of a crowd of soldiers who were playing at "Mora,"
one of the patens escaped, and went rolling into the
middle of the square, making a great sound as it fell.
Xavier, seeing the soldiers hesitating, determined to
brave them, and, instead of making his escape, walked
quietly to pick up his paten, and then, resuming his
usual quick walk, arrived unmolested at his destination,

bearing his treasures to the poor nuns, who were over-
joyed at his success.

But this was only the prelude of the siege. Very
soon fighting began in the streets, and the priests fell
under the Garibaldian swords, who felt that their ruin
was at hand. Nothing stopped the charity of the Abbé
de Mérode. In spite of the balls and bullets of the
French Army, which rained in certain quarters, he
braved the danger, rushing forward to save the wounded,
carrying them in his arms to the hospitals, and caring
for them without distinction of friend or foe. His
extraordinary charity impressed even the Revolutionary
Party, who allowed him for some days to devote himself
to this glorious work in peace. But one evening he
was arrested, with two other French Ecclesiastics, who,
like him, were attending the wounded and dying. One
was Mgr. Luquet, Bishop of Hesebon. They were
thrown into a horrible dungeon, on a level with the
Tiber, where they were exposed to every kind of insult
and ill-usage. The gaoler who brought them their
wretched food threatened them with every sort of horror,
assuring them that if the French succeeded in entering
Rome they would all be massacred before the conquerors could deliver them. In vain the Abbé de
Mérode pleaded his Belgian nationality. No one would
either listen to him or forward his letters. One morning
the daughter of the gaoler, who was only ten years old,
brought the prisoners their breakfast. Shocked at the
misery to which they were reduced, the poor child began
to cry. Xavier took advantage of this to beg her to
take to the Belgian Legation a little scrap of paper in
which he had been able to scrawl some words describing
his imprisonment and the place of his detention. An
hour later his commission was executed. The Minister

F

flew to the Revolutionary Tribunal, and obtained an
order for the instant release of the Abbé de Mérode.
But as he refused to go out alone, they were compelled
to free the French priests also who had shared his
captivity.

On the 5th of July the French troops entered
Rome, and General Oudinot took all the necessary
measures to ensure the public tranquillity. But it
was not enough to win this material victory over the
Revolutionists. The town had to be reorganized, and
the ruins of the siege repaired, besides preparing
everything for the return of the Pope, without
imposing upon him conditions which were incompatible
with his sovereign rights. This was the work of
M. François de Corcelles, a deputy of the National
Assembly, who had been sent as an envoy extraordinary
from France to Rome. His just, wise, and liberal
spirit, the relations of his family with the highest
French aristocracy, and his deep and earnest faith, of
which he made no secret, gave him a peculiar fitness
for this difficult work, which any other diplomat would
have found almost impossible. He had installed himself
during the siege near the Portese Gate, in a house where
he could take account of everything with the extreme
advance guard of the French Army. He entered
Rome with the victorious troops, and at once occupied
himself with the great work of reparation which was
to be accomplished under the French flag. The Abbé
de Mérode joined him directly, and by his zeal, his
incredible activity, and his wonderful tact, greatly
assisted the Ambassador in his arduous task. His
relationship with M. de Corcelles entitled him to
every confidence; but when the diplomat got to know
his young relation better, he appreciated him even

more. Xavier worked hard day and night, and hardly found time to write these few words to M. de Montalembert :—

"MY DEAREST CHARLES,—

"Things are going on better than we dared hope. Rome is regaining its calm by degrees. Corcelles is admirable : pray use all your influence to prevent his return as soon as he wishes. No one but himself could bring about the state of things which we all so earnestly desire. A number of people have already declared their adhesion to the French programme, and the decree suppressing the Republican enemy and flag has been received with supreme indifference. I am running about all day long, from one pillaged convent and seminary to the other, which leaves me scarcely an instant in which to scrawl these few lines to you. I have only one feeling at this moment ; and that is of the overwhelming importance of the prolongation of de Corcelles' mission here. He has so just a spirit, and above all such genuine devotion to the Church and to all that is good and right."

The French Army in Rome soon began to suffer terribly from the heat and fevers of the autumn season. The hospitals were filled with soldiers, and the attendance upon them, even when not dangerous, was most fatiguing and difficult. Xavier then entreated to be raised to the priesthood, so that he might act as almoner to these poor fellows. This satisfaction was not refused to his zealous, loving heart, and in a letter to Mde. de Montalembert he gives her the joyful news.

"ROME, 11*th September*, 1849.

" DEAREST ANNA,—

"As I told you in my last letter, I was anxious to hasten the time of my ordination, so as to be of more use to the poor soldiers who are crowded in the hospitals here. The Archbishop of Mechlin having sent me the necessary papers, it will be on Saturday week, that is on the 22nd of September, that I shall be raised to the priesthood. I have just passed my examination in presence of the Cardinal Vicar, and now no obstacle stands in the way of the great and solemn moment when I shall be made a priest—*a Priest for eternity* after the order of Melchisedec! To-morrow evening I am going into retreat for ten days. Pray hard for me during that time, or at least as soon as you receive this letter. I tremble at thinking how soon I shall arrive at this stage, but I cannot express my happiness at the feeling that I am so near this much-desired term of all my hopes and prayers."

The day after his ordination the Abbé de Mérode said his first Mass over the body of St. Peter in the Subterranean Church, in presence of a chosen body of friends, of whom M. de Corcelles held the first place. His heart overflowed with joy and thankfulness, and this joy quite lit up his face. One would have said that an angel was at the altar, for his modesty equalled his piety. This was the impression of all those who assisted at this his first Mass; but neither time nor habit ever diminished his extraordinary fervour. As he appeared the first morning he offered the Holy Sacrifice, so he was always found for four-and-twenty years—that is, pro-

foundly penetrated with the grandeur of the sacred
mysteries, and by his attitude, his looks and his words,
impressing upon every one around him the deep faith
of his soul in the Real Presence. A pilgrimage to
Loretto was his act of thanksgiving. He went there
with the Abbé de Villiers de l'Isle d'Adam, and found
instantly an occasion for devoting himself to the sacerdotal ministry. A month after his ordination he
writes to his sister from Civita Castellana as follows :—

"*22nd October*, 1849.

" I reproach myself every day, dearest and much
loved sister, for having left you for so long, for so very
long a time without a word from me. The life I have
been leading at Rome has been so busy and so agitated
in every sense, that that, added to my distaste for
writing, which you know of old, has prevented my ever
sending you a decent letter. Now I am at Civita
Castellana since last night, and God only knows for
how long.

" Passing here with the Abbé de l'Isle d'Adam on
our way to Loretto we saw how many sick men were
abandoned in the hospital, for there is a garrison of
1,200 to 1,400 French here. The Abbé, who is very
much occupied with the Roman hospitals, implored me
to come and look after the poor fellows here. I spoke
of it to my Confessor, P. Lacroix, who highly approved
of the idea. The Vicar-General of the diocese at once
gave me the necessary permissions. So here I am,
making my first start as a military chaplain. Although
I only got here last night, I have already two penitents. . . . .

" M. de Corcelles is overwhelmed with work, in the
midst of which he shows the same uprightness of con-

duct, the same elevation of feeling, and the same sound judgment as ever. I admire him every day more and more : it would be really deplorable if he were to leave his post at this moment."

M. de Corcelles' mission, after having been sadly hindered by a letter of the President of the French Republic to Edgar Ney, was singularly helped by a speech of Montalembert's. The great Catholic orator had discussed the conditions which people pretended to exact from Pius IX. before his return, and recalled the ingratitude with which his people had repaid him, the painful experience he had made of Constitutional Government, and the necessity he was under to renounce it for the future. He exclaimed, "It is the crimes, the assassinations which have been committed in the name of Liberty which have driven to despair the hearts most devoted to her cause. You have stopped and turned away the admirable current which inspired us old Liberals with so much confidence and admiration. You have dethroned Kings, it is true, but you have more surely dethroned true Liberty !" Then coming back to Pius IX. and the Roman Expedition, he obtained, by a majority of 467 votes against 168, the supplementary credits for the French Army in Rome, ending his speech with a peroration which has remained one of the finest bits of French eloquence in the nineteenth century.

"History will state that, a thousand years after Charlemagne had gained immortal renown by reestablishing the Pontificate, and fifty years after Napoleon, although at the summit of his power and *prestige*, failed in trying to undo the work of his immortal predecessor, History will say, I repeat, that

France remained faithful to her ancient traditions and deaf to odious provocations. She will say that thirty thousand men, under the command of the worthy son of one of the heroes in our great Imperial campaigns, left the shores of their own country to re-establish in Rome, in the person of the Pope, rights and interests which are both French and European. She will say what Pius IX. himself wrote in his letter of congratulation to General Oudinot—' The French Army has triumphed over the enemies of human society.' Yes, that will be the verdict of History ; for it will be one of the greatest glories of France in the nineteenth century. This glory you would not like to lessen, to tarnish, to eclipse, by embarking yourselves in a tissue of contradictions, complications, and inexplicable inconsequences ? Do you know what would for ever sully the French Flag ? It would be to lift it against the Cross, against the Tiara which it has just delivered ; it would be to transform the French soldiers from protectors of the Pope into oppressors ; it would be to exchange the glorious *rôle* of Charlemagne for the pitiable counterfeit of Garibaldi ! "

The emotion produced in the Legislative Assembly by this speech communicated itself to all Europe. One felt that the letter to Edgar Ney would henceforth be a dead letter: that the return of the Pope was assured, and that he would be free to manage his own estates, for their greater good, as it would seem best to his paternal wisdom. On reading these beautiful words of Montalembert Pius IX. was delighted : tears came into his eyes, and looking round him in the humble room of his exile at Gaëta, he exclaimed, " I have nothing here beautiful enough to send him ; but I will write to him. That will be better." He wrote accordingly on the 13th of November, 1849, and in his letter was this sentence—"Your words will live for ever in the memory of all honest men."

No one enjoyed the triumphs of his brother-in-law more than the Abbé de Mérode, and no one was more delighted at this expression of the gratitude of Pius IX. He wrote to Montalembert :—

"How happy your last triumph has made me I need not say ! A triumph so complete and so glorious ; for now your name is irrevocably coupled with the cause of the Church, not only in France and Europe, but throughout the whole world. I never doubted, even when you were most inclined to despair of the future, that God reserved you for great things. My uncle Frederick when he was going into battle used to say, '*The brave never die.*' How much truer is this of men who, like you, unite the incomparable gifts of talent, conscience and faith, which are so rarely found together.

"After the marvels of which Providence has made us the witnesses during the last few years,-I feel that henceforward it will be easy to hope and to believe with the most entire confidence in the future of the Church, which, after all, is the only serious pre-occupation here below : and still more in the midst of the universal disillusion about things, which I think is a characteristic of our days. As for me, my life as '*fisher of men*' has begun much sooner than I expected. I know very well that I run the risk of young horses who are worked before the proper age ; but I call to mind the words of St. Dominic, who sold his books to give the price of them to the poor, and exclaimed, '*Can I study on dead skins while the members of Jesus Christ are dying of hunger?*' And I feel I cannot abandon so many poor souls who are so terribly in want of spiritual aid. I am the only priest who can come to help the sick in the Military Hospital here, in which many men die every month. I am quite astonished at the faith I have found in these brave fellows; but what a difference there is between them and their officers, not only as regards faith and heart, but even as regards intelligence! I never before was so much struck by it."

In this obscure post of devotion and self-abnegation the Abbé de Mérode laboured on, while Montalembert encouraged and congratulated him, speaking over and over again in his admirable letters of the joy his conduct gave him. He writes from the château of Villersexel on the 28th of November, 1849:—

"My dearest friend, it is so terribly cold in this old château that I have the greatest difficulty in holding my pen. And yet I, who regret you always and everywhere, regret you still more here, where I have come for some days' rest, and where we could have walked and talked at our ease, even amidst the mud and snow, which is a faithful picture of our poor modern society. You are the man, of all my nearest and dearest, and even of all my friends, with whom I sympathize most. And now that it is all over and done, may I own to you without scruple the egotistical sorrow your sacerdotal vocation gave me, inasmuch as it raises a sort of invisible barrier between you and me, as regards the absolute intimacy which reigned between us, as laymen and soldiers, which we both were. At the same time, I do not doubt for a moment that you did the right thing, both for yourself and for us all; *optimum partem eligisti.* Everything that you have done during and since the siege of Rome shows me that the Hand of God is indeed with you and over you. Your present act of

devotedness at Civita Castellana fills me with admiration
and gratitude towards God and towards yourself. I
had been very wrong to blame the prolongation of your
stay in Rome during the Revolution. This has been a
most valuable occasion for you to study both men and
things in their most important elements ; not only the
French Army in its campaign, but the social, political,
and ecclesiastical organization of the Pontifical States.
If, by some happy combination, you should be able to
second or partially direct the work of moral and
Catholic reform, which Pius IX. must now undertake,
if he wishes his Pontificate to be really glorious, I
shall look upon your career in Italy as more useful and
fruitful for good than it could be anywhere else.

" Do not fail to write to me as often as you can, and
to keep me informed of all your plans and movements,
and, above all, of your impressions on the affairs of
Rome and on those of France. I do not write often
myself, for you know how incompatible my life is with
keeping up a regular correspondence ; but you know
also what advantage and what enjoyment your letters
are to me."

About this time the Abbé de Mérode had been transferred as Almoner to the garrison at Viterbo, where he
lodged in the Capuchin Convent, and chose the poorest
of all the cells for himself. But he was never in it except
to sleep on a miserable pallet, which was more wretched
still. His whole day was spent in the exercise of his
ministry. One saw him going constantly backwards and
forwards from Viterbo to Rome, sitting in the soldiers'
carriages to help the sick or convalescent, and bringing
back food, clothes, medicines, and every imaginable
little comfort for his hospital patients. He would cheer
and amuse the men by the hour with stories of his

African campaigns, and won to God in that way the
most rebel hearts. His kindness and affability, mingled
with his brusque, soldier-like ways, his zeal and
generosity, his character, at once so proud and so
humble, charmed every one with whom he came in
contact. People compared the services he was rendering to the French Army with what his brother-in-law,
Montalembert, was doing by his speeches, and M. de
Corcelles, his cousin, by his diplomatic ability. Certainly, no family had ever deserved greater esteem
both from the Pope and the Church.

It was on the 12th April, 1850, that Pius IX.
returned to Rome. Two days later the Abbé de
Mérode came to his audience to implore his Benediction, and to announce to him that his family had
recalled him to Belgium, and that he was about to
place himself in the hands of the Archbishop of
Mechlin, who was his Ordinary. Pius IX., who saw
him for the first time, but who knew very well his
antecedents and the eminent services he had rendered
to the Church during the Revolution, scarcely allowed
him time to finish his sentence, and then, looking at
him with that deep, penetrating gaze which seemed to
read the very depths of his soul, said, " Do you promise
to obey the Pope ? " " Yes ; certainly ! " replied the
young military chaplain, who could not conceive that
there should be any doubt on such a subject. " Well—
but to obey him in everything ? " " Oh, yes ! certainly,
most Holy Father ! " " Well, it is my wish you should
remain here. I will keep you, and make you my
Cameriere segreto participente." At these words the
Abbé de Mérode was stupefied, and could not forbear
some remonstrance. He pleaded his bad manners,
which were the reverse of those of a courtier ; that he

was not fitted for the post ; that his family had recalled
him, &c.   Pius IX. would listen to no objections, and
only dismissed him, saying playfully, " You have promised to obey, remember.   Go and put on your purple
stockings ! "

Xavier de Mérode had, in fact, no choice but to obey.
This sudden elevation astonished no one save himself
and his family.   But the Marquise de Grammont, his
grandmother, could not conceal her discontent.   She
wrote a very sharp letter to her dear Xavier, reproaching
him for having accepted an honorary position, when
he ought to have asked for a humble one in a little
village, saying that he risked damnation at a Court,
and that a courtier's life was not suitable either for his
health, his youth, or his character.   These indignant
remonstrances arrived in Rome so quickly that he had
not had time to explain to her the cause of his change of
position.   He answered her on the 20th April, however, as follows :—

"I reproach myself, dear grandmamma, for not
having written to you myself about the great change
which has come upon my life—from the poor hospital
at Viterbo to the Palace of the Vatican, where I am
attached to the Person of the Holy Father in the
closest and most intimate manner.   But it was certainly from no choice of mine.   His Holiness insisted
I should be in his service as ' *Cameriere segreto*,'
and he spoke to me in so touching a manner of the
duty and happiness of serving the Vicar of Jesus
Christ that I could not hesitate any longer, but placed
myself in his hands, telling him I would do whatever
he wished.   My functions consist in accompanying
him in his walks or drives, saying Office with him,
introducing the persons to whom he wishes to give

audience, and taking his orders. This places me in continual relation with His Holiness, which is a very great consolation. I told the Pope of your extreme displeasure at my being at his Court; he laughed heartily and said: 'I do not wonder that I had so much difficulty in making you consent. I had a powerful enemy to encounter!'

"The Holy Father is of a goodness towards me which makes me very happy. The pleasure of saying Office with him, and of being always able to approach the Stone on which the Church is built, is immense."

His affection for M. de Corcelles made it a duty on his part to let him know the marks of confidence which Pius IX. had shown him.

"ROME, 30*th April,* 1850.

" MY DEAR COUSIN,—

"I am rather cross with you at having had no news of you for so long; so that it is only from the express wish of the Holy Father that I write to you to-day! You know that, according to your wish, I am now closely attached to his person: he willed it so persistently that there was no way of avoiding so great a consolation. I am consequently installed in the Vatican, alongside of those beautiful Loggias of Raphael which you and I used to study together this time last year.

"The Holy Father has told me to tell you that he received your letter, written in the month of March, and that he was full of regret at not having been able as yet to answer the many kind and good things you had said to him. He has preserved the most agreeable recollection of you, and always speaks of you in the most delightful manner. You can fancy what a plea-

sure it is to me to hear him express himself in such
terms of you, my dear cousin! I cannot say how
grieved I was not to see you on the return of the
Holy Father to Rome, to which you had so ably and
efficiently assisted. I suppose there must always
be a ' but ' in everything : your absence and that
of General Rostolan was the ' but ' on the 20th of
April, 1850. I have already written to Montalembert
about what the Holy Father wished me to tell him ;
as also to MM. de Falloux and Molé. He has had
their letters printed as documents to put in the hands
of the Cardinals who are entrusted with the Education
Law, and as soon as he has time he will answer
them."

The Law of 1850 had been passed. It was important
for its authors, and for the conscience of all Catholics,
that Rome should pronounce without delay on the
use to be made of it. M. de Montalembert wrote to
his brother-in-law on the 6th of May on this subject :—

"I hope you will profit by your frequent relations
with the Holy Father to make him understand that,
if in the matter of the Education Law, he were to
side with the *Univers* against M. de Falloux,
Mgr. Dupanloup, M. Molé, M. Thiers, M. de Vatimes-
nil, M. Berryer and myself, it is all over with France
and with the real Catholic party, as well as with
liberty of teaching. Journalism would then become
the master of the Church, as it already is of the
State. Anonymous writers, without mission, without
right, without any responsibility, now exercise an
absolute dominion over both men and things. It is
the triumph of the modern spirit (under the most
oppressive and anti-pathetic form) over the Catholic

spirit of which the mainspring is *reverence for authority.*

" Certainly, the Falloux Law is not perfect, a better one might have been proposed ; but who could have undertaken to pass it ? The whole question lies in a nutshell. There is not a single member who would not tell you that it was absolutely impossible to induce the Chambers to vote for a law of perfect liberty or even of the separation of State from free education. Our only choice was between the Falloux Law or the *statu quo.* The *Univers* did not hesitate to pronounce in favour of the *statu quo,* against which all the efforts of the Catholic party have been directed for twenty years. Such is the ordinary line of conduct of these imperturbable logicians, who fancy that all is saved when they have printed a more or less eloquent article in their journal, and who sacrifice without the smallest scruple the salvation of souls to polemical exigencies.

" As for me, the strongest argument in favour of the Falloux Law is its adversaries. Against it were ranged all the violent, chimerical and absolute spirits from every camp. Especially was it attacked by the enemies of the Church and of Society, who for once joined hands with a handful of Catholics infected by democratic ideas ; and who preach with M. de Cazalis, that the Church is indifferent to the principles of Socialism, and only reproves its excesses. When I read Cazalis' amendment, which excluded the bishops from all the superior and departmental councils, and which was seconded by men like Jules Favre, Lamartine, Lamennais, Victor Hugo, &c., &c., the whole question was settled, as far as I was concerned. The

sympathy of such men with the doctrines of the
Univers in the matter of teaching, will not that open
the eyes of those in Rome whose business it is to
judge of this matter?

"At any rate, do what you can, and keep me
informed of all that is said and done. Elizabeth made
her first Communion at St. Roch on the 2nd of May;
what a grand day that is for a father's heart! . . .
When will you come to baptize your god-daughter,
Madeleine? She is expecting you impatiently. I
want it to be either at Villersexel or La Roche. . . .
I feel sure that you are as much convinced as I am
that we are on the eve of a formidable crisis. Pray
for me and for all our dear ones. I think the danger
has never been greater."

His wishes were fulfilled. MM. de Falloux, Molé
and Montalembert, who had written to the Pope to
solicit his approbation, received through the Nuncio a
letter from the Cardinal-Secretary of State, approving
of their conduct, and warmly congratulating them on
the success of their efforts. A similar despatch was
addressed, by desire of the Pope, to all the French
Episcopate. In consequence, all dissenting voices
were hushed in the Church of France, and the Law of
1850, which was immediately put in force, resulted in
the opening, that very year, of upwards of a hundred
colleges, the scholars from which, for the last thirty-
four years, have filled our army, navy, bar, magistracy,
and endless commercial and industrial professions.
The Law of 1850 was, with the expedition to Rome,
the great triumph of Christian France and European
civilization. It was one of Mgr. de Mérode's greatest
joys, in the first years of his priesthood, to have been

associated with two such undertakings, and to begin his service with Pius IX. during this memorable year 1850, which witnessed the re-establishment of the Pope on his throne and the triumph of freedom in religious teaching.

CHAPTER V.

From 1850 to 1859.

THE return of the Pope to Rome, which inaugurated
the second half of the nineteenth century in the history of the Catholic Church, had been carried out
under the French Flag and under the auspices of all
the Catholic Powers. It was the re-establishment of
social order and of the European equilibrium. The
new régime lasted ten years. One might have fancied
that it had been re-established on a solid and permanent basis, and that the Pontifical States would remain
in their integrity as guaranteed by the Treaty of 1815.
France watched over Rome, Austria over the Marches
and the Romagna. The capital and the provinces
seemed assured against a return of the Revolution by
the concurrence of two Great Powers, who, without

giving umbrage to one another, lent the Pope the
support of their arms and the prestige of their name.
But interior difficulties broke out from the very beginning. A letter from Mgr. de Mérode to the Comte
de Montalembert gives a graphic picture of the state
of things. It is dated the 14th June, 1851 :—

"It seems to me that the actual state of affairs
both here and in France demands that you should perfectly understand how the land lies. Every one is
agreed in blaming the Pontifical Government because
it does not do enough, or does not act quickly
enough. But without reckoning the difficulties which
are inherent in each special reform, the Pope, in his
present position, is deprived of almost all liberty of
action. Look at the situation in which his Government is placed by the French Army. I do not speak of
his relations with the Austrian Army, which are even
more delicate and difficult in some ways, but with this
advantage, that there are no revolutionary influences
among the Austrians, and that the Imperial Government is much more stable than that of the Republic.
One knows, at least, with whom one shall have to deal
on the morrow. But to speak only of our relations
with the French, I do assure you that the position of
the Pontifical Government would be untenable if the
Pope were not to show a gentleness, a sweetness and
a prudence of which it would be difficult to form an
idea, and of which, I may add, only he himself is
capable. The fact is, that everything here is left to
the mercy of the General-in-Chief, who shelters himself
behind the instructions which emanate from the War
Minister in Paris. They take possession of such and
such a building : they arrest such and such an indivi-
dual : and, if I am not misinformed, they will some

day lay hands on the Quirinal and dislodge all the Pope's *entourage*, that is to say, his servants and his civil administrators, including the Swiss Guard, and that on the pretext that the Quirinal would be a good strategical position! Every day the mutual relations are more strained. You know how different French habits and ideas are from Roman ones. Ecclesiastical jurisdiction is a thing absolutely unknown in France. Very often priests are called upon as witnesses before a military council, and have often been shamefully ill-treated by the President because they stated that they could not give evidence on oath before receiving the previous authorization from the ecclesiastical authorities according to Canon Law. From one day to another a Cardinal may be cited before these councils without any regard to his dignity; it is all at the mercy of the first little captain whose turn it may be to preside at the court-martial. I am afraid there is no remedy; but I only mention it to show you the immense difficulties of our position.

" A foolish vanity and an unintelligent self-love blind certain people to such an extent that they do not see that what would most redound to the honour and interests of France would be to treat the Pontifical Government in a chivalrous and respectful manner ; and to maintain its honour and dignity in the eyes of the whole world. Whereas, on the contrary, they make it a point of honour to insult the Pope on every occasion, to mix themselves up with things which do not in any way concern them, to put themselves forward at every opportunity, and to pretend that they are necessary under every circumstance. To carry out this view, they represent the state of Rome daily as most alarming ; they pretend to feel and spread the

most exaggerated alarms ; they are always speaking of
absurd and chimerical eventualities, or of dangers which
are the offspring of their own imaginations. And all
this is said and done to magnify their own importance,
and to prove the necessity of their assuming all the
responsibility of maintaining law and order, and so
setting aside altogether the Pontifical Government.
The result is a permanent state of agitation and irrita-
tion, and au impossibility for the Pope's taking up an
assured and dignified position which would render
the realization of many reforms possible.

"The intentions of the Holy Father are shown every
day; even lately the measures taken with regard to
the Religious Orders have given proof of it. After
his efforts for reform had been paralyzed by the per-
fidious action of demagogues, who tried to denatural-
ize an enthusiasm which was true in its origin and
really founded on the deepest feelings of the people, is
it possible that these hearty and honest intentions
should be paralyzed again by another kind of tactics,
which consists in exaggerating existing evils and
giving birth to groundless anxieties ? The truth is,
that the enemies of the Church and of the Holy
See played on the popularity of Pius IX. at the beginning of his reign, and everybody helped them by
involuntarily conspiring with them. Now they have
changed their note : will they be seconded with the
same blindness as before ? As for myself, it appears
to me that the efforts of Catholics should tend to exact
guarantees for the independence of the Pontifical
authority, and to enlighten public opinion as to the
true state of things. A reduction in the strength of
the Army of Occupation would be essential on many
accounts, and especially to prove what progress has

been made in calm and pacification. I quite understand how careful one must be about speaking of such a thing, for fear that people should fancy there were an intention of substituting the Austrian for the French Army. Already the French have declared that that is the wish of the Pontifical Government, which is absolutely false.

" Would there not be a way of drawing up a convention which would preserve the honour and security of the Pontifical Government, and at the same time regulate the limits of the military authority in the Papal States ? Here is a characteristic case. Lately the King of Bavaria wished to light up the Coliseum with Bengal lights, and leave was given by the Pontifical authorities. But the French police got wind of it, and replied with great bitterness that ' the granting of such permissions rested with them, and that henceforth they reserved to themselves the right of so doing ! ' "

The difficulties which Mgr. de Mérode so well describes were partly caused by the precarious state to which the French Government was reduced. Every one felt it was incapable of maintaining order in Paris, and feared that it could not maintain it in Rome. The *coup d'état* of the 2nd of December seemed at first to be a signal interposition of Providence. Mgr. de Mérode thought so in Rome as much as M. de Montalembert did in Paris. He wrote to M. de Corcelles under this impression, which was the same as that which this event had produced in Europe. But two months after, his language was not the same. He excuses himself for having been badly informed; he writes with reserve; he expresses regrets; at last, he ends by declaring that he has no taste for politics;

and that if politics are to divide honest men, charity should reunite them.

The pledges which Louis Napoleon gave to the Church when he first became Emperor were quite enough to deceive the Catholic Party. Every one knew that he wished to be crowned by the Pope, and that the conditions of his consecration were openly discussed. Among other things there were modifications to be made in the Code Napoléon, to render religious marriage obligatory after the civil one. But the storm raised by the Press frightened the French Government. One morning an official note appeared in the *Moniteur* which took away all hope; as the Government declared that no change would be made in the law on civil marriage, the benefits of which had been appreciated for fifty years !

It was a check for the *Univers*, who had taken the initiative in this question, and who had gone far beyond the desires of those who wished to solve it in a Christian manner. Its attitude on the question of the Classics, its quarrels with Mgr. de Sibour, Archbishop of Paris, the interdict of the Bishop of Orleans, the favour which it enjoyed at that time with the Holy Father, and the violent passions it awoke, both in Paris and Rome, by its polemics, are all a matter of history. Mgr. de Mérode wrote to his brother-in-law in 1853 on this subject as follows :—

"I am delighted at what you tell me of the good effect produced by the Pope's allocution. It is very fortunate that this horrible mess should at last be brought to an end ; but I am very much afraid that it will begin again on some other question. Veuillot himself was only an incident in the matter. The thing is to know if the Church in France is to be

governed purely by the caprice of a journalist, or if it
is to be ruled by established laws and rights? As to
myself, I am far from admiring the politics of the
Univers. I think its articles on Civil Marriage against
M. Sauzet were those of a madman. For the last
three years I have never ceased deploring the Roman
correspondence, which I consider has done more harm
than anything else to the Pontifical Government, not
only from its awkward statements but also from its
falsehoods. But outside all that, it is certain that this
paper is the only organ which affirms certain Catholic
truths which would otherwise remain under a bushel.
If its adversaries hated it only for what was bad in it,
one could still reply that its evils do not deserve death;
but as, in general, it is only hated for what it con-
tains of good, one cannot help siding with it now and
then, without being of the same opinion on all questions. God grant that Catholics may still have time
to dispute among themselves, and that the common
enemy may not make too serious a diversion ! ' '

We must now turn to a young French priest, who
was an intimate friend of Mgr. de Mérode's, and who
had been still more closely united to him during the
siege of Rome, when they vied with one another in
the exercise of the most admirable charity. We speak
of Mgr. Bastide. Born at Ornans in 1820, he was
the countryman of the painter Courbet, and he had
begun his studies with him in the Seminary of their
native town. The two friends met in Paris some
years later : Courbet was studying painting, and
Bastide civil law ; but their intimate relations soon
ceased, for the painter had yielded to the impiety of
the age ; while the young lawyer, a faithful disciple of
the Père Lacordaire, and a zealous member of the

conferences of St. Vincent of Paul, strengthened his faith day by day in the exercise of the most fervent charity.

It was at the foot of the pulpit of Notre Dame that Bastide first conceived the thought of being some day a priest. His family strongly opposed the idea, and thought to have put a stop to it altogether by sending him to Algiers, to his eldest brother, who was a distinguished lawyer, and one of the first Frenchmen who left behind him an honourable name in Africa and a large fortune honestly acquired. But when Gustave Bastide arrived at Marseilles, instead of taking the boat for Algiers, he started in the steamer for Civita Vecchia, and went to study his vocation in the Eternal City. He was less fitted for theological questions than for works of zeal and the labours of a pastor. With a charming face, an agreeable manner, and the sweetest smile, no one could better represent France in that city, where faith is enthroned and the arts have given birth to such masterpieces in her service. Bastide went on at Rome as he had done in Paris, giving to music and painting all the time he could spare from his theological studies. He made a special study of Raphael's Loggias, and delighted, above all, in explaining the " Dispute of the Blessed Sacrament." That was really his masterpiece. He loved to gather strangers round it, and used, without any pretension or preparation, to give them a real apology of Christianity, and that with an eloquence and purity of diction which were inexpressibly beautiful, showing how Raphael had preached and preconized that august mystery which is a summary of our whole faith. He proved his conclusions by comparing this picture with that of the " School of Athens," where all the diversities and contradictions of philosophy are revealed, in contrast to the harmony and unity of the Catholic dogma. While drawing the attention of his audience to each of the personages in these two frescoes he would dwell at one time on their history, at another on their portraits; but never for a moment losing sight of the fact that he had to instruct as well as to please; and that *there* he was less of an artist than a priest and an apostle. This was one of the Abbé Bastide's great pleasures; but the zeal which had transformed it into a duty made him find still greater satisfaction in another work, in which his conduct was really heroic.

When he had finished his theology he had been appointed to the Chaplaincy of St. Louis des Français, by the advice of Cardinal Matthieu, Archbishop of Besançon. He was there when the siege of Rome enlarged the field of his labours. With the Abbé de Mérode he shared the honour of rescuing the wounded from the battle-field and watching by them in the ambulances. This was the origin of their close friendship; and this affection, conceived in the heroic exercise of charity, went on increasing to the end of their lives.

After the return of Pius IX. Abbé Bastide was naturally appointed Chaplain to the Army of Occupation. The great qualities he there showed induced the French Government to offer him the post of Chaplain at Val-de-Grace; but, in spite of this temptation, Abbé Bastide remained at Rome, where he passed all the rest of his life. It was a great blessing for the French Army. The cholera which broke out in 1854 in the Roman garrison showed all the devotedness and charity of the new Chaplain. The hospitals were insufficient to contain the sick, so that ambulances were opened in various parts of the town, and especially in

the Noviciate of St. Andrea, where the Abbé Bastide
shut himself up with his sick soldiers, who, in spite
of all his care, died by hundreds. It is difficult to
imagine the panic which the cholera caused in Rome.
All who could took to flight; and those who remained
shut themselves up in their houses to try and escape
the plague. Mgr. de Mérode and Abbé Bastide,
braving all dangers and prejudices, and taking no
account of their own lives, opposed a quiet courage to
the universal panic and signalized themselves by a
thousand acts of heroism. Every day Mgr. de Mérode,
after having performed his duties with the Pope, flew
to the hospitals, stopping at each bed, cheering and
encouraging the sufferers and distributing all kinds of
little comforts amongst them. Not content with thus
braving the pestilence, he would make an inspection of
the beds and the clothing of the victims. One man
he found had no flannels. Going quickly behind a
curtain, he undressed and stripped himself of his own,
which he made him put on at once; and then rushed
off, hoping he would not be found out.

But the terrible state to which Abbé Bastide was
reduced in the ambulance of St. Andrea touched him
more than anything. The doctors had sunk under
their labours; the infirmarians died and could not be
replaced; and, literally, the poor Chaplain was almost
alone in this terrible crisis, and had to do everything
for upwards of 400 sick men. He administered the
remedies, heard their confessions, received the last
wishes of the dying, and buried the dead. Before
closing their eyes he did not shrink from embracing
them to gather from their lips the names of their
villages, or the last adieus to their mothers; and these
poor fellows, blessing their devoted Chaplain with their

last breath, felt as if they once more saw France, their homes, and all that were dear to them.

This magnificent example was the wonder and the talk of all Rome. No one was prouder of his friend than Mgr. de Mérode. He spoke of him every day to the Pope, telling him all the details of his visits to the ambulances; and the great heart of Pius IX. was deeply moved; he even shed tears of admiration, while blessing and praising God for the fidelity of His servant. But even this did not satisfy Mgr. de Mérode. He persuaded the Pope to go himself and pay a visit to St. Andrea. Pius IX. started alone with his Chamberlain, taking care to say nothing to his Secretary of State, and not letting even his servants know where he was going. It was only after his usual drive that his coachman received the order to stop at the door of that house where death was reaping twenty-five soldiers a day. The coachman was so panic-stricken that he caught the disease and died two days after. The footmen could not understand the Pope's proceedings, so that they were left in the street, and the Pope went into the hospital alone, only being accompanied by Mgr. de Mérode. Pius IX. went to every bed, and saw all the sick, consoling, cheering, and blessing them, with tears in his eyes. He determined to reward Mgr. Bastide, as a General decorates a soldier on the battle-field, and created him, on the spot, his domestic prelate, with the title of Monseigneur. The investiture took place without delay. Mgr. de Mérode stripped off his cloak to put it on the new prelate, and pulling off his violet collar, exclaimed, as a brother soldier would do to his comrade in arms, " Here, Bastide, take these signs of your new dignity. You have won them nobly ! "

The news of the Pope's visit to St. Andrea flew through Rome, and filled every one with fear and astonishment. On his return Pius IX. found the whole Vatican in consternation. Cardinal Antonelli, turning to Mgr. de Mérode, reproached him bitterly. "What a fearful responsibility you have taken upon yourself," he exclaimed, "and to what danger have you exposed his Holiness! Only think, for a moment, that it might have been his death!" "Well!" replied Mgr. de Mérode, "and if the Pope had died on the spot, what death would have been more glorious, or more worthy of the Vicar of Jesus Christ?" Pius IX. approved of his words, and with a bright smile and a tender voice, replied: "You are quite right, Mérode, I have only done what was my duty!"

One sees by this little trait how Mgr. de Mérode knew how to practise and urge others on to heroic deeds. With his devouring zeal and activity he was not content with serving the Pope in an ordinary manner: he wanted to make him loved; to make his reign fruitful in good works, and in carrying out necessary reforms; to make his cause popular, and his name revered and blessed by all his subjects. A man like him was soon weary of waiting for his master in an ante-chamber. Above all, he watched every opportunity to tell the Pope the truth. To criticize abuses is easy enough, but to remedy them is more difficult. His first proposal was with regard to the reform of the prisons, of which Pius IX. at once recognized the necessity, and confided to him the task of carrying it out without delay.

Ever since 1703 Pope Clement XI. had taken steps to improve the state of the prisons by establishing the cellular system, with all the resources which religion could give to make it supportable. A House of Correction for the young was annexed to the Hospital of St. Michel, and was a great success. But the reform did not go further, and the revolutions which had followed had thoroughly disorganized the whole penitentiary system. The women had been transferred to the Thermes of Diocletian. The House was vast, but not appropriate to its destination. The three hundred prisoners who were there incarcerated were placed under the surveillance of what were called " Guardians," who were in reality nothing but old prisoners on parole. The same rooms served for kitchen, refectory, and dormitory. The food given being insufficient, they were reduced to making matches by way of eking out a miserable livelihood. The dirt, misery, disorder, and vice of this prison were simply inconceivable. Pius IX. determined to put a stop to it all, and employed Mgr. de Mérode to work the desired change.

No one was more capable than this Belgian prelate of carrying out his wishes. In his own country there were both model prisons and Religious Orders, specially set apart for the work. He went to Belgium in 1854 for this very purpose, and studied on the spot the admirable penitentiary system of M. Ducpétiaux. He took with him M. Hanibal Piccoli, who was employed in the Home Office at Rome, and together they visited the Penitentiary of Namur, the Reformatory for Boys at St. Hubert, and most of the other prisons. The Brothers of Mercy, instituted at Malines by Mgr. Schœppers, and the Sisters of Providence of Champion, seemed to him admirably suited to fulfil towards both sexes the ministry that was most required of them. As soon as he arrived at Champion he felt, by an interior warning, that he had found the instruments

which God had destined for his great and generous
work. When he first went to visit the establishment
he said to the Superior : " It is you and your Order
which I shall choose on account of your simplicity."

He had scarcely returned to Rome when the Sisters
of Providence föllowed him, and placed themselves
under his orders. Twelve of the nuns were sent to
the prison at the Thermes, and began their work. They
have written down the narrative of their installation,
with all its details, and we give it in all its simplicity
as being the most touching eulogium possible of the
holy prelate whose life we are writing :—

" We arrived at Rome on the 15th of June, 1854, at
five o'clock in the morning, by the Cavaleggieri Gate.
There we found Monseigneur de Mérode waiting for
us : he was dressed as a simple priest, and had a servant with him. He received us with the utmost kindness, and conducted us at once to St. Peter's, to pray
on the tombs of the Apostles. After we had satisfied
our devotion he took leave of us, saying : ' Go to your
dear prison, where I will join you very soon.' At
twelve o'clock Monseigneur came to the Termini, accompanied by Mgr. Talbot, and having collected all of
us twelve sisters, he announced to us that that very
day the Holy Father would give us a private audience.
The Vatican carriages came to fetch us, and Monseigneur was in waiting to present us to the Holy Father.
A short time after he procured us the favour of receiving Holy Communion from the hands of his Holiness.

" Like a loving Father, Monseigneur took care not
only of everything which could give pleasure to us as
his children, but also to put us in communication with
people in society who could help us in our work. He
would take us himself to certain houses, go in before

us for a few moments so as to pave the way for us, and explain to us all the little usages which are strange to new comers in a foreign country.

"The next thing he did was to get a large garden for the prisoners, so as to give them the advantage of fresh air and innocent recreation. The care he took of the health of the prisoners was doubled when it was a question of any of us Sisters falling ill, and many of us at that time suffered from the change of climate and caught the prevailing fever. When any one of us became seriously ill he left no stone unturned to give the patient every comfort and consolation in his power. He was the first to come by our bedsides with words of faith and hope, and with every religious consolation, saying Mass in the sick room and obtaining leave for daily Communion from the Holy Father. And when we got better, thanks to the many remedies which his tender charity suggested, he would send a carriage for us every day and make us take a drive to get fresh air. A little later, he bought for us himself a country house at a little distance from the town, to which we could always send our sick Sisters.

"He occupied himself with the greatest zeal in the reorganization of the prisons, established the most perfect discipline in the House, and took care that it should be observed. The new works he had undertaken necessitated his constant presence, and every day he would come two or three times from the Vatican to the Termini to see how things were going on, and always on foot.

In spite of his innumerable labours and the important duties laid upon him, he never would give up to others the humble post of Confessor to the Sisters, and came regularly on a fixed day to the prison to hear our confessions, and that up to the time of his death. It was in the confessional that one could feel all the beauty of this soul; his lively faith, his ardent charity, his contempt for all the grandeurs of earth, his great appreciation of the vanity of all things here below, and of everything, in fact, which was not God, virtue, duty. If only all the world could have heard his energetic and helpful exhortations to faith, patience, and courage ; and could have realized the extent of his goodness and self-abnegation, and the gentleness and sweetness which made one think of his Divine Master! We may live for a hundred years, and yet never cease weeping over the loss of such a father! He was for us a real St. Francis of Sales—that is saying everything! Nothing escaped his penetrating eye. He had so much sympathy, and so tender a heart, that he never could see any one in trouble without doing all in his power to relieve it. He took the greatest interest in all we did. The humblest Sister was listened to by him, and as kindly received as those of the highest rank and education amongst us. Monseigneur was always grave, yet he had ever a kind and playful word to say to us when we had the happiness of meeting him. For a great many years, every Sunday and feast day, at five o'clock in the morning, in spite of bad weather or other circumstances which made the long walk from the Vatican a difficulty, he never missed coming to the Termini to say Mass for us, and feed us with the Bread of Life as he had already fed us with the Divine Word. Sometimes he was so tired that we used to implore him to take a little more care of himself, but he would always reply, ' How many poor labourers and carters are at work already, and I am not more ill than they are!' His real charity towards his neighbour made him occupy himself with

H

our souls first and then with our bodies. During an epidemic among the prisoners he would not give up to any one else the duty of hearing their confessions, even of the most disgusting cases. His devotedness went to the length of rubbing them with his own hands, and he taught us how we could give back life and warmth to these poor dying creatures. He always recommended us to treat the sick prisoners as if they were one of ourselves, and to give them every little thing which could please them. One poor sick girl, having begged for a few grapes, we went to ask the gardener for some ; but as they were the first of the season, and rare at that time, the gardener said he could not cut them without Monseigneur's leave. When he came that day he heard of this, and instantly went off to the gardener, and came back, bringing with him a basketful of ripe grapes, which, we found, he had reserved for Mgr. de Mérode himself ; but which, instead, served to content the fancy of our poor sick prisoner. His zeal for the ceremonies of Divine worship made him come to the Termini in Holy Week to celebrate the Church offices in our chapel, which he did with the utmost care. He gave us also the most touching meditations on the holy mysteries. The ceremonies lasted two whole hours ; but he took care to arrange a very beautiful Calvary, which made the exercises more interesting to the prisoners, and they seemed only too short. This real father of souls showed the most sensible joy when, either after the annual retreat of his dear prisoners, or on the Feast of the Sacred Heart, or at the close of the month of Mary, he could come and give a General Communion to these poor lost sheep, whom he had brought back to the fold. His ingenious charity suggested to him a thousand little ways for softening the troubles of his penitents, and endless encouraging words and thoughts which were the outpourings of his tender and compassionate heart. If any very strong reason prevented his performing these functions he would take care to send some eminent prelate to take his place, and often even a cardinal. He who is pleased to exalt the humble blessed this work of Mgr. de Mérode's every day more and more; while he, to increase the glory of God, and to show how His grace could act upon the lowest and most miserable of His creatures, often brought the most distinguished persons to visit the prisons. We thus had the honour of receiving in turn all the princes and princesses of Rome and of foreign countries, the eminent prelates who formed the Roman Court, and even the Head of the Universal Church. The immortal Pius IX. did not disdain to come and visit our poor prisoners, to whom he spoke the kindest and most paternal words."

After the witness given by these grateful Religious, we will quote the words of one or two political personages who came to see the prisons reformed by Mgr. de Mérode: M. Lefebvre,* whose visit dates from 1857, writes as follows :—" The House at the Termini is destined for women. The establishment is very large and well-aired throughout. There are two hundred criminals, the greater part of whom, till they came in there, knew no law but their own. Savage and unregulated instincts are directed and looked after by a dozen weak women, who have no other arms than their crucifixes and their beads. But these women are nuns, and, to our glory be it spoken, are Belgian nuns. At the time of our visit, which was quite unexpected, the most perfect order, silence, and quiet reigned in this

* "On the Charitable Institutions of Rome," p. 245.

vast enclosure. Some of the prisoners were walking with a Sister in the garden under a glorious sun. Others were at work in a large work-room. Some were in the chapel. The cleanliness of everything was exquisite. All these violent, ardent, gross natures had been softened and brought into perfect order and submission under the tender, religious influence of these Belgian sisters."

The Brothers of Mercy, who had been brought by Mgr. de Mérode from Belgium at the same time as the Sisters of Providence, were placed in charge of the House of St. Balbina, where the young delinquents of the male sex were incarcerated. Here, again, we will listen to what M. Lefebvre says of the usefulness of this measure :—

" The House at Balbina is a kind of Reformatory for · boys. They are only confined to their cells during the night, and these cells are arranged in a peculiar manner. Vast dormitories have been divided into a series of little rooms about six feet square, closed in front and above by a wire trellis. They have thus combined proper ventilation with complete separation of the boys from one another, as the cells are so arranged that they cannot see each other, and the presence of one of the Brothers in each dormitory ensures silence and order. All day they are together. One set learn a trade, such as carpentering, bookbinding, tailoring, shoemaking, and the like ; the others are taught agricultural work, and labour in a large garden and farm which surrounds the whole establishment. All receive religious instruction, and learn to read, write and count. There are about a hundred of them. This establishment, which is quite out in the country, is gay, bright and beautifully clean. It has more the look of a college than of a penitentiary, and the boys, with their curious wide-awake look, seem to visitors more like lads full of fun and mischief than criminals. They are under the care of the Brothers of Mercy, and, as I need not say to Belgian readers, they are not gaolers, but gentle and devoted masters."

But it is not only a Belgian writer who gives this testimony of Mgr. de Mérode's work ; English, French, Germans—all those who visited his prisons hold the same language. In a secret despatch to M. Walewski, M. de Rayneval, the French Ambassador at Rome, declares that these prisons should be visited by every one, "if only that strangers should admire and if possible imitate the noble and persevering charity of the Holy Father and his ministers." And this diplomat adds—"All that I have said ought to be enough to prove that every measure adopted by the Pontifical Government bears the stamp of wisdom, reason and progress."

An English member of Parliament, Mr. Maguire, after having shown that the Pontifical prisons could bear a comparison with those of any other country, specially dwells on the devotion of the two Chamberlains in the Pope's household who had " devoted their lives to this work," Mgr. de Mérode and Mgr. Talbot. "Mgr. de Mérode," he writes, "has a thorough knowledge of the Belgian system of prisons, which is perhaps superior to that of any other country ; while Mgr. Talbot knows all the improvements which have lately been adopted in England. The first is at the head of all the Roman prisons, which he administers with the greatest ability ; the second occupies himself more with their spiritual care.* The venerable Canon, M. Lamy, in his notice

* Maguire. "Rome, its Sovereign and its Institutions," p. 158.

upon Mgr. de Mérode, remarks "that there is one fact which outweighs all other evidence, and that is, that Mgr. de Mérode's great work survives him; and that the Piedmontese, who have so ruthlessly destroyed so many things, have not dared change the prison system which he introduced. Although those bitter persecutors and haters of all religious orders have driven out the Brothers of Mercy from the prison of St. Michele, to replace them by gaolers, they have not ventured to expel them from St. Balbina; and these devoted Religious continue their ministry of love and' self-abnegation—both at St. Balbina and also in the madhouse and in the asylum for old men, which the municipality has entrusted to them since the invasion."*

The Termini prison, as we have seen, was specially dear to Mgr. de Mérode. He had arranged, embellished and enlarged it; while the purchase of the Strozzi Palace (which he did out of his own money), seemed to be the last sacrifice which his charity could impose upon him for the consolidation of this great work. Even the events of 1870 did not discourage him. At the first rumour of the nuns being about to be turned out of the Termini, he proposed to the Piedmontese authorities to transport the prisoners and the Sisters to the Villa Altieri, outside the walls, which he had recently purchased. His proposal having been accepted, he had the courage to begin again, at his own cost, all the necessary works for the new installation. It was an enormous expense; but he economised his money as little as his labour. The Villa Altieri being quite out in the country did not offer sufficient security for prisoners; so that he built an enormously high wall all round it, which gave it the appearance of a real fortifi-

* "Mgr. de Mérode," by Canon Lamy, 1874.

cation. He added two wings to the palace, raised it by a story, built two staircases in white marble, each of a hundred steps ; and built a beautiful chapel above, both for the Sisters and the prisoners, which he went on decorating and embellishing up to the last hour of his life. A spacious court, planted with trees, and a good garden, serve for air and exercise for the prisoners. No one can imagine, on going over this house, that it is a prison. It keeps the name of the Villa Altieri, and an air of comfort and satisfacton is seen on the faces of all the prisoners whom one meets. It seems rather as a home offered by religion to the unfortunate, of which the whole tone is happiness and calm. The Director-General of the Italian prisons on a recent occasion said to the Superior of the Sisters of Providence—"Mother, we do not come to inspect but to admire."

If Mgr. de Mérode's foundations were sometimes criticized by narrow-minded people they won, on the other hand, unmixed admiration from all those whose opinion was worth having—not content with praising they imitated him. Cardinal Pecci, now Leo XIII., was among those who appreciated his reforms the most. When he came to Rome for the definition of the dogma of the Immaculate Conception, he had long conversations with Mgr. de Mérode on the subject of the prisons, of children, and the poor in general, who were the great objects of his pastoral solicitude. He determined to do in Perugia what Mgr. de Mérode had done in the Eternal City, and to give the same consolations to the miserable prisoners in his diocese. This meeting was followed by a still more agreeable visit, of which Mgr. de Mérode wrote the following account to his father :—

"*10th December,* 1855.

"I have been to Perugia to see Cardinal Pecci and
the two establishments of the Brothers from Malines
and of the Sisters from Namur, whom he has summoned to his diocese to direct these two houses.   The
good Cardinal, in spite of his apparent coldness,
shows the greatest zeal in his diocese.   He has put
his seminary on the best possible footing, and is now
restoring his fine cathedral.   He is anxious also to put
on a new and better footing the many charitable
institutions with which the town is filled.   I found
in him an incredible activity.   On every side fresh
streets and roads are being opened and new gates
made in the ramparts. . . . . . The Cardinal received
me with the greatest kindness, and talked of his residence as Nunzio in Belgium with the most affectionate
remembrance.   He charged me to tell you how precious the recollection of your kindness was to him as
well as that of all the de Mérode's."   .   .   .

In the midst of the touching care which Mgr. de
Mérode took of the Sisters of Providence, God had
reserved to him another paternal and spiritual consolation which flesh and blood made still dearer to him.
He found himself entrusted with the education of his
young half-sister, Mlle. Albertine de Mérode, whom
certain circumstances brought to Rome and placed
under his direction.

Albertine was born at the Château of Trélon on the
7th of June, 1839, and was the only issue of Count
Felix de Mérode's second marriage.   She was only
eight years old when her mother died.   This pious
lady on her deathbed recommended her to the care of
her half-sister, Mde. de Montalembert, saying, "You

will bring her up with your own girls, and she will be happy even without me." This charge was scrupulously fulfilled. The most delicate care was given to Albertine, and her education was begun in the midst of her nieces, who were to her as sisters. Nothing at that time presaged her future life. Her good heart, solid judgment and real energy were paralyzed by an indecision and a timidity of character which were carried to excess. If she had to make acquaintance with any stranger or even to come into the drawing-room, she would hide herself behind her eldest niece, while no one could ever draw a word out of her. She grew up like this till she was seventeen, without any kind of pre-occupation. When she was told to think of and to pray about her future, she would answer, "Pray ! Yes ; but think, no ! I am too young for that ! "

"Others, however, thought for her," writes one of her contemporaries, who is now a nun of the Sacred Heart at the Trinità dei Monti, "and especially her half-brother, Mgr. de Mérode, who was settled in Rome, where his devotion attached him to the service of the Holy Father. Full of affection for this sister, whom he called his little Benjamin, he could not wish for her a better lot than what he had chosen for himself ; and having been raised to the honour of the priesthood, he earnestly wished Albertine to have a religious vocation. But he did not dare hope for it. Besides that, he felt he really knew her very little ; for Albertine, with her extraordinarily shy and reserved nature, had never done anything to break the ice. Divine Providence, however, brought about closer relations between them ; for the doctors having decided that the warmer climate of Italy was absolutely necessary for her delicate health, Mgr. de Mérode obtained

leave for her to be admitted into the Convent at the
Trinità as a free boarder. The Superior tolerated this
exception to her rules from her great respect for
Mgr. de Mérode and his family; but she made the
condition that it should only be for three months, and
that Albertine and her governess should have little or
nothing to say to the other pupils in the house. At
first this clause was easily observed, as her visits to
the many monuments and interesting sights of Rome
took up all her days. But when Albertine was once
more quietly settled in the Convent her excellent
spirit was so much appreciated by the Superiors that
they could not refuse to admit her among the other
boarders. Her new life saved her from all the difficulties of deciding upon anything, and her natural
indecision being set aside by having to follow a fixed
rule, her strong and amiable qualities very soon developed themselves.

"It was really a pleasure to see her during the hour
of study, or at recreation, when she was the life and
soul of every game. One might have fancied she was
an old pupil, who had been always brought up at
school. In the classes she delighted everybody by her
simplicity, never showing off her superior abilities or
the varied knowledge she had acquired in the previous
excellent and careful education she had received.
The cordiality of her relations with her companions
won all hearts; she was completely above any of the
littlenesses of vanity or the puerilities of childhood, or
the frivolities of a worldly spirit. It was especially when
she received the riband and medal of the Children of
Mary that Albertine showed all her zeal. She strove
continually to bring back the giddy ones to a proper
spirit, to soften the turbulent ones, and to uphold,

though with great delicacy and tact, the authority of the mistresses. She was especially noted for her love of the poor, enhancing the merit of her abundant alms by a singular modesty, imploring the Sisters never to let the sufferers know the name of their benefactress. When given the charge of sacristan to the Children of Mary, all other occupation seemed to fade in interest before that one. Mgr. de Mérode and the other prelates at the Roman Court ended by interesting themselves in this important sacristy; and when Pius IX. came to the Trinità, with his usual tender playfulness, he would ask if anything were wanting? and if everything were in order? 'for,' he would add smilingly to Albertine, 'you know we must go and pay it the necessary canonical visit.'"

On the 7th February, 1857, a telegram announced to all Rome the death of Count Felix de Mérode, which was so sudden and unexpected that his son and daughter could not arrive in time to assist at his last moments. The death of this great man and noble citizen was felt by all Belgium as a national calamity. In every newspaper mention was made of his great share in the foundation of Belgian nationality, and of the modesty and ability with which he had refused the crown himself to place it on the head of a prince who would have the support of all the Great Powers of Europe. Successively Minister for Foreign Affairs, for War, and for Finance, he had only left the Government in 1839; but he had remained the firm, frank, and devoted councillor of King Leopold, and his most faithful friend and servant. He was also the intrepid champion of all Catholic rights and liberties. Only eight days before the short and cruel malady which deprived the country of his services he took an active part in a debate in the Chambers on freedom in Religious Education. The discussion was not yet over, when the news of his death came to drive his colleagues almost to despair. M. Charles Rogier, the head of the Opposite Party, claimed the right to do him honour and justice in a speech delivered to a crowded house, and warmly applauded on all sides; while the President of the Assembly wrote the following letter to Count Werner de Mérode :—

" It has been unanimously resolved to-day that the Chambers shall assist in a body at the funeral of a colleague so universally honoured and so deeply regretted. Wishing to associate the whole country with the sorrow of your family, the Members have also decided that the business of the House should be suspended on that day.

" This public manifestation of feeling, which is without a precedent in our annals, is more than justified by the long and glorious services rendered to his country by Comte Felix de Mérode.

" He has worthily paid the debt which so great and historic a name imposed upon him.

" As the courageous Founder of our Independence and of our Nationality, as a Veteran in our Parliamentary ranks, which he so powerfully helped to create, as a man of the highest intelligence and ability—above all, as a man with the warmest heart and the holiest private life, he carries away with him the regrets, the esteem, and the affection of all his fellow-countrymen. The greatness of his career raises his death to the height of an irreparable national loss. May the thought that this event is so deeply felt by the whole country help to soothe your legitimate sorrow ! The Chamber of Representatives is the organ of the general

feeling, and unites its tears with yours. Religion alone
can dry them and console us."

His obsequies were celebrated on the 11th of February, 1857. All Belgium was represented there. All
the newspapers throughout Europe sung his praises;
and, some months later, when the Père Lacordaire was
blessing the marriage of the Vicomte de Meaux with
Mlle. Elizabeth de Montalembert, the granddaughter
of Comte Felix de Mérode, he took the opportunity to
speak of the grand qualities of this man " as the only
one in this century who saw the throne at his feet in a
revolution which freed his country from the yoke of a
stranger and yet refused it : and who, after having been
the Father of its reconquered Liberty, defended for
twenty-five years his memorable work; a statesman
even greater from his conscientiousness than from his
genius; more remarkable for his fidelity than for the
brilliancy of his eloquence ; and who, having won all
parties by the force of his honesty, reconciled them
once more at his tomb, and obtained a regret so
universal that his death was raised to the dignity of a
triumph."

Monseigneur de Mérode brought back to Rome, with
the remembrance of so great and good a father, all
the consolations which faith gives to such great
sorrows, and with the additional care of superintending Albertine's education, who was now nearly eighteen.
He brought her back with him, and her orphan state
made this little sister even more dear to him than
before. He watched this soul with the most paternal
solicitude, hoping always to find in her some germs of
a supernatural vocation. Every Sunday he gave up
more important occupations to come and spend his
afternoons with her at the Trinità, and Albertine used

frequently to return his visits.   She had often thus the
happiness of seeing the Holy Father.   Pius IX. liked
her, called her by her Christian name, sent her many
little presents, laughed at her playfully for her shyness,
and sometimes combined with Mgr. de Mérode to put
her timidity to the proof.   One day, especially, he sent
her some beautiful pineapples.   The next morning
Mgr. de Mérode placed his sister in one of the rooms
in the Vatican through which the Pope was about to
pass, so that she might thank him.   "But," she exclaimed, in great distress, "what in the world shall I
say, all alone, when the Pope comes?"   "Say whatever you like," replied her brother, laughing, and went
away.   Poor Albertine fell on her knees at the end of
the gallery, trembling with fright and waiting for the
passage of the Pope and his suite.   As soon as he
came near Mgr. de Mérode hastened to say : "Most
Holy Father! here is my sister, who has prepared a
beautiful little speech to thank your Holiness."
"Well," replied graciously Pius IX., smiling and
stopping, "here I am to listen to it!"   What she
said is not known, for it is certain no one heard a
word, and the Pope good-naturedly did all the talking
for her ; but he did not forget her excessive timidity,
and one day when talking of her said : "It seems to
me she is a good little creature, full of activity and
life, and very gay and bright ; and I believe she is not
wanting in talent.   I say, I believe, for never have I
been able to make her speak ; she has always kept me
at a distance!"   The next day he said to her brother :
"Yes, she is a good girl, for whom we must find a
really good husband ; not a creature without faith, and
without any zeal for doing good!"   Albertine had, in
fact, reached the age when she had to make up her

mind as to her future life. She was just twenty; and in the month of September, 1858, she left the Trinità. "I feel sure you will carry away an imperishable recollection of this convent," wrote her brother; and he never spoke a truer word. Her health had been reestablished by the Roman climate, and she made her entrance in the world with that faithful and courageous love of duty which was one of her characteristics.

Mgr. de Mérode had at that time accompanied the Pope as Chamberlain in the journey he had undertaken to visit the Marches and the Romagna. This journey, which was begun on the 4th of May, 1857, lasted for four months, and was one succession of triumphs. The Arch-Duke Maximilian of Austria, the Grand Duke of Tuscany, the Duke of Parma, the Duke of Modena, all came in turn to present their homages to Pius IX. The welcome which the Holy Father received from his people was hearty and spontaneous, and in no way constrained or equivocal. Received, as he was, with acclamations and praised to the skies, he seemed less the legitimate sovereign than the father of his subjects. One might well believe that the foreign bayonets which guarded these provinces were only a useless display, so completely did the Pope live in the heart of his subjects, and this unanimous feeling found expression in every town and village by the mouths of thousands of people of every class. The breath of the Revolution, however, had passed over these provinces, and especially over Bologna; but before Pius IX. all this was changed. Even the few who might have been discontented with these popular demonstrations were wise enough to keep silence; while the mass of the people wished for nothing so much as the consolidation of a reign which was at

once paternal, prudent, and really liberal.   Pius IX.
had kept all the promises he had made in his *proprio
motu* of the 18th September, 1849, by which he had
inaugurated his personal Government.   By showing
himself in this way to his people he could only increase their affection for him, and give greater weight
to his words.   His noble face, his good figure, his
great virtues, the sweetness and kindness of his
manner, the happy knack he had of always saying the
right thing with a playful grace and goodness which
were specially his own, his earnest desire to ameliorate
the condition of his subjects, and to carry out wise
reforms, both in the finances and the municipal
administration of his kingdom, all served to rally
round him the respect, love and sympathy of all the
countries through which he passed.   His faithful
Chamberlain took care to point out to him the different
ways in which effective changes for the better could be
made : he took notes of everything, and in familiar
conversation he omitted nothing which could enlighten
the Pope as to the truth and ensure both the popularity and durability of his reign.   We will give one
or two extracts from his correspondence during that
famous journey, which will thoroughly paint his impressions :—

"MACERATA, 12*th May*, 1854.

" Our progress is wonderful.   The Holy Father
has been everywhere received with genuine enthusiasm,
but here especially the illuminations have been quite
beautiful.   Joy is in every heart and on every face.
Nothing can be more touching than the expression of
all these poor people when they meet the Holy Father.
The Pope made a public eulogium of the ladies of the

Sacred Heart at Perugia, advising the Bishop to entrust his new school to them." . . .

"*16th May,* 1857.

" MY DEAR WERNER,

" I have hardly time to scribble a few lines before our departure for Fermo and Ascoli. We lead the most out-of-door life possible. Three Masses every morning, including mine, and sometimes four, with two or three benedictions of the Blessed Sacrament, sanctify our days. Then there are refreshments and ices five or six times a day, with dinners and suppers which are interminable, and audiences given to hundreds of people. The reception everywhere given to the Holy Father is the most touching thing imaginable. I am very much astonished at all I see and remark in these Pontifical States, which are represented as so abandoned and so miserable. To see the solemn magisterial receptions, the Bar and the Universities all in their robes, to behold the magnificence of their works of art, the beauty of the decorations they have set up for the passage of the Pope, the fireworks and illuminations in every town, the admirable country roads through which we drive, with the constabulary so well dressed, in boots and leggings, as you saw them at Viterbo, and the careful cultivation of all the fields and vineyards, one asks one's self how it is possible for this poor Pontifical Government to have such a bad reputation ? The fact is, that the country is rich far beyond what any one believes, and it will be found out when valued by the railroads. We find everywhere those admirable Sisters of St. Vincent de Paul, at Foligno, Perugia, Camerino, Macerata, Loretto, Terni, &c., &c. What

I

a prodigy of grace it is that France, who fifty years ago destroyed all the convents, is now re-peopling the whole world with these holy women ! "

"22nd May.

"Here we are at Ancona. The receptions are always equally satisfactory. Here we have met the Austrians for the first time ; they have no garrisons in the other towns : all were on their knees on the ground as the Pope passed, in the most respectful attitude. This evening the port is illuminated ; yesterday we had a concert given by the Austrian band, escorted by soldiers carrying lighted torches. Every day there are fresh rejoicings : concerts, illuminations, fireworks, &c., mingled with visits to all the convents and hospitals. I am very glad to have seen all this, but shall be glad to be quietly at home again in the Vatican."

"BOLOGNA, 1st *August*, 1857.

"Here we are at last at Bologna, with a little more calm and tranquillity, which I assure you we have not had for a long time. The Holy Father was admirably received this morning. He celebrated Mass in the Cathedral, and then crowned an Image of Our Lady, which is much revered by the people of Bologna, under the title of *Madonna del monte della Guardia*. After this important ceremony the Pope addressed the crowds who filled the church in the most touching and admirable manner. He explained the sense of the coronation of the Blessed Virgin, which he had just performed, as being only the expression of the feeling in the hearts of all. He implored the grace of God upon himself and his people, and the help of her who reigns 'in the midst of the lions and the leopards,' according to the words of Holy Writ; that is, amidst evil men and sinners, that the hardness of their hearts might be overcome. He implored the Mother of Mercy to give us one day that crown of immortality of which she is the guardian for her divine Son. Finally, he promised to remember the people of Bologna, and asked their prayers for him, as long as it pleased God to leave him here below—for him, the poor Vicar of Jesus Christ, ' so feeble and unworthy of his great mission ! ' . . . This allocution was short, but excellent, and drew tears from every eye."

The Pope before returning to Rome held a consistory at Bologna on the 4th of August. The functions which fell to the lot of Mgr. de Mérode on this occasion gave him a higher idea than ever of the importance of the Church amidst the ever-changing events of this world. He wrote to the Comte de Montalembert as follows :—

"BOLOGNA, *3rd August*, 1857.

" To-morrow we shall hold a consistory here, and I have to make the demand for the pallium for the Archbishop of Seville. Who would have believed in 1842, when, on my return from Madeira, I passed the Holy Week at Seville, that fifteen years later it would be my duty to ask the Pope for the pallium for the Archbishop of that city! The man who then filled this see was Cardinal Cienfuegos, who was exiled to Alicante by Espartero. He was pointed out to me by the Belgian Consul as a sort of ' pauvre honteux,' at this place, and I went to pay a visit to the venerable old man. Thus earthly things pass and succeed one another ; but the Church remains ever the same—glorious, stable, and triumphant."

The victories of the Church are always mingled with cruel trials. The triumphant journey of 1857 had a mournful morrow. From the 1st of January, 1859, the Emperor of the French gave signs in his speech to the Austrian Ambassador that war between France and Austria was imminent. That was enough to make wise heads understand that Italy would be the theatre of that war, and the Pope its victim.

CHAPTER VI.

From 1859 to 1860.

The War in Italy—Invasion of the Romagna—The Policy of
Pius IX.—M. de Corcelles sounds General de Lamoricière
—Mgr. de Mérode engages him for the service of the Holy
See—Journey of the General and the Prelate—Arrival at
Rome—The State in which he found the Pontifical Forces
—The Pope appoints Mgr. de Mérode War Minister—
Prodigies of Activity and Zeal—The Results—Aggression
of the Piedmontese—Battle of Castelfidardo—Siege of
Ancona—Defeat of Lamoricière—His Heroism and his
Glory.

THE Italian Campaign which opened on the 1st January,
1859, and was signalized by the battles of Magenta and
Solferino, had been closed in three months by the
peace of Villafranca.   It seemed as if the Pope would
have nothing to fear for his Roman States.   Napoleon
had declared him President of the Italian Confedera-
tion, and simple-minded men, who saw in him only a
defender of the Holy See, thought he was faithfully
acting on the policy of Charlemagne.   But those who
read in the heart of the Emperor, thought quite
differently.   They remembered his revolutionary antecedents, his enterprises against the temporal power,
his imprisonment under Gregory XVI., and the generous pardon he had obtained from him.   Every one
knew that he was bound by oath to the *Carbonari*.

No one could forget that during the Paris Congress Count Walewski, his minister, had brought forward the Roman question among those which were to be deliberated upon. The Orsini bombs which burst on the Emperor's head in 1858 had not succeeded in killing him ; but, which was more decisive, had reminded him of his promises. The assassin, before mounting the scaffold, had written a menacing letter, and the *Moniteur* had printed it by order of the Government. All these circumstances combined should have warned Europe that by tearing in pieces on the battle-field the Treaty of Vienna Napoleon III. had equally changed his policy with regard to the Holy See, and that the days of the temporal power were numbered.

The peace of Villafranca was only a lure, which did not even last to the end of the year. Hardly had the defeated Austrians retired behind the Mincio and abandoned the Romagna, than the Revolution seized upon its prey. The delegates of the Holy See, being no longer protected by foreign bayonets, were compelled to quit Bologna, Ravenna, Ferrara, and Perugia before a handful of Revolutionists. Thus, Milesi was carried off from Bologna in Count Pépoli's carriage (he being the head of the insurrection), on the pretext of saving his person. In the same way Ricci at Ravenna and Rendi at Ancona were forced to quit their posts, barely escorted by a few constables, and not a shot was fired ! The movement spread throughout Umbria ; Perugia was abandoned ; but, under the somewhat tardy orders of the Cardinal-Secretary of State, the first regiment of the Roman garrison left that city, marched upon Perugia, took it back by assault, and thus stopped the march of the Revolutionists, who, without that exploit, would have quietly flown from town to town up to the very gates of the Vatican.

The retaking of Perugia was a good sign. It would have been easy at that moment to take back the other places, for they were only held by a few wild young fellows, who would have quickly yielded to the approach of regular troops. The League called of "Central Italy," which gave a body to the Revolution, was not yet formed. Orders were sent from the Cardinal-Secretary of State to General Schmidt to send a battalion of his regiment to General Kolbermatten, and this officer, as soon as he had received the necessary reinforcements, was to attack and reconquer the Romagna. Schmidt, however, excused himself, on the plea of the state of his troops, and the order was revoked. During this time the League was regularly constituted (20th of August, 1859), the Revolutionists were strengthened in the different towns they had occupied, and the Piedmontese, called in by them, took possession of these cities without having to strike a blow. Committees were organized to decide by vote whether the Romagna should give itself to Piedmont: it was all done in a few weeks. The Duchies of Parma, Tuscany, Modena, and Piacenza shared the same fate, in spite of their sworn oaths to the Pope. Money stirred up the Revolutionists and bought the votes; treason opened the gates of the cities, and the peace of Villafranca, more murderous than any war, gave up thus into the hands of Piedmont more than two-thirds of Italy. To complete their victory the Piedmontese had only to drive the Bourbons from the Two Sicilies, and to steal from the Pope the Marches, Umbria, the patrimony of St. Peter, and the town of Rome. Pius IX. could then judge what the friend-

ship of the Emperor was worth.   Everything was lost
outside, for Napoleon had been clever enough to divide
or to paralyze all the Powers to whom the Holy See
could look for help.   Prussia saw, with a secret satisfaction, the weakening of the temporal power. Austria,
to whom nothing but Venice remained, seemed to be
little interested in the cause of the Papacy, which she
had weakly defended.   Russia, in whom the Cardinal-
Secretary of State had placed too much confidence,
looked upon the Pope more as a spiritual rival whom
she could humble than as a temporal king of whom
she should embrace the interests.   Spain, convulsed
by internal conspiracies, had nothing left but sterile
wishes for a Pontiff whom she loved, and who had
boldly declared himself for the cause of Isabella.   His
abandonment by the Great Powers of Europe was
visible, and if France had not already withdrawn her
flag from Rome and Civita Vecchia it served only to
cover the small territory which it pleased the Emperor
to leave under the authority of the Pope, until the day
when he should choose to abandon him altogether.
This very equivocal protection gave rise every day to
fresh difficulties.   Now the Emperor threatened to
withdraw his troops ; then he complained that his services were not sufficiently appreciated.   Mischievous,
though unacknowledged, pamphlets were circulated
under cover of Imperial authority ; certain impertinent
words were attributed to a French Prince, who spoke
of limiting the temporal power to the gardens of the
Vatican.   Among the officers of the Army of Occupation one set showed the deepest piety, and were filled
with the utmost respect and veneration for the successor of St. Peter ; while another openly accused him
of incapacity.   How was all this to end ?   Clever men

guessed but too well; politicians concealed the truth; the French bishops did not dare explain themselves openly. A word from Mgr. de Mérode described the state of things exactly : " The Emperor protects us as they shore up a house with the intention of demolishing it."

Then the most illustrious speakers and writers of the era strove to move public opinion in favour of the Pope. On the 25th of October, 1859, Montalembert put pen to paper and declared that the French people were responsible before Europe, before posterity, and before God, for all that the Government did or allowed to be done. He said : " It may be that this ancient and holy edifice may perish, after it has resisted the storms of centuries. It may be that this sacred principality may be submerged in the common ruin of all the most ancient rights of Europe, so obstinately attacked at this moment, and so miserably defended. All this is possible—for everything is possible here below. . . . . . But it would be at the same time a fault and a crime ; a folly and an injustice. It is the fashion among our great journalists, who are so courteous towards the strong and so disdainful towards the weak, to mock at the tears and the thunders of the Vatican. Ah ! we well know that the tears of the Pope only touch the hearts of his docile children, and that his thunders frighten only those whom they do not menace. But believe this—that the former will not remain always sterile, nor the latter powerless. The mouths of men will not be closed for ever. A thousand voices in the Church and in History will repeat the *non licet* of the Gospel. Listen well—*non licet.* These words seem to be nothing ; yet they are everything. They may prevent nothing at the present moment, but they will determine everything in the future, both in the judgments of God and in that of men. It did not prevent Herod from doing what he chose; but, after all, who would wish to be Herod? It did not prevent Pilate, while he washed his own hands, from yielding to the passions of a people blinded by rage and self-confidence; but who would be the Pilate of the Papacy?"

After Montalembert the flower of French liberators entered the arena. Monseigneur Dupanloup refuted with indignant eloquence the pamphlet entitled "The Pope and the Congress." The best writer in the *Débats*, M. de Sacy, declared himself the champion of the temporal power; and the Permanent Secretary of the French Academy, Villemain, published his admirable pamphlet, entitled "La France, l'Empire et la Papauté." The Pope had thus rallied to his cause all the princes of Christian literature. This would have been everything in old times: even in 1860 it went for a good deal.

Pius IX. felt this strongly, and Mgr. de Mérode helped him to understand it still better. He sent eloquent praises to Sacy and Villemain, desiring his Chamberlain to transmit to them the expression of his gratitude. He thanked Montalembert by a blessing as affectionate as it was solemn, and wrote with his own hand the following words at the bottom of a letter from Mgr. de Mérode to his brother-in-law:—

"*Benedico ex corde com. Carolum de Montalembert et totam familiam suam. Dirigat semper Deus cor ejus, et ut bonus miles Christi prælict prælia sua usque in finem.*"—Pius P.P. IX.

M. de Montalembert answered: "My dearest Xavier,

I am really afraid of doing something impertinent by sending the enclosed response to the words which the Holy Father deigned to add to your letter of the 8th January. For one cannot write to the Pope as one does to the first-comer, which I remember having said to M. de Turgot, then Minister for Foreign Affairs, when this good and simple man came to me at the end of November, 1851, to ask me to write to Pius IX. and tell him that there was going to be a *coup d'état*, but to assure him that this event would in no way injure the Catholic cause, and would deserve the approbation of His Holiness. I am glad to be able to add that in giving you the news I took care to guard myself against any such guarantee.

"Whatever may happen, I send you my letter, that you may do with it absolutely what you think best. But I attach a great deal of importance to one thing, which may appear to you unreasonable. The words which the Holy Father has had the goodness to send me will be a valuable relic to my posterity. But their value would be sensibly increased by the *date*, which he has forgotten to put. Do see, then, if it would not be possible to induce His Holiness to have the great condescension to write himself on this precious sheet of paper the date—1860. This year will probably witness the renewal, under a new Napoleon, of the great crime which was the ruin of the first; and will, moreover, be for ever memorable by a great example of apostolic courage and intrepidity."

The illustrious writer did not deceive himself. He observed also that the Holy See was in a worse position now than in 1849, and even than in 1809. "Why?" he asks. Because in 1849, and even in 1809, public opinion in France and throughout Europe sympathized with the Pope, while in 1859 it was hostile to him. It was from that undeniable hostility, fostered by the sects, that the Emperor drew the needful audacity to act as he did. He added : " Public opinion is, most certainly, neither infallible nor omnipotent ; but it is a great power, and he would be a fool who did not take it into account, even if he were the Vicar of Jesus Christ Himself—who is the first among mortals."

It was about a month later that Mgr. de Mérode persuaded the Pope to throw off, by a bold stroke, this odious unpopularity, and to rehabilitate in the eyes of the whole world the title of " Soldier of the Pope." He had often made jokes on the line taken by the Army of Occupation, making his hearers understand that the zeal it affected to show hid some ulterior design : " General Goyon makes a great fuss about his patrols. Whole companies are sent through deserted streets to sweep perfectly solitary pavements. No one is more clever than this excellent General at making people believe that those who wish to drown us are precisely those who are saving us from the water. The General acts in good faith. He behaved wonderfully at the departure of the Sardinian Minister, Minerva. The Emperor could never have found any one who could play more naturally the part which is assigned to him."

The clear-sightedness of the Prelate was great, but his generous boldness was greater still. He thought that they must profit by the equivocal conduct of the Emperor to organize a means of safety which would be more sure than the Army of Occupation. On the one hand, the full treachery and meanness of the Italian conspirators would not be shown at once ; on the other, the French Catholics might force their

Sovereign to keep his flag flying over the Castle of St. Angelo, while negotiations could be opened with Austria and Spain and time would be gained. But this precious time must be utilized to organize independent troops, which could be recruited throughout Europe, and must be entrusted to a general of known bravery and renown ; one, in fact, capable of holding his own with the leaders of the Italian Revolution. Rome had in her Swiss Guard and her Carabineers both good soldiers and faithful captains. With an illustrious chief a really strong army could be formed sufficient to resist aggressions both from within and from without.

Such was the idea of Mgr. de Mérode. He opened his whole heart to the Pope, who entered fully into his views. He spoke of Lamoricière in his conversations with Pius IX. ; told him the history of his life, and suggested that he might, perhaps, accept this important post in his service. Mgr. de Mérode could answer for this great and generous heart. He had known him in Africa—his wife was a near relation— and when the *coup d'état* of 1852 had condemned him to exile in Belgium, it was to Count Felix de Mérode's that he had gone, where he had received the warmest welcome. There were, besides, two other reasons which would incline Lamoricière to take up the Papal cause. As a soldier, he groaned over his present inactivity ; but this inactivity had given him time for reflection, and had brought him first to the study and then to the practice of his religious duties. Father Déchamps, who died Cardinal Archbishop of Mechlin, had conquered this great and upright soul for Jesus Christ. He was no longer Cavaignac's Minister, objecting to the Roman Expedition and refusing to take the command of the Army of Occupation there. Little by little all the prejudices of his early education had been set aside. He prayed earnestly, went to Confession and Holy Communion, and brought up his family in all the practices of a docile and fervent faith. In fact, he had become a noble Christian soldier.

This was enough to ensure his being a faithful soldier of the Pope's. M. de Corcelles was entrusted with the delicate mission of sounding him on the matter. He continued in active correspondence with Mgr. de Mérode, and Pius IX. placed in him unlimited confidence. His letters, his writings, his views on the Pontifical Government, were warmly appreciated. The old Ambassador of 1849 expressed himself with the Christian frankness which had won for him the friendship of the Holy Father. In the month of October, 1859, he had seen General Lamoricière on his passage through Paris. He met him in company with General MacMahon, who had come, with the modesty of an old lieutenant, to give him an account of the Battle of Magenta. Having finished his description, M. de Corcelles turned to Lamoricière and asked him what he thought of the command of the Pope's Army. "I think," replied the hero of Constantine, "that it is a cause for which I should be happy to die."

This said everything. It only remained to put the heroic wish into execution. A correspondence was entered into between M. de Corcelles and Lamoricière. They made use of conventional language, and, had their letters been intercepted, they would only appear to have referred to agriculture. But the details of the enterprise required an active personal intermediary; and for that purpose Pius IX. chose Mgr. de Mérode.

Never was a business more discreetly or rapidly conducted. The astute Prelate concealed his mission, but not his person. He stopped a few days in Paris, and thought it would be wise to ask for an audience of the Emperor, as the official Protector of the Holy See. The interview was courteous on both sides, and the conversation began pleasantly, but towards the end the Emperor said : " Well, Monseigneur, I don't hear that things are going on very well at Rome." Mgr. de Mérode replied instantly, while bowing, with that inimitable look and tone of which those only who knew him well can form an idea, " Hé, sire ! in what country are things going on well ? " The Emperor twirled his moustache, saluted his somewhat inconvenient visitor, and the audience was at an end. " This was the only time," writes the Marquis de Ségur, " that Mgr. de Mérode saw Napoleon III."*

Two days later Mgr. de Mérode arrived at the Château de Prouzel, where Lamoricière was living with his brother, Count Werner de Mérode. It was on the 3rd March, 1860. He was not expected, so that his visit might appear to those who heard of it only a family affair. He left his brother with Mde. de Lamoricière, took the General aside, and alluding to the correspondence with M. de Corcelles, immediately delivered the Pope's message. Lamoricière bowed and said : " When a father calls upon his son to defend him, there is only one thing to be done, and that is to go ! " Mérode then spoke of the dangers to which the General might be exposed. Lamoricière answered, " I have neither fear nor hope." Then began a most touching conversation between these two great souls. Mérode could only admire the faith, piety, and dis-

* " A Winter at Rome," by the Marquis de Ségur, p. 132.

interestedness of the great General ; whilst Lamoricière
felt himself more and more inspired to make the sacrifice,
when he heard from Mérode of the unlimited confidence
placed in him by the common Father of the Faithful.
After a combat of generosity between the cousins, they
embraced, and all was settled. Mde. de Lamoricière,
taken into their confidence, approved of everything, and
the next morning the husband and wife offered to God
their noble resolution and generous sacrifice in the
little church of Prouzel.

On the 19th of March the General, though hardly
recovered from a sharp attack of gout, left home after
only saying *au revoir* to his people, who had not the least
idea of where he was going. He had answered one or
two intimate friends, who tried to dissuade him from
the idea, with the words : " One does not discuss a
father's appeal; one simply obeys." He wrote to
General Bedeau : " I have told my wife to tell you the
line I have taken. I have really no hope but in God ;
for after what I see and know human strength is not
enough for the work I have undertaken."

Under pretence of a journey to Belgium he took the
railroad to the North from the Amiens station, having
as his companion a young and resolute friend of his,
M. Francis Cattoir, whom he had invited ten days
before to Prouzel. To him he confided, while crossing
the frontier, his beloved African sabre, which he never
would leave behind him. Father Deschamps waited
for him at Brussels in a little apartment which had
been privately secured for him by the Marquis de la
Boissière.* After some hours spent with that illus-

* This old officer of the Royal Guard in the time of Charles X.
had been settled in Brussels since his marriage to the niece of
Comte Felix de Mérode, Mlle. de Thicnues.

trious Religious, of whom God had made use to bring
him back to the Faith, he took the train to Cologne
with Pius IX.'s Chamberlain. There Mgr. de Mérode
took the famous sabre from Lamoricière and hid it
under his cassock, to pay a visit to the cathedral, and
place their journey under the protection of the Magi.
It was impossible for one of the de Grammonts' grand-
sons to forget that his ancestors in the twelfth century
had mounted guard over those great relics during their
passage through Franche-Comté. In memory of this
glorious service, the knights of his family alone have
the right to enter this magnificent chapel in Cologne
Cathedral with their swords by their sides. The
travellers passed from Cologne to Munich in the
strictest incognito. At Vienna the Apostolic Nuncio
gave them the most cordial welcome. But whilst they
were talking to him the French - Ambassador was
announced, the Marquis de Moustier, whose wife was
first cousin to Mgr. de Mérode. They consequently
escaped by a back door, hurried their departure, and
embarked for Trieste. By the 27th of March they
were at Ancona, before the French police had discovered
Lamoricière's departure. Thus this mysterious journey
was accomplished, the secret of which had been so
faithfully guarded, and of which the success was so
important to the cause of the Royal Pontificate. The
King of the Belgians, when he heard of it, owned
that Mgr. de Mérode had conducted the whole affair
quite admirably, and that it did immense honour to
his diplomatic ability.

The arrival of the travellers at Ancona was like a
thunderclap to the Revolutionists. It was hardly believed in the rest of Italy, than, already, Lamoricière,
having visited the citadel, the ramparts and the

K

barracks, and drawn up a plan to unite the ports with
the arsenal, had flown to Rome, where he arrived in
the night of the 1st and 2nd of April, and placed himself under the Pope's orders, with the sole condition
that he should never be expected to take arms against
France. The Pope received him with the joy and the
pride of a Father who had placed all his hopes of defence in this, the most valiant of his sons. But the
French Ambassador feigned great indignation, and
threatened to withdraw the garrison. After a good
deal of disagreeable correspondence, it was agreed that
the Pontifical Government should ask permission for
the General to serve in a foreign country. Pius IX.
did not hesitate to take this step, which was, however,
very repugnant to Lamoricière. The authorization was
granted, and the General who had proudly said, " I
have given my sword to the Pope and recommended
my soul to God; but I wish to maintain my honour
and to hold nothing from the Emperor," did not hesitate, when once his position was established, to enter
into relations with General de Goyon, who was the
Commander-in-Chief of the French division of the
Army of Occupation in Rome. This officer, who was
full of respectful admiration and esteem for Lamoricière, took care to keep clear of political passions, and
did all he possibly could to facilitate his task. On the
9th of April Lamoricière took possession of his command by an order of the day which might have been
borrowed from the history of the Crusades. " Soldiers ! "
he exclaimed, " the Pope, Pius IX., having deigned to
summon me to defend his menaced and misunderstood
rights, I did not hesitate for a moment to take my
sword again ! " He ended with these words : " Revolution, like Islamism in old days, now menaces

Europe ; and now, as then, the cause of the Papacy is the cause of civilization and of the liberty of the whole world."

If the choice of the General was a happy one, his task was not the less arduous and difficult. Lamoricière could not reckon upon Cardinal Antonelli's help in this work. The Secretary of State had concentrated all power in his own hands ; but he had not the knowledge necessary to enable him to recruit, discipline, or place an army on a war footing. His great ability made him a valuable Minister in time of peace, but not in time of war. M. Keller, writing of him, says : "Possessing an extraordinary keen perception, an astute diplomatist, disgusted with the reforms in which he had co-operated in 1847 with a kind of ardour, having an unlimited confidence in the efficacy of temporizing in all matters, and of offering only a passive resistance, fully persuaded, unfortunately, that the Holy See, in its weakness, could do nothing to save itself, and that, while waiting the course of events, it should place all its hopes in the interference of the Great Powers of Europe, the Cardinal had shown infinite skill in eluding all the demands for reforms which had been made by the French Government, and at the same time overwhelmed the French authorities with attentions and caresses." His diplomatic services had been great : in the conferences of Gaëtà he had been thoroughly appreciated, as well as in the publication and appropriation of the *motu proprio*, and in the skill with which he had served the Pope during the last ten years. All these were incontestable titles to the gratitude of the Holy See : but Pius IX. felt that if he were to have recourse to arms for his defence, he would need a new Minister ; and he chose Mgr. de

Mérode. Antonelli, not believing in the success of the experiment, only saw the discontent that it would create. But the Pope was, after all, his master, and the Cardinal knew how to obey. M. Keller continues: "He bowed before his Sovereign's decision without placing any apparent obstacle in the way; and although he strove to retain in his own hands the post of War Minister, he at last consented, at the request of the General, that this office should be entirely detached from his Secretariate, and be confided to Mgr. de Mérode."* It was just that the Pope should give a War Minister to Lamoricière who had been so instrumental in placing him in his present position.

Mgr. de Mérode at once issued the following Order of the Day :—

"His Holiness Pope Pius IX. has deigned to appoint me as his War Minister at a solemn moment and under circumstances when not only Italy, but the whole Christian world, is moved at the dangers which threaten the patrimony of St. Peter, and has associated itself with noble enthusiasm in the cause of the Vicar of Jesus Christ. A very grave and arduous mission has been entrusted to me, and that is to watch over and supply the wants of the Pontifical Army. I will use every effort to accomplish this task, with the most tender veneration towards the Holy Father, and the most ardent solicitude for his generous children, whose fidelity, in the midst of such great trials, is the surest guarantee for the future."

What the new War Minister promised, he more than performed. To understand fully both his herculean labours and his merit, we must bear in mind what the Pontifical Army was when General de Lamoricière

* "General de Lamoricière," by M. Keller, ii. p. 244.

came to take the command. Let us listen again to
M. Keller (11 c. p. 320) :—

"The Pontifical Army had only eleven battalions of
600 men, who were armed with old rifles, and were
badly clothed, badly fed, sleeping on straw, and
thoroughly demoralized by the evacuation of the
Romagna. Desertions had reduced the cavalry to a
simple handful of dragoons. The artillery existed but
in name, and their cannon were either obsolete or useless for service. There were neither ambulances, nor
military trains, nor any material for a campaign. This
was not surprising when we remember that since the
Treaty of Tolentino, the Papal soldiers had never fired
a shot except against brigands; and, until 1859, no
one ever dreamed of their being called into active
service. All the efforts to stem the Revolutionary tide
had been carried on either by France or Austria. Now
Austria had retired within her own frontiers; and
France was continually warning the Holy See to look
after her own safety, and that as speedily as possible :
while that safety was menaced both from the north and
the south."

In the face of so imminent a danger as this, General
Lamoricière had no other resource than his own genius,
his military experience, his devotion towards the Holy
See, and the active and intelligent zeal of the new
War Minister. What they did in four months is
incredible. The General began the very first day to
organize his staff. The men whom he chose deserved
all his confidence. There was M. de Pimodan, late
Colonel of Cavalry in the Austrian service; M. de
Chevigné, an officer of the Duke of Modena's; M. de
Lorgeril, who had won his spurs in the African campaign; M. de Bourbon-Chalus, whose devotion to the

Church's cause filled him with a courage which made
him ready to brave martyrdom itself. Mgr. de Mérode
also pointed out to him several officers of the old
Pontifical Army worthy of selection: Count Palfy,
an Austrian captain; the Marquis Lépri, the most
studious of the Noble Guard; Comte Dodici, Lieut.
in the 1st Regiment of the Line; and above all, M.
de Mortillet, Captain of the 1st Foreign Regiment,
whose merit was evident to the commonest observer.
Lamoricière made him Chief of his Staff with the
rank of Commandant; associated him with all his
plans and thoughts, both in good and evil times,
and shared with him all the heroism and dangers of
the enterprise. We must not forget also to mention
M. de Charette, whose name, so glorious already in
Vendée, was to be crowned with still brighter glory,
first in the service of the Pope and then in that
of France; M. d'Albivusse, then sergeant-major, but
who left Rome with a colonel's epaulettes; Quatrebarbes, who flew from Ancona to place himself under
Lamoricière's orders; and Blumensthil, who commanded the French Artillery at the Fort of St. Angelo.
Blumensthil sent in his resignation and renounced
all his previous rights in France to espouse the cause
of the Pope. This was the very man whom Lamoricière
wanted. He had fought all through the Crimean War
and passed through all the grades of pontoon and
artillery service. Lamoricière at once put him at the
head of the Pontifical Artillery. This force at that
moment existed only on paper. Its magazines were
placed under the windows of the Vatican, behind the
Belvedere Museum. The whole place was full of
rubbish and was occupied by coachmakers and artists.
It was difficult to realize that this was the famous

foundry from whence the finest cannon and the best
church bells had formerly been issued; besides
(curiously enough) the metal plates of the column in
the Place Vendôme. To give room for the new trade
which had invaded this place, all that remained of the
old war material had been thrown into the cellars.
They were dragged out from thence, with great
trouble; and made a sorry exhibition enough on the
green sward of the Belvedere! It was enough to
discourage any one but Lamoricière. At a moment's
notice, all the men and things which crowded up the
foundry were turned out: the roof repaired: the
partitions taken down: new forges set up with all the
necessary implements, and workshops organized for
the armourers, wheelwrights, carpenters, turners, and
coopers. The workmen were chosen among the
artillerymen as far as possible, and were formed into
a special corps. Everything had to be improvised:
persons, material, work-tables, &c.; yet within a month
all had been organized, and the establishment already
rendered important services to the new army.

During this time the War Minister organized all
the necessary camp material and what was needed for
the ambulances and for the Army Hospital Corps.
He also presided at the recruiting. A forced con-
scription was repugnant to the Pope as well as to the
character of his people; so that they contented themselves with voluntary enrolment. Lamoricière's example was enough, and there was no need of an appeal
to arms, imitated from that in the days of the
Crusades, which had been suggested by certain over-
zealous counsellors. Soldiers arrived from all points
of the Catholic world. Austrians, Swiss, Irish,
English, French, Dutch, and Belgians offered their

services with the most ready zeal. But it was
necessary to study their characters and habits, to
know which to employ, with discernment. Men were
certainly not wanting, but formed soldiers were.
The Austrians were the most numerous. Upwards of
six thousand presented themselves. But the officers'
brevets had been given at Vienna without sufficient
examination; and they had the fashion of giving
the epaulette to whoever brought with him forty men.
The Swiss, who had for a long while formed the personal guard of the Pope, were more solid; but the
rival feelings in the different cantons brought about
lamentable divisions; and the Revolutionary Propaganda had already sown its seed among them. The
Irish, though firm in their faith and incapable of
treason, would only obey officers of their own country.
France and Belgium had also sent brilliant and noble
contingents, if one only regards the names of the
volunteers, and their personal bravery; but one set
quarrelled with the officers of the French garrison;
the others, like Cathelineau, who supported themselves, wished to choose their own officers and have
a special flag and a cross on their sleeves. A brave
captain of the French Army, M. de Becdelièvre, who
had taken the command of the French and Belgian
Contingent, could not master these difficulties, and
sent in his resignation. This picture of the actual
state of things will enable our readers to judge of
the courage, patience, and tact required of the War
Minister. Mérode took his orders from the General,
made his conditions with the volunteers, drew up the
lists, reserving to himself the choice of the officers,
forbid any special flag or cross apart from the rest of
the army, and ended in six weeks by forming these

young recruits into one body under a common law and all ready to obey the General's orders. We must add to this herculean task the re-establishment of the cannon foundry at the Vatican; the re-organization of the arsenal, and the construction of a new riding-school. Wherever he could find relations or old friends he roused their zeal to labour in the good cause. Not content with the formation of the Corps of Franco-Belgians, he showed to each one of the recruits a truly paternal solicitude. He sent to Belgium for the best rifles and guns, formed an admirable battery of artillery, studied every branch of the service, took in every separate want in every separate department, and laboured for twenty hours a day, following Lamoricière's example; the result of which was, the formation of a whole army in an incredible short space of time.

After having clothed, armed, and equipped his men from head to foot, it was even more vital to feed them well. Lamoricière insisted on the bread being brought to his own table to be tested. At the first mouthful he found that it was bad, had it analyzed, and discovered that the flour was mixed with stones, alum, and other substances. On inquiry it turned out that the contract had been given to a certain great man, who had exacted such profitable terms for himself from the bakers that they were well-nigh forced to cheat. This Lamoricière would not stand for a moment. He announced that he should himself be present at the distribution, and would send back all that was not good; and if the contractor were not dismissed, he added that he would send in his resignation. Mérode obeyed him, and the bread henceforth was excellent.

When Lamoricière was at Loretto, he congratulated
the War Minister on the goodness of the bread, who
answered, laughing: " That he could only attribute
it to the influence of the statue of Sixtus V., which
was in the centre of the square of that town, and
whose presence, by the remembrance of the past, inspired the rogues in the country with the wholesome
fear of the gallows, which that great Pope never failed
to employ when needful."   But, unhappily, these are
not days when thieves are hung, and those who had
enriched themselves at the Pope's expense only too
easily obtained pardon and mercy from the paternal
goodness of Pius IX.   The incorruptible honesty of
the General and the War Minister disconcerted them
at last.   Mérode got rid of some, and by vigilance and
severity compelled the others to change their conduct.
At the end of two months everything had been altered.
By the end of May the Pope had eighteen thousand
men under arms, well armed and well clothed, only
too happy to serve his cause, and each and all ready
to shed their blood in his defence.

But, not content with his military programme, the
War Minister pushed forward, at the same time, the
execution of the public works and of the civil and
administrative reforms which were to complete the
organization and defence of the Pontifical States.   He
opened out new roads, and laid down 120 kilomètres of
telegraphic wires to Viterbo, Perugia, Urbino, Gubbio,
Spoleto, and Civita Castellana.   He had all the plans
drawn up for the railroad which was to unite the
Adriatic to the Mediterranean by way of Florence;
created a topographical office attached to the Staff and
to the War Office; and made new stations everywhere
for the postal and telegraph service.   He added to

that a Commission of Inquiry as to the state of the bridges and high roads, and also as to the administration of the police in the Pontifical States; on the capacity and zeal of those employed in such functions; and on the honesty and probity of all those who had the handling of the public money, among whom great peculations had been long suspected.

Lamoricière's correspondence with the War Minister deals with all these questions, whether civil or military. It reveals, like all the rest, the ardour of their fidelity to the Holy See, and the disinterestedness with which they carried on their work. The War Minister sometimes hesitated; then the General reassures, counsels, encourages, and at times even reproaches him. The style of his letters is that of a soldier, full of frankness and honour, going straight to the point, and often full of wit and Gallic humour. One day the General excuses himself for having left certain letters of Mérode's unanswered:

"In spite of the bad state of my hands, I must send you a few words to-day. I owe you a great many answers; but to some I will content myself by replying in the following aphorisms. The first is pagan, the second Christian, the third Mussulman; but I hold all three to be orthodox:

"1. *Æquam memento rebus in arduis*
       Servare mentem.

"2. *Suaviter in modo, fortiter in re.*

"3. The heart of he who governs should be like the sea, which never allows itself to be troubled by the storm."

"Above all, let us be calm," he writes on another occasion to Mgr. de Mérode. "You have had all to do, and you have done it well: the feeding and clothing of the troops, the organization of the staff, the territorial and military circumscriptions, the transmission of orders and reports, &c., &c., &c. . . . . You have perhaps done these things too much at a time; but it was necessary they should be done, and you have done them well. Be content.

"You tell me you have not the habit of command. I may answer that you have given a great proof of this by being surprised that, having suddenly changed all the works of your machine, you find that everything does not act with the perfection you expected!

"But do not be so impatient. All is doing well, and will do better still, later on, I hope, if God protects us, and prevents Satan from sowing discord between the only men who can do any good."—(3rd May, 1860.)

The General was thoroughly outspoken, both as to the capacity of his officers, and as to the fidelity of the civil functionaries; pointing out those who were open or secret traitors; and characterizing others who were sincere enough but weak, and who, though wishing for the safety of the Pontifical Government, thought they had the right to serve it badly. "They are very much astonished," he adds, "when they are asked to do their duty. I do not speak of those who think they have done enough for the Pope and the Church when they have satisfied their consciences by acting up to the letter of the law. This is the quietism of Fénélon, which I thought was condemned by Rome. I prefer Bossuet's formula, which declares that we must show our love of God by acts of service. . . . . Above all, we must determine to practise the maxim, *Rather serve than please.* I promised you always to speak the truth. One must look it bravely in the face, without being shaken by opposition ; and work without stopping at all we can do to remedy the evil, placing our whole confidence in God, and trusting to Him to accomplish the rest."

With these feelings Lamoricière was alike above criticism and praise. He gave the same advice to his friend Mérode, telling him " that he always put in the same pigeon-hole, without reading them, all the letters in which he was glorified, menaced, or calumniated." He had given as a title to this collection the words, " Abuse and compliments."

His magnificent contempt of public opinion and of human meannesses was fully shared by the War Minister. He only thought of the great work in which he was engaged, and every moment of his day and every step he took were employed in some needful action or reform. He put Perugia in a state of defence, fortified Pesaro, emptied the citadel of Spoleto of its prisoners and prepared it for the reception of fresh troops. Viterbo was the object of equal care. He sent eight thousand men there, built new stables for the cavalry and artillery horses, established magazines for military stores, and made the workshops supply all that was necessary for the garrison. Both in Rome and throughout the Papal States, the help of the monasteries and convents was demanded, and the Religious Communities hastened to place at the disposal of the War Minister all the buildings necessary for the common defence.

Lamoricière went from town to town and from garrison to garrison to strengthen the defences of the Pontifical States. He found Perugia infested with the Revolutionary fever ; Gubbio more faithful ; Fano well defended by its little garrison. There he received

a despatch from M. de Courcy, the French Consul at
Ancona, announcing to him that he had been condemned to death by the Revolutionary Junta, or Head
of the Secret Societies. He only smiled and said:
"For a long time I have been threatened in a like
manner; but I hope that God, who preserved me in
1848, will not abandon me to-day, and I am ready to
accept whatever His Divine Providence may appoint
for me."

The town of Ancona was a special object of anxiety
to him. When the Austrians had retired from thence
they had left seventy magnificent cannon and bronze
mortars, which they offered to the Pontifical Government for a nominal price. A most foolish idea of
economy made the Cardinal reject the offer. These
seventy pieces of artillery were painfully transported
to Trieste by coasting vessels, just before Mérode became War Minister. He positively shed tears at this
short-sighted policy—a regret which was fully shared
by Lamoricière, who felt that his defence of the town
was thereby paralyzed. He resolved, nevertheless, to
make Ancona the basis of his operations, believing that
it could hold out for a long time even against superior
forces, by setting up a lighthouse, enlarging the port,
repairing the walls, and giving, above all, to the
inhabitants of Ancona the means of developing their
commerce. He found the population greatly embittered
against the Pontifical Administration. The General
listened attentively to their grievances and lost not a
day in having them redressed. He induced Mgr. de
Mérode to enter into negotiations with a French company to make a railway, ordered the construction of an
aqueduct to convey fresh water into the town, and
started steam-mills to ensure the subsistence of his

troops. The quays were widened, the lighthouse built, the port enlarged, water and bread were at once cheapened, and the discontent of the population was changed into an honest joy ; and whilst the wild beast of Socialism groaned at the implacable enmity of Lamoricière and cursed the powerful Soldier-Priest who had suddenly created this brave army out of the earth, honest men became reassured, the weak and timid came forward, the bad hid themselves, and everywhere arose a hope of a happy and prosperous future for the town.

It had always been the opinion of Mgr. de Mérode that the Pontifical States could defend themselves, provided they had an illustrious chief, good soldiers, and faithful and resolute civil functionaries, and this conviction was shared by Lamoricière. "You may be sure of this," he said, "that the true state of things here is not known in France. The immense majority of the people are in favour of the Pope. In France they see the Revolution through spectacles which enlarge everything. If the Austrians had only warned the Pontifical Government that they were going to evacuate Bologna, and if there had been time to send two thousand men there, the four Legations would have been preserved to the Holy See."

After three months' experience the opinion of the General was even stronger. But that we might not again see the disgraceful sight of the Papal Delegates or Governors being carried off as in 1859, he demanded that the men appointed to these high functions should be of a brave and resolute stamp. To support this theory he used to tell a rather amusing story. In 1831 Cardinal Mastai-Ferretti, uncle of Pope Pius IX., filled the See of Riéti. During the insurrection in the

Romagna a certain Sergognani put himself at the head of a band of Revolutionists and menaced the town. He had Colonel Armandi with him and his two pupils, two young Princes, one of whom became afterwards Napoleon III. On hearing this, the Governor, trembling with fear, flew to the Bishop's House and said, "Eminence! I am going to start for Rome, for the revolution is at hand." " Go as fast as you can," replied the Cardinal, " for your face would be enough to bring it!" The Governor departed, the Bishop called his flock together, made them a stirring speech, had the gates of the town closed, and prepared everything for defence. The band was received with some well-directed shots, and whilst thus kept at bay Cardinal Bernetti, Secretary of State, had time to send troops to deliver the town. Thus Riéti was saved by its Bishop.

This anecdote gave energy and pluck to the Governors in 1860. Almost all remained at their posts. Mgr. Bella was besieged in the Fort of Pesaro, and Mgr. Apollini, made a prisoner at Macerata, was carried off to Turin. But they began to understand that the tactics of evacuation without fighting would never save the position ; that their honour was involved in resistance even unto blood ; and that the first duty of a Governor was to give confidence to his people by his presence, his wise measures and his example.

The Revolutionary Party had tried from the first to hinder Lamoricière's work by launching some troops in the province of Viterbo. But Pimodan pushed forward to meet them, defeated and drove them back in a few hours, and by this brilliant cavalry charge gave to the affair of the " Grottos " a real importance. From that day the Italian Revolutionary bands gave up all further attempts, until they had the assurance of support from one of the Great Powers. The administrative and military organization of the Pontifical States was about, therefore, to destroy the hopes of the Revolution. In a few months more, the prey, watched by Piedmont, would be no longer within her reach. A great blow must be struck. It was decided that, without loss of time, Piedmont should be assured of the secret complicity of France, should lead Lamoricière into error by a diplomatic trick, and then attack him unexpectedly and crush him for ever in an ambush.

Napoleon III. connived at the whole plot. Cialdini went to find him at Chambéry, on the 4th of August, 1860, and asked for his authority to invade the Papal States. The answer has become an historical fact, *"Do it, but do it quickly."* Armed with this passport, Piedmont instantly sent her columns to the front, under the pretext of opposing the entry of the Revolutionary bands, but in reality to carry out her own designs. A letter from Mgr. de Mérode to M. de Corcelles, dated 28th August, points out the danger, but still expresses confidence in the genius and lucky star of Lamoricière : "It is true that Garibaldi's hordes have been multiplied like the sands of the sea, and surround us like an ever-rising tide. But in proportion as the danger increases, so do our fortifications and military preparations ; so that the actual state of things remains much the same. The courage and energy of our General only increase with the danger ; neither among the foreigners nor among the Italians is there a shadow of discouragement. The very name and face of Lamoricière inspire them with unlimited confidence. He has just dismissed the Governor of

L

Sasso-Ferrato, who was a traitor. Every one feels protected and backed up ; the enemy is kept in check;
and, in spite of the immense dangers, every one hopes.
In fact, no one can imagine that Lamoricière can be
beaten ; although no one can guess what he will be
able to do to prevent defeat."

But the invasion became more menacing. Garibaldi
disembarked in Calabria, and rebel bands sprung up
on all sides in obedience to his voice. This news
greatly troubled Mgr. de Mérode, who had previously
been full of joy at the reforms carried out between
him and Lamoricière. He had just received a depu-
tation from the inhabitants of Lodi, who came to
propose to erect a statue to the General, out of gratitude for the road he had just decreed between
Lodi, Orvieto and Spoleto, whereby he had shortened
the two days' journey of these poor people to four
hours' march. The Prelate listened to the long story
of their municipal quarrels, and closes the letter in
which he had described the affair by saying, " Now,
we ourselves shall have to pass through the fire. Let
us hope that we shall be able to say with the martyrs :
' *Et non sum æstuata.*' The army organization im-
proves. Every day and almost every hour shows
signs of real progress."*

A few days later, Mgr. de Mérode went to Terni to
see the manœuvres of the Franco-Belgian battalion
and to consult with Lamoricière. He spoke of the
" phantasmagoria of the Italian Revolution," adding
that all the Garibaldian boasting would fade away
before the genius of his friend. But Lamoricière was
fully alive to the dangers of the situation, and was
thinking of his soul and those of his comrades. " My

* Letter to Comte Werner de Mérode, 30th August, 1860.

dear Mortillet," he said one day to the Chief of his Staff when sitting down at table, "we must put our consciences in order. You know that I have never before tormented you on that point; but now is the moment to settle one's affairs. It won't prevent our drinking a glass of Bordeaux together to-day!"

In the midst of this Christian gaiety, Lamoricière prepared himself for everything. He took the Pope's orders and declared Ancona, Viterbo and Spoleto in a state of siege. The provinces of Frosinone and Velletri were placed in the same position. Wherever the municipalities were hostile, they were dissolved and their leaders imprisoned. The General wrote on the 7th September to Pius IX. upon this subject in the strongest terms: "We must make war on the traitors within our walls, who are no less dangerous to the Holy See than the Garibaldians outside." Pius IX. yielded to his representations, though with tears, and ordered the arrest of the guilty parties. Then General Fanti sent an ultimatum, in the name of Piedmont, which in cynicism and hypocrisy was un-exampled. On the 8th he had reassured Lamoricière. On the 10th Fanti declared to him by his aide-de-camp that the Piedmontese troops would at once occupy the Marches and Umbria "if the Pontifical troops continued to oppose themselves to the expression of the national will." The General replied that he certainly should not evacuate the provinces, which he had received the mission to defend, without a fight; and sent the following despatch to the Cardinal-Secretary of State:— "General Fanti's letter needs no comment; it is the fable of the wolf and the lamb. War, then, must follow unless Europe should intervene." This document is worth its weight in gold, and will delight the

French papers when published. It shows to what
means they have had recourse and to what arguments
they are reduced before they dared violate our
frontiers." But the War Minister, trusting to the
words of the French Ambassador, continued to reassure the General. "A Regiment of the Line had
just disembarked at Civita Vecchia," he said, "and
the Emperor Napoleon had written to the King of
Piedmont to declare that if he attacked the Papal
States, France *would oppose it by force.*" In these
terms Mgr. de Mérode telegraphed to Lamoricière. It
turned out that the actual words of the Ambassador
were, "*that France would be obliged to oppose it:*" a
miserable quibble, which reflects still greater discredit
on the Emperor, and which honest men like Mérode
and Lamoricière could only interpret in one way.
Who could have believed that France only meant a
diplomatic opposition? and that even that would only
consist in a temporary withdrawal of the French Ambassador from Turin?

Lamoricière, deceived like Mérode, wrote asking for
supplies to provision Ancona. "I leave Umbria to be
defended by the French," he wrote. He had reckoned
also on assistance from Austria, and so concentrated
his troops between Ancona and Loretto, where he prepared to make a stand. But on both sides he was
deserted. The French never attempted to defend
Umbria: Pesaro only held out for twenty-four hours:
General Schmidt gave up Perugia without striking a
blow: Colonel Kanzler, who strove to defend the road
to Sinigaglia, had the greatest difficulty in preventing
his men from being cut to pieces, and had to fall back
on Ancona. Two Piedmontese Divisions had encamped before Loretto, on the heights of Castelfidardo,

and at the same time their fleet began to bombard
Ancona. To carry Castelfidardo and defend Ancona
were the two duties incumbent on Lamoricière with
his small body of troops, already exhausted by a five
days' march! He had arrived at Loretto on the 16th,
and Pimodan had joined him on the 17th. That day
the General and all his officers went to Holy Communion in the Holy House, and their example was
followed by a great number of their men. Thus prepared, they determined to give battle on the morrow.

The heights of Castelfidardo were already crowned
by the infantry and artillery of the enemy. Lamoricière gave orders to Pimodan to storm the position and
carry the two farms called *" dei Crocetti,"* while at the
same time another body of men were to keep open the
road to Ancona. We will give the details of the fight
in his own words :

" In the first place, Pimodan, with his well-known
bravery, himself led his Franco-Belgian Corps to the
assault. The first farm, though hotly defended, was
carried : about a hundred prisoners were made, among
whom was a superior officer. The guns were placed in
position to defend the conquered ground, and two
howitzers, under the orders of Lieut. d'Audier, were
brought up under a galling fire in front of the farm
house, in which manœuvre he was assisted by the Irish
Contingent. These brave fellows, having fulfilled their
mission, joined the sharpshooters, and during all the
rest of the fight distinguished themselves by their
courage.

" Four other pieces of the Richter battery arrived
soon after on the heights. This battery was very ably
directed by Colonel Blumensthil, and did great damage
to the enemy. Captain Richter, though with a ball in

his thigh, remained in the middle of the fire : Lieut.
d'Audier, with his howitzers, though terribly exposed,
supplied, by his courage and his thorough knowledge
of his work, the sad inferiority of our artillery to that
of the Piedmontese.

" The two last battalions of General de Pimodan
had crossed the river and had been left in reserve, at
1,500 yards in the rear, hidden by a small wood.

" The moment was come to attack the second farm.
General de Pimodan formed a little column under the
orders of the Commandant de Becdelièvre, composed
of Franco-Belgians, of a detachment of Carabineers,
and of the 1st Regiment of Light Infantry. This little
column advanced resolutely, in spite of the musketry
fire opened out upon them from the farm and the
wood. They went on thus for about 500 yards in the
open, but when about fifty yards from the hill which
they were about to scale, so terrible a fire was poured
upon them from two ranks of men in a regular line of
battle, and so many of our brave fellows fell out of the
ranks in consequence, that they were compelled to
retire. The enemy pursued them, but just as they
got near our men faced them, and received them with
so well directed a fire, and then with such a vigorous
bayonet charge, that, though infinitely superior in
numbers, the enemy fell back about two hundred yards,
which enabled our soldiers to reform and regain the
position they had left. The fire of our artillery, which
was admirably directed, protected this movement.

" From the position I occupied I could judge of all
the phases in the fight, and I heard that General de
Pimodan had been wounded in the face. I ordered
two of the foreign battalions under Colonel Allet to cross
the river and advance to the height of the reserves of

the first column. The 2nd Foreign Battalion and the battalion of the 2nd Line Regiment received orders to form in échelon behind, under the orders of Colonel Cropt. Then I went to the farm to judge of the state of things. Although wounded, General de Pimodan would not give up his command. The enemy had lost a very large number of men, but our losses also were considerable ; and, relatively speaking, were more serious than theirs. I saw that the two battalions and a half, which were all that the General had with him, were not sufficient to carry the second position. I sent to get the reserve under Captain Lorgeril, and replaced them by two of the 1st Foreign Battalions, which I deployed so as to expose them less to the enemy's cannon, though they were fifteen hundred metres off. Lastly, I sent the order by Captain Palfy for the cavalry to cross the river and follow the march of our columns on our right flank. Whilst these dispositions were being made the enemy tried to retake the first farm on two sides, in spite of our artillery fire, and their skirmishers endeavoured to take our reserves in flank. Major Becdelièvre, gathering together all that was left of his battalion, dashed down upon them and forced them to retire to the wood from which they had emerged. The movement ordered to the infantry was well and faithfully executed. But hardly had the 1st Foreign Regiment been deployed, than I saw that a panic had been produced in their ranks by the noise of the shells and the wounds of two or three of their men who had been hit. The officers, I am bound to say, shared fully in the panic of their men. In vain did I try to reassure them. The brave Colonel Allet did all that was in his power, but was not more successful than I had been : the result of which was, that in a few moments both battalions, without having fired a shot, turned tail and fled. The second échelon of the reserve, which had not a single wounded man, followed this sad example. Whilst I was sadly witnessing this, the 2nd Pontifical Corps of Bersaglieri came up to the farm where General de Pimodan remained. To their praise be it spoken, that in the midst of all the confusion and disorder this excellent corps, commanded by the brave Major Fuchman, remained firmly at their posts and defended the position entrusted to them with the greatest bravery. I cannot say as much for the 2nd Battalion of Sharp-shooters, who, seeing the flight of the Swiss, hastened to follow them, and ran down the steep hill up which they had just climbed. Our artillery, six pieces of which alone were in the battery, got entangled in a cross road from which an embankment on each side made it difficult to emerge. The panic was shared by a portion of the artillerymen. One set wanted to turn with their battery and fly, which the narrow road made impossible. The others simply cut the traces of their horses and fled across the fields. I tried in vain to rally a portion of the Foreign Infantry behind the walls of the houses, where they were completely sheltered from the artillery fire, but it was useless. Colonel Cropt and Colonel Allet, who were on horseback in the midst of the fugitives, had not the least influence over them, and even their officers seemed stricken with terror.

" I advised the two Colonels to try and collect the fugitives behind the banks of the Mussone, and to lead them to the conflux of the Aspio, where there was a ford which would bring them on to the Umana Road. Then I returned to the house where the fight was raging. I had just arrived there, when I found the brave General de Pimodan mortally wounded and about to be transported to the ambulance, which had been established near the river. I exchanged a few sad words of farewell with him. This last misfortune, more irreparable than all the others, aggravated our position, which was already terribly compromised."

The Marquis de Pimodan, feeling that he was mortally wounded in three places, called out to his Zouaves, "Never mind me! Let me die! Go and do your duty!" "Vive la France! Vive l'Ardèche!" cried Montravel, dying by his side; while Chalus, with the contrition of a real Christian hero, said, "I have often offended God, but I have shed my blood for His honour and glory, and I feel that God will have mercy upon me!" A little further on Nanteuil sunk in a morass, where four balls and two bayonet thrusts ended his brave career. Young and old fell side by side; all were ripe for heaven. Beccary was but 17, d'Héliaud 18, Du Manoir 19. They fell with their eyes turned towards the Church of Loretto, where they had so lately received the Bread of Life. These heroic deaths formed the first page in the history of the Papal Zouaves. There were three hundred of them, and three months had sufficed to teach them their trade. The evening of that fatal fight at Castelfidardo there were only one hundred and six left, with Becdelièvre and Charette: Becdelièvre, who, when persuading them that morning to go to confession, had exclaimed, "Let us go before God with pure souls;" Charette, who, seeing those brave boys falling one after the other, cried out, "Heaven has opened its gates this day for many amongst us!"

All this was some consolation for poor Lamoricière

and de Mérode; and the latter was never weary of
telling the Pope all the sad but deeply interesting details of that fatal day. In the midst of the General's
grief, as he watched, with tears, the litter which was
bearing away Pimodan, he perceived that the smoke of
the fight and a fringe of trees had concealed from the
enemy the disgraceful flight of his two battalions; so
that he decided to rally all the forces he could muster
and retreat to Ancona. But the cavalry had dispersed,
and barely more than forty-five of them, with 350 of
the infantry, followed him into the town.

It was half-past five o'clock in the evening when
Lamoricière arrived at the gates. " I have no longer
an army ! " he exclaimed to Major de Quatrebarbes,
as he wrung his hand. Then he called together his
officers, and told them that as long as the Pontifical
flag floated from the citadel, nothing was despairing
or lost. There, the intervention of the French was
momentarily expected. The French Consul at once
showed Lamoricière the despatch sent to him on the
11th September by the French Ambassador at Rome.
It was more explicit than the one which de Mérode
had communicated to the General. The words were :
" Orders have been given to embark fresh troops at
Toulon, which cannot fail to arrive soon. The Emperor's Government will not tolerate this culpable
aggression on the part of the Sardinian Government."

At the request of M. de Quatrebarbes, a messenger
from the Consulate was sent off, post-haste, to carry
the document to General Cialdini. He offered to
give him a receipt for its safe arrival; but when the
Frenchman insisted, in the name of his country, on
obtaining a cessation of hostilities, Cialdini replied:

" You have been deceived. We saw your Emperor,
fifteen days ago, at Chambéry, and we know what we
are about." Several of Lamoricière's men, who had
been made prisoners at Castelfidardo, expressed their
astonishment, in presence of Cialdini, at having been
thus abandoned by France. "By France!" exclaimed
the Piedmontese General. "But she is with us!
All we have done is with the permission of your
Emperor!"

If ever there were a defeat more glorious than a
victory it was that of Castelfidardo; as the battle of
Thermopylæ resulted in the glory of Leonidas and his
300 Spartans.

For ten days longer Lamoricière held the place
where he had concentrated his last troops and his last
efforts. Admiral Persano bombarded Ancona with a
large fleet, armed with upwards of 100 guns; while
the town was equally invested on all sides by land.
The churches, the Archbishop's Palace, even the
French Consulate, were riddled with shells. But the
enemy paid dearly for the ground gained near the city,
and never succeeded in retaining any important position. The Piedmontese were driven back day by day
by the heroism of the Pontifical troops, who were continually making vigorous and unexpected sorties.
"Yet," as Lamoricière wrote in his memorable report
of the siege, "the prolonged bombardment of Ancona
did not bring a single vessel to our aid, not even from
those neutral Powers who, under similar circumstances,
generally send ships to protect their own Consulates
and men of their own nations. For eight days the
roar of the cannon was heard at Venice, on the coasts
of Dalmatia, and even at Trieste. The telegraph was
not silent, and Europe knew well enough what was

happening under our walls; yet no sign of help or
sympathy was given us from any quarter."

During this terrible siege the Pope, without waiting
for the result, determined to honour the memory of
Pimodan by magnificent obsequies. M. de Corcelles
and Mgr. de Mérode went to Civita Vecchia to receive
his body, which was brought back by Sigismond de
Mirepoix, his brother-in-law, and Prince Henry de
Ligne. De Rossi wrote the inscription for his tomb,
and Pius IX. gave to the dead hero the title of Duke
de Castelfidardo. Mérode wrote on the 27th September, 1860 : "We still keep Tivoli, which cuts the road
to the Piedmontese, and saves the two provinces of
Frosinone and Velletri up to the Neapolitan frontier.
But this will only last till the regular troops come
down upon us. It is quite clear that the French
Government is determined that the Revolution shall
be accomplished. General de Goyon contents himself
with the occupation of Frascati to please the French
Ambassador, who is in *villegiatura* at the Villa Conti,
and protected by French cannon. The officials are
ready for anything; for, to be in a state of grace in
the eyes of the Emperor, is to kiss the foot and hand
of the Pope, while all the time they are despoiling him
of everything; yet they are ready to re-establish things
as they were, if circumstances should arise to make it
expedient. Not only are they prepared to forswear
their previous assertions, but they are content to have
no opinions for the present, and are ready for anything
and everything : this is the habitual state of their
consciences. . . . .

"Look at all the heroic efforts of Lamoricière
swallowed up by a conspiracy organized by a man
whom people fancied was simple and good! His

plan seems to be, by means of this Piedmontese
invasion, to leave nothing to the Pope but the patrimony of St. Peter. When the Revolutionists have
arrived at the frontiers, people will feign to cry out
' Stop ! ' while they allow them to enter in on all
sides. In the meantime, the General has repassed the
Appenines with the determination to defend Ancona to
the last. God knows what he will be able to do !
Until now he has really worked miracles, and no one
is more capable than he is of remedying all the
miseries of the country ; while he has organized an
army capable of resisting all these Revolutionary bands,
unless backed up by regular forces. All Umbria is now
invaded up to Spoleto. Not one of the soldiers would
desert his flag, in spite of all the efforts and temptations
offered by the enemy to induce him to revolt. You can
fancy the agony of mind we are in here, when we think
of those brave fellows shut up in Ancona and exposed
to a double danger : on one side, the danger of death,
which they seem to court with reckless generosity ; on
the other the danger of ridicule, with which our per-
fidious enemies are hoping to stifle the Papal cause.''

But it is not for himself, it is for those who are
in the heat of the strife that his heart bleeds and his
eyes are filled with tears. He passes his nights in
pleading for them before God, and makes his sister-in-
law the confidant of his sorrows :—

" No meditation could make me more fully understand, or more deeply feel, the immense graces which
God has given me, in permitting that I should be
placed, as I am, in the midst of the events which are
being now accomplished. You can guess how much
we are suffering, and I am ashamed of not suffering
more with all those brave and generous souls, of whom

the world takes little heed, but who are sacrificing
themselves so nobly in the suite of Lamoricière.
Our General is, without doubt, by his actions and
example the greatest preacher I know. How I wish
you could have seen, as I have done, these young
fellows, belonging to the highest classes of society,
coming day by day to be enrolled in the Papal Army
and embracing all the hardships of a soldier's life
with the greatest courage and cheerfulness! They
serve the Church with a devotion, a simplicity, and a
faith which I can best explain to you by quoting the
speech of the young Duke de Sabran, nephew of that
General de Pontévés whom I was so fond of, and who
was killed at Sebastopol: 'I do not know if we shall
be called upon to fight; but, even if not, I shall
always be too happy to think I have carried a knap-
sack in the service of the Vicar of Jesus Christ.' I
quote his words; but I could tell you of hundreds of
others, and the lives of these young fellows are in
keeping with their speeches. Their piety does not
hinder their zeal; nay—what am I saying?—it only
makes them more perfect soldiers.

"Well, to think of all these young heroes with
Lamoricière, shut up in Ancona, separated from all
friendly relations and exposed to such terrible dangers,
is to us the greatest torment you can imagine. I
think of them day and night, exposed to defeat, to
hunger or thirst, to violent deaths, to the most extreme
and varied dangers; while we are sitting quietly here,
and clasping the hands of those traitors who have
prepared all these snares for us, while they pretended
to be our friends. How hard life sometimes is, and
how bitter are such trials!"

He wrote these lines at five o'clock in the morning,

adding that the despatches had just announced to him
the attack of Montefiascone, and that the Governor of
Viterbo besought him, by telegram, to forbid any
resistance to the two thousand Revolutionists who were
besieging the place. The capitulation of Ancona put
an end to the struggle. On the morning of the 28th
the enemy's batteries, advancing to within 250
yards of the ramparts, demolished them entirely,
and the fire of the Papal artillery could no longer
pretend to check them. This unequal struggle
lasted an hour and a half. " Then," wrote the General,
" one of the enemy's shells set fire to the powder maga-
zine, which exploded. The quays were much injured,
and the walls to which the chains were attached being
thrown down, all the defences of the port were destroyed.
A breach five hundred yards wide had been made in
the fortifications, and the other side of the town could
offer no serious resistance. The enemy was on the
point of landing on the quay and carrying the town by
assault,.without our being able to prevent it. Then I
was obliged to hoist the white flag on the citadel, and
all the forts repeated the signal. I sent Major Manzi
immediately on board the admiral's ship to treat about
the capitulation. It was half-past four in the afternoon, and the fire immediately ceased on both sides."

This was the end of the General's report. Major
Quatrebarbes went up to the citadel and found him
walking alone in the casemate. The officers of his
staff respected his silence. From time to time he
stopped, his eyebrows were contracted, and his dark
eyes flashed lightning. " On how many men can I
reckon," he asked Quatrebarbes, " if the capitulation
should not be accepted?" " On 1,000 or 1,200,
General." " That is enough for the intrenched camp

and the citadel. By abandoning the town we might, if necessary, prolong the defence for forty-eight hours. It would be my duty to do so if there were the vaguest hope of succour. But, as it is, it would be a useless suicide." . . . .

The next morning Lamoricière, with his staff, went on board Admiral Persano's frigate. He only remained there a few hours and then embarked in a merchant ship, which landed him at Genoa on the 7th of October. There he found a letter from the Pope fitted to console that brave heart. "The enemies of truth and justice," he wrote, " may choose to misrepresent facts ; but all good Catholics and all honest men will look upon what has lately passed in the Pontifical States as a triumph for the Church. We have seen, thanks to your activity, zeal and intelligence, an army organized in a few months— a small one, it is true, but more than sufficient to repress the Revolution, had it not been encouraged and fostered by powerful hands and by regular forces incomparably superior to ours in numbers, and aided by all the means which fraud and lying could suggest."

Mgr. de Mérode came in for a large share of the praises addressed by Pius IX. to Lamoricière. But he never thought of his own work, and only complained bitterly and openly of the deception practised upon them by the French Government in the despatch of the 11th of September. He wrote to his brother : "The Emperor has played us false. I have not answered the Ambassador on the accusation of falsification. The whole question is so clear and simple that I cannot understand how they can pretend to muddle it. When they talked of ' *opposing the enemy by force*,' and embarking troops at Toulon to come to our aid, how was it possible to imagine they meant nothing by it ?"

Now, all this mystery has been cleared up. The despatch from the Duc de Grammont to the French Consul at Ancona was not only authentic but sincere ; and the Ambassador was the first to be taken in. When the Home and the Foreign Ministers, MM. Thouvenel and Billaut, heard of the invasion of the Papal States by the Piedmontese, Napoleon III. was at Marseilles, preparing to embark for Algeria. He had left no instructions whatever. The two Ministers, taken by surprise, telegraphed to the Emperor for orders, but received no reply. Then, being entirely ignorant of his secret thoughts, they telegraphed in the sense which they thought most conformable to his previous policy and the public interest. They were entirely ignorant also of what had passed in the interview at Chambéry. When they found out the truth, they had nothing left for it but to disown the telegram, or rather to change its sense ; and M. de Grammont, in his note to Cardinal Antonelli of the 25th October, only said, "That there never had been a question of making war with Piedmont" ; an excuse which had neither sense nor object. It was necessary now to negotiate for the deliverance of the Pontifical Army, who were prisoners. Mgr. de Mérode arranged with the Pope that M. de Corcelles, accompanied by an officer of the Staff, M. de la Guiche, and by a Colonel of the Pontifical Army, should undertake this delicate mission with the Piedmontese Government. This negotiation was happily accomplished and the prisoners were released, meeting Lamoricière at Rome, to whom they gave the most enthusiastic reception.

Lamoricière's return to Pius IX. was that of a hero who comes to console himself in the arms of a Saint after the adversities of fortune. The War Minister gives

M

the following account of the great and salutary impression which his return to Rome produced :—

"We knew nothing whatever of the General's movements," writes Mgr. de Mérode, "since the 29th of September, that was, for a fortnight, when on Sunday last he suddenly reappeared like another Jonas. He is preparing a careful report of all that has passed, which will be a most interesting document. I do not think that at any period of his life he displayed more genius than during the siege of Ancona. To understand fully how great were his difficulties, we must remember that it is only during the last six months that he has been able to prepare, organize and instruct his little army in all its branches. You cannot imagine how his arrival in Rome has stirred up every one's courage."

De Mérode then protests against the lying reports which had been given of the fight of Castelfidardo and of the treachery of the Italians.

"There is not a word of truth in all this," he exclaims, "and the result of these false statements is to diminish the merit of the General, who knew how to inspire every man under him with the strongest sense of duty. There were certainly differences between one army corps and the other, both in point of courage and in powers of resistance ; but that is a very different thing from treason."

The victorious Piedmontese had allowed the General to come to Rome from Genoa to see the Pope, to make his report, and consult with him as to the state of affairs. After his audience of Pius IX., during which that great Pope forgot his own disasters to console the warrior who had sacrificed his glory in his cause, Lamoricière shut himself up with his Staff to draw up his report, which history will call the description of

the last Crusade. The Pope revised it himself, but
changed only a few words in it; and Europe declared
that Lamoricière wielded the pen as well as the sword.
After having performed this duty he asked for a ten
months' leave of absence to revisit France. Pius IX.
offered him the post of War Minister, which he refused.
His defeat had given some advantage to those who had
complained of his inviolable probity, and he did not
feel that he had sufficient influence to conquer local
prejudices, and especially to overcome the old routine.

The employment of force had always seemed to
Antonelli both useless and dangerous ; and the creation
of an army composed mainly of foreign volunteers had
not pleased many of the Romans. What they could
hardly forgive to Lamoricière, who, until now, had been
victorious in every battlefield, how would they accept
it, when he had been beaten at Castelfidardo and
Ancona ? He retired, therefore, only keeping the title
of Commander-in-Chief; but he entreated the Pope to
leave the War Office in the hands of Mgr. de Mérode,
who was to be the soul of the little army which was
about to reform itself and repair the catastrophe which,
for the moment, had destroyed all their hopes.

Pius IX. wanted to give Lamoricière the title of
Count. He refused it, saying he wished to be called
nothing but Léon de Lamoricière. The Pope then sent
him the Great Pontifical Order of Christ, ennobled, in
this instance, by the terms in which it was conveyed,
and which were as truly Christian in thought as they
were beautiful in their antique simplicity :—

" I send you one thing, at least, which you cannot
refuse—the Cross of Christ, Who will be, I hope, your
reward and mine."

France wished to offer Lamoricière a sword of honour,

which he refused, saying, with a military modesty:
" A sword of honour is given to a general for a great
victory, for the capture of a strongly-defended town by
assault, or for having valiantly defended and held a
fortress besieged by the enemy beyond the time when resistance seemed possible. Now, as is too well known, I
have done nothing of the sort. The provinces I was
defending have been invaded ; the towns taken ; our war
material is lost, and the whole army has been carried
into captivity.

" If, since our disasters, the moral position of the
temporal power has been improved; if confidence and
strength have returned to the defenders of the right,
while a spirit of division and uncertainty reigns in the
enemy's camp; if France, that noble champion of the
cause of God, has not ceased to feel her heart beat with
those generous impulses of devotion which have never
failed her in moments of peril, we must not look to the
hand of man in all these matters. But I cannot forget
that a General who has done nothing but save the
honour of his flag, does not deserve, and cannot receive,
any reward."

When, ten years after Castelfidardo and Ancona,
the Emperor who had said to Cialdini, " *Do it, and do
it quickly*," was abandoned by fortune and lost his
first battle, it was not difficult to see in these reverses
the judgment of God, whose vengeance ever falls on
those monarchs who have betrayed and deceived His
Church. It was on the 4th of August, 1870, the very
anniversary of the famous meeting at Chambéry, that
Napoleon III., after twenty years of prosperity and
grandeur, was defeated at Wissembourg. Only a
month later his army, his empire, his dynasty—all
was lost. Prussia, with God's permission, had acted

more quickly even than Piedmont with the leave of the Emperor. Napoleon III., as miserable as he was guilty, escaped neither abuse, nor defeat, nor captivity. His posterity has been destroyed, and the Hand of God has smitten his whole race. But the destruction of the Pope's temporal power, of which he was the principal author, leaves, after fifteen years, great sufferings and great ruin. The Pope, having lost his independence, the European equilibrium has been broken; and the punishment of the nations who have given a helping hand to this iniquity will be prolonged long after the fall and death of its monarch, who, whether he wished or simply permitted it, will be looked upon, by the verdict of history, as its principal cause, and as one upon whom the greatest responsibility rests.

CHAPTER VII.

From 1860 to 1865.

The State of Affairs after Lamoricière's Defeat—The Re-
awakening of Catholic Feeling—Peter's Pence—The Work
of Mgr. de Mérode—He reorganizes the War Office—The
Pontifical Zouaves—The Military Hospital—The Pretorian
Barracks—Difficulties between Mgr. de Mérode and
General de Goyon—The Affray of 1862—Return of M.
Drouyn de Lhuys to Office—Montebello and La Tour
d'Auvergne—Their relations with the War Minister—
Intervention of M. de Corcelles—The Affair at Orvieto—
Public Works executed by Mgr. de Mérode—How he
encourages the Religious Vocation of his Sister Albertine
—His Journey to France—His Impressions—The Conven-
tion of the 15th of September, 1864—Encyclical of the
8th of December—The feelings of the War Minister—
Acquisition of Land—The opening of several new Streets
—Mgr. de Mérode presses Lamoricière to return to Rome
—The Death of the General—The War Minister is replaced
—The astonishment felt at his disgrace.

THE heroic devotion of Lamoricière, so far from being
sterile, began to bear fruit as soon as people had recovered from their surprise at the sad events of Castelfidardo and Ancona. The confidence previously felt
by French Catholics in the Emperor had been rudely
shaken, and if some were still blind, their discontent
and mistrust found vent in the public Press, while
they were not silent in the Chambers. The Episcopate also opened its mouth : some publicly, like Mgr.

Pie, Bishop of Poitiers ; Mgr. Dupanloup, Bishop of
Orleans ; Mgr. Plantier, Bishop of Nîmes, whose
talent and courage enlisted the sympathy of all : others,
like Mgr. Parisis, Bishop of Arras, and Mgr. de
Bonnechose, Archbishop of Rouen, addressed themselves to the Emperor and his Ministers. Their
language was as strong and as Apostolic ; but whilst
their colleagues roused public opinion, they strove in
vain to touch the heart of the Sovereign. The Senate
was the only arena open to the Cardinals, but there
their complaints and warnings did not fail to find an
echo, and the force and dignity of their words commanded the attention and respect of the whole country.
The cause of the temporal power, abandoned by the
Emperor, could now at last be freely discussed and
defended. To sustain it efficiently, money and men
were needed. Peter's Pence was established firmly in
France, in Belgium, in England, and in America.
All the Bishops recommended it in their pastorals,
and the clergy joyfully collected it in their respective
parishes. All the principal families in each country
put themselves at the head of the movement, and the
first sums received by Mgr. de Mérode were from his
parents and friends.

Men of good will, not content with giving money,
offered themselves to fill the ranks in the Pontifical
Army, which the Prelate was recruiting. The young
nobility of France was weary of doing nothing. The
Comte de Chambord had congratulated Lamoricière
on his heroic devotion, and the General took advantage of this opening to make his friends understand
the honour and glory of being called upon to defend
the patrimony of St. Peter. With such encourage-
ments the recruiting became easy, and the Pontifical

Army thus rapidly acquired both strength and solidity.
The Irish and Austrians had retired ; but the 106
French and Belgians who had survived the disaster of
Castelfidardo became, in two years, under the name
of Zouaves, a magnificent battalion of 1,500 men.
Becdelièvre, the heroic commander of Castelfidardo,
could only sympathize from a distance with the fame
of this picked body of men ; but the brave Allet was
their colonel, and Lieutenant-Colonel de Charette
animated them with that French zeal and generosity
of which he was himself so noble a specimen.

It was difficult to complain when the War Minister
himself set such a living example of devotion and
self-abnegation. As priest and soldier he possessed
all the virtues of both professions. Never did there
exist a man who more thoroughly forgot himself and
encouraged the sacrifices of others by his own. He
had kept his apartment at the Vatican, it is true, but
he was scarcely ever in it save at night. He rose
every morning of his life at four o'clock, and his first
hours were devoted to God and his own soul. When
he had celebrated the Holy Sacrifice, made his meditation, and all his other pious exercises, he would
go off to his office in the Piazza della Pilota. He
generally went on foot by the shortest way, unless
he had some work of charity to see to, or some abuse
to remedy. Caring nothing for etiquette, but only
anxious about his duty, he generally arrived at the
office before his clerks, and the most industrious
among them found him reading despatches and preparing the work of the day, however early they might
arrive. The office-keeper had no trouble in announcing visitors, for he would meet them half way, passing
from one department to the other, dictating half a

dozen letters at a time, and always in that firm, nervous style which betrayed his resolute character. His relations, his friends, strangers or petitioners, found him always the same, full of his work, prompt in reply, understanding instantly the whole bearing of a case, impatient only of unnecessary delays, deciding in a few minutes on the most important affairs, and rendering to all that fair and brief justice which was so much in favour with our ancestors. Those who were fond of intrigue, or given to peculation, or actuated by ambition, found small favour in his eyes, and were not often satisfied with the short audiences he granted them. But he would forgive a great deal to those who were frank and straightforward—even personal abuse. A woman whose husband had been removed from his post for very valid reasons, came to the War Office one day and overwhelmed the War Minister with reproaches. At last he said: "But really, madam, you do not know what you are saying. You speak like a madwoman!" "I mad! Well, that is a good joke! No one ever said that of me! But it is you who are mad, Monseigneur, and everybody says so!" Upon which Mgr. de Mérode burst out laughing, and, to console her, gave her a hundred scudi.

He went on steadily, in fact, in spite of abuse and contradiction, reforming abuses, hindering peculations, and putting his hand to everything where vigour of administration was required. He went himself into every detail, inspecting the meat, tasting the bread, and insisting upon everything in the barracks being properly supplied. The smaller was the Papal budget the greater pains he took in its management, and in getting rid of those who would take advantage of the

Pope's kindness to rob and despoil him. The Marquis de Ségur describes him in his office and among his employés as a man of exquisite politeness and consideration for others.

"The most military of all," he writes, "was their Prelate Head. He was a mixture of a Soldier, a Religious, and a high-bred nobleman. Tall of stature, thin, and with long members, he was incessantly in movement, and his whole frame spoke as well as his lips. But this activity excluded neither distinction nor dignity. Everything in him spoke of his high birth and noble race. His eyes, one of which was higher than the other, sparkled with wit and reflected all the impressions of his ardent soul. His clearly-defined profile showed the energy of his will. But in religious ceremonies, when he officiated or when he was praying, his attitude and his features, in fact his whole expression, took an unexpected and striking character of majesty. His restless agitation seemed suddenly to be arrested under the visible action of Divine Grace. His very look breathed faith, love, and calm. His whole person seemed to adore; and in those moments his striking resemblance to St. Louis de Gonzagua and St. Charles Borromeo, of whom he had many of the features, was most remarkable."*

After the Marquis de Ségur, we will listen to M. Cochin, in his " Souvenirs de Rome " :—

"What one feels about Mgr. de Mérode is, that though he may not be always a wise man, he is something very near a Saint. His noble birth, his military bravery, his quick and witty spirit, his universal activity, his extraordinary energy, and, above all, the

* " A Winter at Rome," by the Marquis de Ségur, pp. 125, 126.

holiness and humility of his life, and his wonderful
self-abnegation, make Mgr. de Mérode a most remarkable and totally unique character. He is a kind of
mitred general, whose sword is with difficulty restrained
by the scabbard of his cassock. He is both a hero and
a saint, with a peculiar and remarkable face which it
is impossible to forget when one has once seen him.
Add to this, theological theories pushed perhaps to an
extreme, struggling in his brain with a modern spirit,
as if two different persons were in the same body, he
seems at one and the same time a Spanish Inquisitor,
a brilliant French officer, and a loyal Belgian citizen.
I do not think that the Pope has a more faithful and
devoted friend, nor a more useful instrument. To see
him sleeping on a board, passing his winters without a
fire, rushing into every corner of Rome, reforming the
prisons, founding endless charitable institutions, building barracks, setting up fountains, and the like, one
says to oneself that Mgr. de Mérode is, in all Rome,
the only true friend of real progress. . . . . I am not
one of those who blame him for having worked so
hard to give the Pope an army. . . . . Small as it
may be, this little army is enough to prevent the oldest
monarchy in existence from sinking in silence, without
a word or a cry which will echo through history. I
am not capable of judging of its military value, though
the camp at Porto d'Anzio seemed to me admirable ;
and I do not know anything more beautiful and disin-
terested than the sight of those young men, most of
them of noble birth, who have come to spend their
time, lose, perhaps, their place in their own country,
brave ridicule, and expose themselves to death, to
mount guard faithfully at the feet of the successor of
St. Peter. But whatever may be the military value

of these young cosmopolitan regiments, I can bear witness to their moral and political value, and at the same time realize the enormous practical difficulty of grouping, retaining, and disciplining this little army, and providing it with all the necessary material. All the honour of this great effort is due to Mgr. de Mérode."

We must take exception to the justice of the words "a Spanish Inquisitor." Mgr. de Mérode was incapable of hurting a human being; and his "inquisition" only extended to whatever concerned the Pope's service. He certainly would never have consented to burning a guilty man; but he would find pleasure in rebuking him, or in shutting him up for a day or two for the good of his soul, and, above all, in making him disgorge his ill-gotten gains.

The more careful he was of the Pope's budget the less attentive he was to his own interests. His personal revenues were spent entirely in alms, or in public works, to profit the cause he so faithfully served. Among the most important and useful establishments which signalized his ministry, we must reckon the organization of the Military Hospital. An institution of this kind was entirely wanting in Rome. The sick soldiers were carried to the Hospital Santo Spirito, and separated by curtains only from the civilians. The War Minister rightly judged that they were not at all pleased at being confounded with beggars, and that, to raise the Papal service, the army should be treated with special consideration. He accordingly got a division made in the Hospital of Santo Spirito, bought with his own money two adjoining houses, divided the sick from the convalescents, and, with great skill and many sacrifices, arranged bath-rooms, a pharmacy and a school of surgery, which was provided with all the necessary instruments. A military superintendent was placed at the head to direct the administration, and a body of Infirmarians, instituted by Mgr. de Mérode, were put under the orders of the Sisters of Charity, to whose loving care the sick were confided.* Mgr. de Mérode, in writing of that hospital, says: "It is on my way to my office at the Pilota, so that I go there for a few moments every day. I hope that the Sisters are as pleased with me as I am with them: It is impossible to show greater delicacy, economy, and devotion than those holy Sisters in their loving service. They thought the Pontifical Government more utterly ruined than it really is. It is quite true that we go on, through a series of disasters, past, present, and to come, with an ease and a tranquillity which is something marvellous. They told me lately that a traveller, sitting at the *table-d'hôte* of the 'Minerva Hotel,' said that he fancied, when he arrived at Rome, he should find the Pontifical Government at its last gasp: instead of which he saw everything going on as smoothly and quietly as possible. In fact, our vigour is such that one might wish some of it to those pretended infirmarians who are always busying themselves with the supposed extinction of the Pontifical Government, and who, perhaps, are nearer their own demise."† The new hospital was not only a great delight to the soldiers, but also an example to the administrators of the civil portion of the hospital, who soon made several useful reforms in their regulations, ameliorated the food of their sick, and thus

---

* The Sister Superior was Ma Sœur Lequête, sister of the Bishop of that name, and an admirable woman. She became afterwards Mother-General of the whole Community.

† Letter of the 1st September, 1861.

profited largely by the initiative set on foot by the War Minister.

To complete his good work, Mgr. de Mérode established underneath the hospital, in the street "*Borgo Santo Spirito,*" a school for the soldiers' children. He entrusted it, as well as the hospital, to the care of the Sisters of St. Vincent of Paul, and soon upwards of one hundred and· twenty young girls were gathered round them, in whom Mgr. de Mérode took ·the most paternal interest. It was not only an asylum for virtue and a protectorate for young girls from the evils of barrack life, but a busy workshop in which excellent needlework was turned out. Mgr. de Mérode bought them a number of sewing machines, the first that had been seen in Rome. The children found in this school not only the means of gaining an honest livelihood, but an elementary instruction suited to their position, and a careful training and enlightened protection which was extended to their families. The War Minister often visited them, knew the names of each, and made their parents equally feel the good effects of his all-powerful benevolence.

To undertake these establishments, and, above all, to carry them on, he had received generous assistance from every quarter. Lamoricière also came to help him to establish an arsenal for military constructions, which was directed by Colonel Blumensthil. "We have set up two steam-engines," writes Mgr. de Mérode, "which work a vertical saw as well as a circular one, and other machines to work and polish iron. With all this we can do a quantity of fresh things, which keep alive our men, develop their intelligence, and enable our little Pontifical Army to pride itself on its progress. Our soldiers feel that the public no longer consider them good for nothing. So we go on, and I think it is wonderful, considering the political *régime* to which we have to submit. It is true that the men of the present day are forced into a state of resignation which prepares them admirably to expect and accept everything. One does not ask oneself any longer : Shall we consent to such or such a thing? Shall we wish for such a form of government ? or, such a territorial agglomeration ? One has to content oneself with guessing at what our masters wish for, and he who arrives at discovering this impenetrable secret would be perfectly satisfied ! " *

Lamoricière also helped him in a work of still greater importance for the defence of Rome. That was the purchasing, in 1862, of a piece of ground outside the Porta Pia to form a camp and a field for manœuvres, on which spot a barrack was also built.

All this was done with Mgr. de Mérode's own money. The canonization of the martyrs of Japan having brought to Rome, in the June of that year, an immense number of strangers, as well as Cardinals and Bishops, he took the opportunity for the blessing of the first stone of the new barracks, and invited not only the Sovereign Pontiff, but the higher clergy, Ambassadors and Ministers, the Roman nobility, and all the strangers of distinction who were at that moment in the Eternal City. There were the representatives of two worlds grouped round the Vicar of Jesus Christ. The army was ranged in battle array in the Pretorian Camp, and the crowds overflowed on all sides of the barriers. It was the Archbishop of Dublin who officiated. When every look had been turned with respectful admiration towards the Throne where Pius IX.

* Letter of the 6th October, 1861.

had taken his place, each one pointed also to the Prelate who had organized this magnificent fête, and who had thus given to the whole world the sight of a city where the work, activity, and devotion of one Minister seemed to ensure happier days for the Sovereign Pontiff, and some security for his temporal power.

His little army was rapidly being completed. It amounted now to 10,000 men, and the spirit which animated them became every day firmer and stronger. They could now be shown to strangers; they could stand fire; and one might reckon on their fidelity as much as on their valour. In 1862 Garibaldi, with his red shirts, tried a skirmish which did not redound to his honour. While he was recovering from a wound received at Aspromonte, Lamoricière wrote to the Pope that he was ready, at the first appeal, to return to Rome and take the command again of the Pontifical troops. Pius IX. thanked him warmly, and praised the Zouaves in his reply :—

" The abandonment of our frontier by a part of the French Army left us in great peril. But the Zouaves having come to replace them in a strong body, everything was saved, to the great honour of our Army, which remembers having been formed by you, and which, if small in number, is strong in its discipline, in its courage, and in its love for its Sovereign."

The Pontifical Army thus held itself in readiness to act, but during this time of expectation trials were not wanting to the Minister who had created it, and who loved it as a father. Mgr. de Mérode was naturally jealous of the honour of his soldiers : he considered himself as their sole judge, and this jurisdiction was sacred to him. The Army of Occupation had then at its head an aide-de-camp of the Emperor's, General de

Goyon, who was as faithful to his master as Mgr. de Mérode was to the Pope, and who was ever ready to take offence and to consider that he represented the Emperor in person. Loyal and frank, but obstinate, the epigrams of the War Minister affronted him, and instead of laughing at them as others did, he took them all seriously and became terribly embittered against him. A conflict was inevitable. One day two soldiers, one French and one Pontifical, had a quarrel in a public square; the Frenchman was wounded, and the Papal Zouave managed for some days to escape the police. The War Minister, at last, having caught him, warned General de Goyon that he was going to have him brought to trial. But the General claimed the prisoner, so that he might be brought before a French court-martial. As he insisted, Mgr. de Mérode went to him and tried to convince him that it was the duty of the Pope to judge his own soldiers. All his reasoning, however, was in vain : General de Goyon exclaimed that with any one else he would have drawn his sword. "I would rather have a dozen sword-thrusts," answered de Mérode, "than sacrifice my subordinates and give them up, bound hand and foot, to judges who are not theirs." They parted in this way, and General de Goyon seized the culprit, and even the head of the Pontifical prison, and shut them up in the Fort of St. Angelo! However, the French court-martial, with greater wisdom, unanimously acquitted both prisoners. The wise M. de Corcelles, to whom Mgr. de Mérode gave a detailed account of this affair, did not fail to give his cousin a warning as to how the best cause might be spoiled by slightly intemperate language. The War Minister answered as follows :—

"A thousand thanks for all you have said to me,

N

which is so affectionate as well as so true and just.
Your letter is a real balm to soften, heal, and enlighten
my wounded spirit.   If I do not entirely yield to
your loving remonstrances, do not think it is from
obstinacy.   I say 'entirely,' for, as regards the
greater part, *habes confitentum reum.*   I know very
well that hastiness and a show of temper only spoil
matters, and my nature, I am well aware, needs correction on that point.   But there are questions of
dignity, honour, and justice with which one cannot
compound." . . . He then goes on to describe the
affair, and ends with the words : "How is it possible
to consent to what has been asked ?   How declare
that the Pontifical tribunals are incompetent to
judge Pontifical subjects guilty of crimes committed
on Pontifical territory ?   The question which is at the
bottom of the whole thing is, that, by acting as they
have done, the Pontifical authority has been entirely
ignored ; and whether, if such an insult to Papal
authority be accepted by us, to the prejudice of a
Pontifical subject, who has the right to appeal to his
own Sovereign to obtain justice, we should not commit
a real weakness if not a crime.   I own to you, therefore,
that if what has happened were to begin over again,
I should sing the same song to the same tune,
though I might put on mufflers ; and I am sure that
if we could have a quiet talk together you would be
exactly of my opinion."

The annexation of the kingdom of Naples to Piedmont was the next step dreamed of by the Revolution
towards Italian unity.   But the Revolutionists wished
to eat their artichoke leaf by leaf, and after each
fresh annexation came a moment's respite.   On the
15th October, 1862, M. Drouyn de Lhuys received

the Portfolio of Foreign Affairs. His return to office marked a policy favourable to the Holy See. M. Lavalette was recalled from Rome, and replaced by Prince de la Tour d'Auvergne. Instead of a Revolutionary who had openly declared that he hoped to be the last Ambassador accredited to the Pope, a Prince had been sent whose name was dear to the Church, one who had formed part of the mission of the Duke d'Harcourt and of M. de Corcelles, and who had participated in 1850 in the negotiations of Gaëta. It is true that General de Montebello, who had succeeded General de Goyon in the command of the Army of Occupation, was not always on good terms with Mgr. de Mérode. But the choice of the new Ambassador, and the return to power of M. Drouyn de Lhuys, seemed to presage a future good understanding between the French and Pontifical authorities. The Holy Father had just appointed a commission to inquire into the necessary administrative reforms, and the French Government promised to give every assistance in this laborious work. But then came the Orvieto affair, which upset all calculations.

The Pontifical authorities had seized, on the Viterbo frontier, some sacks of corn which certain speculators had smuggled in to avoid the Custom House dues. All of a sudden, a troop of Piedmontese soldiers, violating the Papal frontier, seized the patrol which was guarding the smugglers, and imprisoned them at Orvieto, after having made them submit to many insults. General de Montebello instantly ordered their release; but on condition that the sacks of flour should be restored to the smugglers. Mgr. de Mérode could not bear that his men should thus be exchanged for sacks, or that the violation of the Papal

N 2

frontier should pass without notice, and complained
bitterly in consequence. M. de Corcelles addressed
the following temperate letter to the War and Foreign
Ministers to appease matters, and this at the request
of Mgr. de Mérode himself :—

"The character of the French General and his
religious feelings suit the present state of affairs ; but
he is often influenced by his Staff, who think that the
main thing to do is to please the Army and keep to the
point of honour. That argument may be used on the
Pontifical as well as on the French side. The War
Minister thinks himself equally obliged to satisfy his
little Army and not to expose it to unnecessary humiliations.   If there were a little less sensitiveness on
both sides it would be far better. . . . . Mgr. de
Mérode has been accused, in turn, of being a Legitimist
and an Orleanist, of having a Belgian infatuation, and
an antipathy to France; of wishing for civil war, and
of Ultramontane fanaticism!   The simple truth is,
that he is solely a devoted servant of the Pope.   Nor
do I know any one who is a more ardent and ingenious
lover of progress.   When there was a fear of Rome
being given up to the Piedmontese, he may have
spoken hotly ; but those know him little who fancy
that a policy favourable to the Holy See would not
have had his warmest approval.   I cannot give a better
proof of this than his anxiety to bring the Orvieto
affair to an end without anything disagreeable to M. de
Montebello.   I hope that a new method will be adopted
to obtain what has hitherto been refused to threats ;
and that on both sides they will give up altercations to
which one can only apply the words of a writer of the
last century, 'Little things are the grave of greater
ones.' "

The War Minister was not a man to allow his energy to be absorbed in petty quarrels. Whilst the Cardinal Secretary of State was disputing as a clever diplomat with the French Ambassador, and exchanging notes in which his policy of compromise and expectation obtained nothing, Mgr. de Mérode pushed vigorously forward all public works which could conduce to the improvement of the city and of the Pontifical States. To him we owe the magnificent road from Subiaco to Frosinone, the new prison and the schools at Civita Vecchia, the fountain of Agnani, where the water is raised by a machine to the height of two hundred and fifteen metres, and many other equally useful works.

Mgr. de Mérode had sent some Zouaves to garrison Agnani : this was the saving of that little town. Situated on a hill, the only drinkable water they possessed was what was collected in a few cisterns or tanks, which, in time of drought, was sold at ruinous prices ; while the poor were compelled to seek in a neighbouring valley for the water of a little stream and bring it up the hill with incredible fatigue and loss of time. Among the items in the military budget presented to the War Minister was one for thirteen francs forty-five centimes a day for the carriage of the water necessary for the troops. " And what does the population do ? " inquired Mgr. de Mérode. And then he found out the distress of the poor, who had to climb painfully up this hill four or five times a day to bring the necessary supply of water to their homes. He at once consulted Padre Secchi, and they found that there was an hydraulic machine in the plain below the town which worked a flour-mill. This machine was of sufficient power to work also certain pumps placed on the height above ; and then, by means of canals cut to

the length of four thousand metres, the town of Agnani
was fully supplied with water. The whole cost was less
than a hundred thousand francs, which was partly de-
frayed by the munificence of the Pope ; and the works
were carried on with the exactness and promptitude
which characterized everything undertaken by Mgr. de
Mérode, who determined to give the inhabitants an agreeable surprise. Certain of success, he induced Pius IX.
to come to the inauguration of this great work. The
curiosity of every one was surpassed by the result. At a
given signal the water flowed into the town from all sides
amidst the cheers of the crowd and with the Benediction
of the Holy Father. Mgr. de Mérode, who thought
oily of the public good and the interests of the Pope,
attributed the whole glory of the enterprise to Pius IX.
The neighbouring villages, many of which were in a
similar condition, quickly adopted the same system of
machines and pumps. This did not suit the views of
the proprietors of the cisterns, who had made such a
large profit by the sale of water. But the War Minister
laughed at his critics, and was abundantly consoled by
seeing comfort, cleanliness, and health reign in this
little corner of the Papal States.

It was also by his advice that the Pope resolved, in
the month of June, 1863, to make a tour in the few
States still remaining to him. He went to all the
villages on the Neapolitan frontier, by roads which were
almost impracticable, accompanied by Mgr. de Mérode
and an escort of Noble Guards. The journey ended at
Ceccano, on the Neapolitan frontier. A diplomat, who
was a spectator of the Pope's reception, relates an
adventure which happened towards the end of his tour,
and which was looked upon as a political manifesto :—

"We left Naples by the seven o'clock train. The

weather was beautiful, and never did the Roman Campagna look more green and lovely, or the sky more clear and transparent. At half-past ten we came to the frontier station, where we got donkeys to convey us to Ceccano, which was all dressed as for a grand feast. The village street was nicely sanded; red and white and yellow draperies hung from every window. Triumphal arches and festoons of evergreens had been erected at all the cross-roads and in the public squares. All the houses had been freshly whitewashed or painted a few days before, which, in that bright sunshine, gave a festive look to the village which I shall never forget. The peasant women, with their snow-white head-dresses picturesquely arranged on their heads, théir scarlet petticoats and black velvet bodices, looked at us in astonishment from their beautiful large eyes. There was not a single stranger in Ceccano save ourselves. Amidst all these peasants in their Calabrian costumes I did not see a single frock-coat or middle-class clothes. We were the only spots on the landscape, and the peasants stared at us as if we were savages. The two little inns at Ceccano were full to overflowing. All the neighbouring villagers had come in. The Holy Father had slept in an old house built out of the ruins of an ancient castle, at the extremity of the town.

" We were resting in one of the little rooms of the inn after a frugal breakfast, when one of the Pope's officers came to conduct us to him. Mde. d'Ideville, escorted by myself and Chateaubriand, hastened to walk through the little hamlet till we reached the house where the Pope was resting. Some one had recognized us and told him we were in Ceccano. The Pope received us most kindly, and asked for news of Rome, as if he had left his capital for a long while.

He spoke of his journey, and the pleasure he had had in visiting these villages, whose inhabitants had never seen a Sovereign Pontiff for ages.

"'I have been so touched at their eager welcome,' he added : 'if you had been here this morning you would have seen all the population of the villages on the other side of the Liri, kneeling on the opposite bank the moment they caught sight of me. You know the Liri is the barrier between the States of the King and those of the Church. But we are not dreaming of conquest, and our powerful neighbour has nothing to fear. That is why I was vexed at a little incident which has just taken place. Mgr. de Mérode will show you the hero of the adventure. He is a peasant boy of fifteen. At the very moment when I came back to this house we heard some shots fired from the other side of the river, and at the same time perceived a little Neapolitan swimming across to us, and braving the balls of the Italian soldiers, to come and get his Pope's blessing. He was not hit, however, and his faith, or perhaps his imprudent curiosity, has been rewarded.'

" On taking leave of the Pope we saw in the courtyard the little Neapolitan, still wet through, but who was eating his breakfast very gaily while telling his adventure to the Guards. The Italian authorities had feared, though quite wrongly, a hostile political manifestation on the part of the Neapolitan population. They had contented themselves, however, with a pious demonstration in favour of the Pope ; and nothing could be more touching or more natural than the eagerness of these poor people to receive, even from a distance, the blessing of the great Father of the Faithful, of whom they had so often heard."[*]

* " Journal of a Diplomatist," by H. d'Ideville, p. 83.

If anything could add to the pleasure Mgr. de Mérode felt in serving the Pope it was when an opportunity occurred for surprising strangers, removing some of the prejudices of heretics, and showing him to the whole world as a Sovereign who was continually occupied with the welfare of his subjects. Here is an instance of this :—

"ROME, 22*nd October,* 1863.

" We assisted to-day, by the purest of accidents, at a very interesting ceremony. We were driving to the Porta Portese, on the banks of the Tiber, at a spot where a suspension bridge had just been thrown over the river—one which, when necessary, opens to allow merchant vessels to go up and down the Tiber.

" We saw from a distance a number of men in carriages and on horseback, close to the bridge, and, on drawing near, found it was the Pope and his suite. We had arrived unexpectedly at the inauguration of this new work, which the Pope had come to bless, at the same time congratulating the engineers and workmen on its success. Everything was done with the greatest simplicity. There was neither a tent prepared, nor flags, nor speeches. The Pope had contented himself with announcing his visit at four o'clock, and those most interested had come to meet him. The whole thing was shown to Pius IX., and four men, with astonishing ease, raised and lowered, in succession, this immense drawbridge, to the surprise of all the assistants.

" Mgr. de Mérode, full, as usual, of energy and initiation, went from one group to the other, explaining the mechanism with his ordinary ardour and volubility. Every one surrounded the Pope ; peasants — men, women, and little children—scrambling and rolling

over the mounds of grass, so as to be able to catch a
look or a word from their beloved Father, or striving
to gather scraps of his conversation. A certain number
of strangers and tourists had stopped their carriages
on their way to the Campagna, and were enchanted to
be able to assist at this unexpected sight. All of a
sudden I saw Mgr. de Mérode say something, in a low
voice, to the Sovereign Pontiff, and then walk quickly
towards an Englishman whom we had met the day
before, and who was Minister of Public Works in
England.

"'Ah! at last I have caught you!' exclaimed
de Mérode; 'you will not have to wait long for the
audience you asked for of the Pope. I am going forth-
with to present you to His Holiness.'

"'But,' objected the Englishman, looking at his
grey coat, his straw hat, and his sun-umbrella, 'I am
not in a proper dress, or presentable!'

"'Oh, what does that signify?' replied the Prelate.
'You have been taken unawares; the Pope will excuse
you. Come along!' And at the same moment the
English Minister was presented to Pius IX.

"'I am very glad to see you,' said the Pope,
smiling; 'especially at this moment. You will be
able to say, on your return to town, that the Roman
Pontiff is not always saying his prayers, surrounded
with incense, monks, and Religious. You will tell the
Queen that her Minister surprised the old Pope in the
middle of his engineers and workmen, helping to
inaugurate a new bridge over the Tiber, and explaining fairly well,' added Pius IX., laughing, 'the
mechanism of this new invention.'

"The Pope went on talking to him in this way for
some little time, and the Minister did not leave His

Holiness without kneeling for a moment for his blessing." (*Journal of a Diplomat*, 108.)

The interest felt in the Papal cause went on increasing, and the maintenance of his temporal power
became, in France, one of the first articles in the
Catholic programme. The elections for the Legislative
Body, on the 31st of May, 1863, took, for the first time
since the *coup d'état*, a decidedly religious character.
It was a question of keeping or rejecting the ninety-
two Deputies who wished to bring forward, in the
address to the Emperor, an amendment favourable to
the Holy See. Other great servants of the Church
came forward to stand at the elections in order to
defend this great cause. Such were M. de Montalembert and M. Werner de Mérode in the Department of
the Doubs. The struggle was severe; and, if the
universal suffrage preferred to the first M. de Conegliano,
and to the second M. Latour du Moulin, twenty-two
thousand electors showed by their votes how earnestly
they wished to induce the Empire to return to the old
paths of Catholicism and public liberty. The numbers
of malcontents had increased; the clergy rallied to a
man round those noble candidates; and the people
began to detach themselves more and more from a
Government which was refusing to protect and defend
the Vicar of Jesus Christ.

Two of the daughters of the House of de Mérode,
an aunt and a niece, left the bosom of their families
at this time to become nuns. The first was Mlle.
Catherine de Montalembert; and, a few months later,
Mlle. Albertine de Mérode. Both entered the noviciate
at Conflans of the Ladies of the Sacred Heart. Mgr.
de Mérode, who had followed his sister's career in the

world, had been greatly edified at the abundance of her alms, at the great charity she showed towards the poor, and at the fidelity with which she kept to all her little practices of piety. He had also been struck at the obstinacy with which she had refused all proposals of marriage ; but he did not dare conclude from that fact that she had a vocation for the cloister, and used to joke with her on the *rôle* of old aunt and chanoiness which she seemed to prefer. But her disgust at the world became stronger, and the thought of uniting herself for ever to God in religion became daily sweeter to the young girl's heart. She confided her feelings to her brother, and her letter reached Rome at the same time as the tidings of the unsuccessful French elections. " Do not hide your wishes any longer," he writes to her, " but draw still closer the links which bind you to God. I have not seen the Pope since I received your letter, and have not, in consequence, been able to ask him for his blessing ; but I will do so this very day. Yesterday he was condoling with me on the loss of the two elections ; but I am sure he will now rejoice at your triumph over flesh and blood." It was indeed as he said. Albertine won a complete victory in the order of Grace, over the repugnances of nature, and her election, blessed and ratified by Pius IX., drew her to the noviciate of Conflans in the month of October, 1863.

M. de Montalembert heard this news at Maîche, where he had come to rest after his electoral fatigues, and to enjoy the sympathy which the whole population showed him for that which they considered a victory rather than a defeat. " Les Moines de l'Occident," his great work, occupied a large portion of his day. But in the course of the afternoon he gave himself up to his friends and visitors, and regained both health and strength in the mountain air. He answered Mgr. de Mérode's letter with the faith of a Christian and the courage of a Crusader, while not failing to remind him that it was to him that his family owed the first example of self-sacrifice :—

" I leave all political questions aside to speak to you of Albertine, whose vocation was such a surprise to me, and, at the same time, inspires me with such respect. I never should have thought her capable of taking so energetic a decision. She was so undecided and so timid ! But how marvellous are the ways of God ! This young girl, whom I had for ten years under my roof, and who came every morning into my library with my own daughter, never let me suspect for a moment that one day I should have to look upon her with that feeling of veneration which so generous a sacrifice demands—the renunciation of her liberty, her will, her ease, her pleasures, her youth, her whole life, in fact ! Although this act of hers has not touched me to the heart like that of Catherine, it has not failed to move and sadden me a good deal ; for to the blanks which death creates around us as we go on in life, it is sad to have to add the other blanks left by those young lives who are gone to bury themselves in the cloister. This sadness may be disputed on higher grounds ; but it will not yield to the most conclusive arguments, and we may say in truth, ' The heart has its reasons which reason does not recognize.' It is you, my dearest Xavier, who first opened out the path of devotedness and self-abnegation to these young Christians by your own noble example, for they are of the same blood as yourself. Help, then, with your prayers those whose hearts are torn by these cruel separations, which Religion may bless, but which to poor human nature are so bitter and repugnant. On the 26th of this month the Bishop of Orleans will give the habit to Catherine. I dread beforehand the emotions of that day, and entreat of you to help me to go through them by your remembrance of me before the Altar of God.

"I see you have as little consolation from General de Montebello as you had from his predecessor. I have just read his insolent order of the day, destined to tarnish the sacred weakness which he is expected to protect. I found, a day or two ago, in the Prophet Isaiah a text which seems to me to sum up in an admirable manner the whole history of the two Napoleons—'*Posuimus mendacium spem nostram et mendacio protecti sumus.*' I hope that the person who is employed to open my letters will take a note of this text and communicate it to his Superiors. I recommend it specially to M. Duruy as an epigraph to the course of cotemporary history, which he pretends to impose on all the youth born under the reign of Napoleon III. With which words I embrace you fraternally, recommending myself anew to your sacerdotal compassion."

Montalembert's previsions were but too well verified, though with occasional respites and certain apparent changes of policy, which made some persons hope for better days for the Pope. So passed the first few months of 1864. The Roman sky seemed to have cleared, and the War Minister, intent on his plans of improvement, opened out great floods of air and light in the darkest corners of the Eternal City. The first work he undertook was to clear the space by the Church of Sta. Maria degli Angeli. This church, built by Michael Angelo out of the ruins of the Thermes of Diocletian, was served by the Carthusians, and their

cloister is one of the most solitary and yet attractive
spots in Rome. But the soil had been raised several
yards, and one could only get at this masterpiece of
the great sculptor by going down a great number of
steps, as if one were entering a cellar. Mgr. de Mérode
lowered and levelled the ground, created a beautiful
square before the church, and thus opened out this
wonderful creation of faith and genius to the admiration of the whole world.

But he only rested from one work to undertake
another, and he did not hesitate, when his funds
were exhausted, to contract debts in order to make new
streets, with every sanitary and hygienic condition.
Men of business were amazed at his boldness; his
relations remonstrated with him on his extravagance;
his enemies declared he was ruined, and rejoiced in
the fact. Nothing stopped him. He had guessed
the future, and his boldness was blessed by God. The
space near the Termini had been hardly cleared when
he bought all the land situated between that and the
Quirinal. This ground ended at the railway station,
and its value, which at the time was very small, was
rapidly doubled, and even trebled. Mgr. de Mérode
traced out the streets now called of "Florence,"
"Turin," and "Palermo," and had them drained
and paved at his own expense. He brought to this
work the same ardour and energy which he showed in
everything else, whilst, with the passion of an archæologist, he carefully gathered up all the remains of
ancient Rome which the pickaxe of the workman
revealed at every turn. A diplomat returning from
hunting, surprised him in the midst of his labourers,
who had just discovered a beautiful arch, of the
existence of which no one had had the least suspicion.

"Well!" exclaimed de Mérode, "can you understand this taste? Is it not superior to your sport? We have both been hunting; but my enjoyment is purer than yours, for I have discovered what was before unknown."

The War Minister sought, above all, the public good. To make the quarters of the town where fever generally reigned more healthy, to enlarge and open fresh streets, to spread ease and comfort among the population—such were the projects worthy of a great Pope which he felt bound, as his Minister, to propose, direct and carry out. It was necessary to do much on credit, and people accused him of having ruined himself in consequence. But just the contrary happened. His speculations enriched him immensely, and what he had bought for a small sum he sold again at a high price; so that he was rewarded for having thus served Rome and the Pope with as much skill and ability as prudence.

During the summer of 1864, the Pope and his Court removed to Castel-Gandolfo. Pius IX. enjoyed going over the whole neighbourhood, making it the object of each drive to see a different village, church, or convent, and being received everywhere with heartfelt enthusiasm. He determined, on the 15th of August, to visit Genazzano, one of the most famous sanctuaries in Italy, situated on a hill in the diocese of Palestrina. They assured him that it was impossible; that the road was bad and unfinished. "Well!" replied the Pope, "then it is all the more necessary to facilitate the visit to this sanctuary of the faithful. I will have the new road finished at once. I will not give up my pilgrimage to our 'Holy Mother of Good Counsel' at Genazzano, and my wish will facilitate the access to this mountainous country, whose inhabitants are now deprived of proper means of communication."

The engineers whom the Pope had summoned to set about the work respectfully suggested that there was not time enough to finish it by the day he had pointed out. " That's all very fine," exclaimed Pius IX., laughing. " Fortunately I have some one about me who knows how to overcome difficulties. If you give it up, I shall tell Mgr. de Mérode to make the road, and you will see it will be done before the 15th of August." The engineers were silenced, and made up their minds at once that it must be done, and the War Minister, to facilitate the work, placed two hundred soldiers and part of the material of an artillery train at their disposal. But while the Pope thus reckoned on the zeal of his devoted Minister, de Mérode himself was nearly carried off by an attack of that terrible fever called "*perniciosa.*" His devouring activity made him disregard the ordinary precautions taken by Romans in the summer. One saw him at all hours, with a temperature of thirty-two degrees, superintending the military constructions, walking on foot from the Vatican to his office, remaining exposed to the most burning sun, and then going into the coldest churches or subterranean excavations—in fact, braving those great alternations of cold and heat which are the real danger of the Roman climate. The people of the country are far more prudent. They always try not to provoke violent perspiration, and, above all, not to check it suddenly. Besides that, Mgr. de Mérode did not believe in the malaria, and was always laughing at the precautions the Romans are continually taking against the fever. His incredulity nearly cost him his life.

Being with the Pope at Castel-Gandolfo, he thought
he might very safely leave all his windows open at
night. But he forgot that they looked upon a lake;
and the miasma and damp air from the water gave him
the fever. In a few hours his state was despaired of;
he was delirious, and then fell into that state of stupor
which precedes the last agony. The country doctor at
once realized his danger, and applied the most urgent
remedies. But M. Castano, a friend and companion-
in-arms of Mgr. de Mérode, and who was the head-
surgeon of the French Army, was telegraphed for, and
arrived by the first train. There was still time. Mgr.
de Mérode, however, did not know him; his agitation
was extreme, he was purple in the face, and his fore-
head streaming with perspiration. Pius IX., hearing
of his state, followed the doctor into the room, and
came up to his bedside. The sight of the white dress
produced an extraordinary effect on the sick man. He
recognized the Pope, and tried to kneel at his feet.
This brought on a happy crisis. The Holy Father,
greatly touched at this sign of filial piety, took him in
his arms, and leant his head against his heart, calling
him his "beloved son," with that Italian accent which,
with its "*tu*," gives such a peculiar tenderness and
charm to the loving words of a father or a friend. He
overwhelmed him with caresses, reproaching him for
not having taken sufficient care of a health so precious
to him, blessing him over and over again, and then
saying, "No—no! my son. God will not allow the
Church to be deprived of your services. I want you
more than any one; and you must live to be the consolation of my old age."

The Pope spoke the truth. His prayers, added to
the energetic remedies of Dr. Castano, checked the

fever, and prevented a relapse, which would have been fatal. Two days later Pius IX. could say with a joyful exclamation, "Thank God, we have saved him!"

The news of the death of Mgr. de Mérode was reported for some hours in Rome, and produced a most painful sensation. The Democrats themselves were more touched than one could have imagined, with their feelings about him. The military frankness of the War Minister, the elevation of his character, the integrity of his life, and his burning charity, had won for him the esteem and respect of all good and honest men. The Army especially was full of consternation. No sooner was his recovery ascertained, than there was but one heart and one voice to thank God. But the warning had been sufficiently grave to entitle the War Minister to a holiday, and to make the Pope insist on his leaving Italy for a short time. Leaving Rome on the 21st of August, he went to see M. de Sartiges at Albano before starting for France, and the Ambassador asked him if he did not think it would be wise for him to ask for an audience of the Emperor as he passed through Paris? He thought that an interview between these two men would be very important both for France and for the Holy See. People at the Embassy said: "Stripped of his prejudices against the Emperor, Mgr. de Mérode is a very remarkable man. Above all, he is so straightforward and so thoroughly honest! In spite of his eccentricities, what an admirable priest he is! What self-abnegation he shows! and what charity! Some people in Rome do not like him; that is, there is a certain clique—a *camarilla*—who dread him. They fear his frankness, which they characterize as 'brutal'; and the ascendency which his eminent virtues and devotedness have given him over the mind of the Holy Father."

Mgr. de Mérode did not refuse to take this step; but the Emperor would not see him, and he was not surprised. It was at this very time that the French Court was having a secret understanding with that of Turin to fix the terms of the Convention of the 15th September. Mgr. de Mérode said justly : " One does not care to receive people whom one is about to strangle."

The War Minister passed his few weeks' holiday in France with his own family, and with one or two intimate friends. He revisited Maîche, Villersexel, the Château of Bournel, and Roche en Brény, where Montalembert was still working at his " Monks of the West." He enjoyed his stay there immensely, and carried away the pleasantest impressions of his visit, with the recollection of the conversations he had had with his brother-in-law on all Church and State matters. A few months after he wrote to him :

" This is the first year, I think, that the Feast of St. Elisabeth has passed without my writing to you; but that does not mean that I have forgotten you ! My heart, on the contrary, is quite full of recollections of Roche en Brény, which place altogether has an inexpressible charm for me. One sees in your home, at one and the same time, a life which is both bright and serious, and an association of good things, both material and spiritual, which harmonize wonderfully with each other. Your old pine woods and your books, your writing-table and your strong walking-sticks, your inscriptions and your chapel, create the most charming pictures in my mind, which are continually recurring, without speaking of the persons, great and small, who give life to the whole. The thought of the life-long absence of your dear Catherine was before me, during the two days I passed at La Roche, like a bleeding wound which one

does not dare look at. I had been a little bit afraid,
when we first met, of our disagreement on certain
points ; but I found it to be much less than I had
fancied. It is in the nature of things in this world
that a host of questions should be judged from a number
of different points of view by different minds. The
only important thing is that these appreciations of the
same subject should be founded on the same love of
truth, of justice, and of right. The elect who will meet
one another in Paradise will have had in this world the
widest divergences of opinion ; but our good God will
assign to each his place. A few days ago we were
reciting, in choir at St. Peter's, the Hymn of the
Dedication, which in our Vatican edition has escaped
the corrections of Urban the Eighth :—

> ' *Illuc introducitur*
> *Omnis qui, ob Christi nomen*
> *Hoc in mundo premitur.*
> *Tunsionibus, pressuris   Expoliti lapides*
> *Suis Coaptantur locis.   Per manus artificis,*
> *Disponuntur mansuri   Sacris ædificiis.*

By dint of *tunsionibus* and *pressuris* we shall end in
being so moulded as thoroughly to understand one
another. Certainly our Lord does not spare you your
share ! "

When Mgr. de Mérode returned to Rome, the news
of the Convention of the 15th September, 1864, between the Marquis de Pepoli and M. Drouyn de
Lhuys, had already become known. This act put a
stop to the French occupation at the end of two years,
and left the Pope to provide for his own security and
virtual existence at Rome. Pius IX. openly expressed
his displeasure, and he had very good reason for his

complaints, for the Treaty which concerned him most
had been drawn up and signed without his participa-
tion. It was looked upon as a virtual abandonment of
the Pope and of his temporal power. Certain diplomatic notes strove in vain to minimize its real importance. In a despatch published in the *Moniteur*, the
Emperor, by means of M. Drouyn de Lhuys, declared
that Florence, as a capital, was not to be looked upon
as merely the first stage, but as a serious guarantee;
and that France had reserved to herself all liberty of
action in the case of a Revolution in Rome. When
this news came, the Second Secretary at the Embassy
rushed to Mgr. de Mérode and exclaimed, " Well,
Monseigneur, what do you say now? Has not our
Government at last spoken out? As for me, since I
read this, I am more proud of being a Frenchman,
and my mind is more at ease." "Say you are less
ashámed!" replied the War Minister, smiling and
embracing him. "I found our fiery Prelate very calm
and reasonable," wrote M. d'Idéville. "How easy it
would be to come to an understanding, if only he were
Secretary of State! Is he not a Frenchman? The
Emperor and our Government would not have a
warmer partisan if Mgr. de Mérode were once convinced that the Emperor was firmly resolved to
maintain the temporal power of the Pope, even in its
actual limits."*

But this confidence was wanting, and the Pope himself had lost it altogether. M. de Sartiges had said to
his Secretary, "As you are going to see the Pope, tell
him to trust us and the Emperor." The Secretary
repeated exactly this message to Pius IX. "Yes,"
replied the Pope, "I am not wanting in confidence

* "Journal of a Diplomat," by the Comte d'Idéville, p. 269.

or trust, but it is in God alone, and not in men. He alone never deceives us."

It was in the midst of these continual apprehensions that the French occupation continued for two years. The nearer the end of that time approached, the more Mgr. de Mérode's little Army attracted public interest. Every one asked if it would be large enough to protect the Holy Father from all danger. The War Minister answered for its fidelity; and presenting it to the Pope, on the occasion of the Christmas festivities of 1864, he used this noble language :—

"Most Holy Father! The officers of the Pontifical Army are happy to be admitted to the Royal Presence of your Holiness, so as to offer him in person the homage of their veneration and fidelity. If the years that have passed have not yet brought about the triumph of the cause to which they have devoted themselves, yet each day has been signalized by fresh acts of magnanimity on your Holiness' part, for you have continued to defend, with invincible courage, those sacred rights which are also the rights of all true Catholics. Your actions find an echo in the whole world, and fill your soldiers with love and admiration. For they justly feel that, under these difficult circumstances, the service of your Holiness is of all duties the most honourable and the most glorious." The Pope replied by showing his defenders the sword which he had blessed according to usage, but which he could no longer offer to any Prince : "I keep this sword, for there is not a single Christian Sovereign to whom I can send it. I look everywhere around me, and I see no army in the world drawing its sword for justice and the right, saving yourselves. You only, a feeble remnant, gathered round your Sovereign, serve a just

cause, for you bear the sword to defend Truth and the
Right. Be proud of this fact. I say once more, in
the wide world you are the only ones!"

Pius IX. had just performed one of the greatest acts
of his reign by the publication of the Encyclical
Quanta cura and the *Syllabus*. This Encyclical, dated
the 8th December, 1864, was the condemnation of
modern errors, of which the Syllabus gave the
catalogue. Never did a thunderclap fall more suddenly. Whilst the French Ministry was deliberating
on the conduct they were to hold, two Prelates—
Cardinal Mathieu, Archbishop of Besançon, and Mgr.
de Dreux-Brézé, Bishop of Moulins—published the
Encyclical in their Cathedrals, and, in consequence,
deserved to be summoned before a Council of State,
who had the melancholy courage to condemn them.
But all the remainder of the Episcopate adhered to
the Encyclical, and the Pope found nothing but docile
spirits and submissive hearts in the clergy of two
worlds. The laity, who were at first astonished, ended
by yielding. Montalembert was the first to set the
example, and declared "That, after the warning he
had received in 1832 by the Encyclical *Mirari vos*,
which condemned Lamennais, he would not have recourse to any subtle distinctions to escape a fresh
remonstrance, and that he had nothing to do but
simply to obey."

This subject was, during a whole year, the cause
of incessant discussions in the Eternal City as elsewhere. De Mérode willingly shared in them; but,
instead of long dissertations, he would throw a brilliant
word into the strife; and this word, full of wit and
cleverness, sharp, bitter, and pointed, often had more
effect than the gravest arguments. One day, for in-

stance, when some one was talking of the great Revolution, and drawing a distinction between the causes which had inaugurated it, and the frightful crimes which had been committed in the name of Liberty, Mgr. de Mérode simply shrugged his shoulders, and said, with a sarcastic smile, "1789 is the toilet of the condemned!"

By an equally clever answer, he made his hearers understand the difference between a thesis and a hypothesis. The Encyclical condemns the pretension of looking upon modern liberties as necessary, but it recognizes the right in Governments to make certain concessions, when circumstances render them needful. "Well," exclaimed one day Mgr. de Mérode, "no one admires the Belvedere Apollo more than I do. But when I want to have a pair of shoes, it is not on the foot of the Apollo, but on mine, that my shoe-maker takes the measure. There you have the thesis and the hypothesis!"

M. de Corcelles had come to pass the winter in Rome with his old friend, continuing his *rôle* of counsellor and moderator. The more he was devoted to the Pope, the more he tried, under circumstances which every day became more difficult, to make his good offices act as an agreeable go-between with the War Minister and the French Ambassador. The Holy Father answered a Catholic address by saying: "What distinguishes us from our enemies is, that they hate and curse us, and we bless them." M. de Corcelles affirmed the necessity for the temporal power: "A corner of territory is necessary to the independence of the Sovereign Pontiff." M. de Sartiges announced on the 7th of March, 1865, that the French troops would depart altogether in twenty months. The Ambassador was sometimes sad, sometimes threatening. Pius IX. remained perfectly calm, whilst his War Minister tried to imitate his tranquillity and his silence, which cost his impetuous nature a good deal. But the presence and counsels of M. de Corcelles were a great help to him. When he went back to France, that excellent friend of the Pope's did not conceal his views, and his conversations determined M. Thiers to pronounce that famous speech in the Chambers on the 16th of April, on the discussion of the Address. Eighty-four votes were recorded for an amendment in favour of the temporal power. This was an imposing minority in a house of only 249 members. But his speech was more important than the vote. He said : "The Pope is an earthly Sovereign with a kingdom, which he possesses in the most regular way and by the most legitimate titles. His is the oldest Government in Europe, for it is a Government which has been a thousand years in existence. I do not speak of his spiritual kingdom, which is far more ancient ; I speak of his actual temporal power, which is a fact not to be denied, for a thousand years. It is a perfectly regular Government, which has always been respected, and has a right to that respect.

"Well, what has happened? First, we took away one part of his kingdom—the Legations. The excuse was that the Austrians had retired from them. It was quite natural that they should fall back before our troops ; but instead of giving them back to the Pope, we gave them to Italy ! What reason did we give for that ? People said : ' The country is too much advanced to be governed by representatives of the Roman Court.' Well, and what happened after ? The Marches were invaded, and what reason was given for that ? 'It is the high road,' they said, 'to go to Naples. We must have a territory which is free to pass through.' 'After that, there was a little army, composed mainly of Frenchmen, and which defended Umbria, with the full consent of the French Government. What was said to the Pope ? 'You have an army of mercenaries—for that is the way they spoke of Frenchmen in a nation which was a faithful ally of France—we cannot suffer such an army in Italy. They came, therefore, with very superior forces, and expelled these pretended '*mercenaries*,'—who were serving the Pope, remember, with the full consent of France, and then they invaded the whole of Umbria !

"What remains to the Pope after these three invasions ? Nothing but the little province which is called the Patrimony of St. Peter.

"Then they quietly say: 'Oh, the Pope would not make concessions. He shut himself up in his *non possumus !*'

"Well, gentlemen, I ask you again, are there two kinds of justice ? Are there two languages ? Is there one justice for one nation and another justice for another? How ? Here is a regular, legitimate Sovereign, who has the oldest and strongest of titles to his kingdom, and you deliberately and successively take four-fifths of his States ; and then, because he remonstrates, you say: 'He is an obstinate old man ! He shuts himself up in his *non possumus !* He won't consent to anything !'

"In the name of Heaven, *what is it that you expect him to consent to ?* . . . . . and, still further, look at this famous proposal of conciliation—on what footing do you pretend to establish it ? What remains to the Pope ?—a fifth of his kingdom ! Well. And you ex-

pect him to sacrifice the remainder, under the specious
plea of ' wishing him to return to the simplicity of the
Apostles.' It must be owned that of this spirit you
do not set him a very brilliant example ! "

Such words, spoken by such a man, made an immense sensation, and rather cooled the ardour of those
who had declared that the temporal power was at an
end, and that all that was needed was the formula to
announce it. On his side Mérode did not lose a
moment. The Pretorian Camp was finished, and the
Pope had himself assisted at its inauguration, which
an eye-witness describes in the following terms :—

" The Holy Father, at six o'clock, was to visit the
Pretorian Camp and Mgr. de Mérode's new barracks,
while he was to hold a review of his little Army afterwards. That afternoon we accordingly turned our steps
in that direction. The new barracks were gaily decorated with flags and flowers, and covered with the
Papal arms.

"According to an excellent usage in Rome, the access
was free to all. Very soon the Pope arrived with his
War Minister, who made him examine into and go
over everything. Presently he mounted into the gallery, and every one present received him with the
warmest acclamations. Before leaving, the Papal-
King blessed his little Army, which was formed in
square in the old Pretorian Camp. Cavalry, infantry,
artillery, all were there—and all, in truth, in admirable order and with a thoroughly military appearance.
The bugles sounded, the drums beat—everything was
perfect. Then the Holy Father, with his beautiful
voice, which vibrated through every heart, gave his
Benediction to his Army. Every one knelt and joined
in the responses to the prayers. Then Mgr. de Mérode

on foot, and the staff on horseback, conducted the Pope
to the gates of the Camp, vulgarly called Macao, and
the troops defiled before him. An old Swiss General,
de Baumgarten, was at the side of the Pope, and Mgr.
de Mérode, seeing me behind the staff, with M. de la
Haye, dragged us forward and said: ' You must come
and see our march past. You will be as the National
Guard by the side of a Priest-War Minister. This is
all, alas! that remains of our brave little Army—this is
all that is left to us!' "

But Mgr. de Mérode left an imperishable monument
in that Pretorian Camp—in his barrack, which was
80 metres long, 50 large, and 30 high. It was
arranged on the most careful hygienic principles, with
dormitories for 1,000 beds, and covered halls for
manœuvres in wet weather, the walls being built of
tufa and bricks. It was built in ten months, and 700
men, both civil and military, were employed in it.
The rapidity of the work did not impair its solidity.
The cannon, on the 20th September, 1870, beat in
vain on those walls, and scarcely left a trace. The
whole cost was only 430,000 francs. The critics
accused the War Minister with having built the
barracks outside the town. They did not foresee that
the railway station would soon create a new town on
the Esquiline Hill, and that the new quarter would
need a military establishment. After the barrack
came the stables for 300 horses, canals of water, the
old drainage put into thorough order, wells dug to
supply the fountains and the like. Mgr. de Mérode
himself superintended everything, directing, correct-
ing, and overlooking the whole works, so that nothing
was scamped or neglected. The Sovereign Pontiff expressed his highest satisfaction with Mgr. de Mérode's

work, and publicly thanked him and all the officers
who had carried out his orders.

The remembrance of Lamoricière hovered over the
little Army. He only awaited a word from the Pope
to come back and take the command of the troops.
It was God Who called him home, whilst he held himself in readiness to respond to the appeal of His Vicar.
He had several times had crises of suffocation, which
threatened to prove fatal; but for the last few months
the gout, from which he suffered, had diminished, and
nothing about him announced a speedy death. The
10th of September, 1865, was the last day of this
beautiful and glorious life. He was at Prouzel, and
was about to rejoin his wife and two daughters in
Anjou. He had gone to bed and was sleeping quietly
when a terrible crisis of suffocation woke him at two
o'clock in the morning. " Send for the Priest ! " was
his first cry. The Curé hastened to his bedside, and
found him dying. He had unfastened the crucifix
which was hanging on the wall, as he had buckled on
his sword to serve France and the Church in old times ;
and his lips were pressed upon that image of his
Redeemer. He was without the power of speech ; but
his look and his actions spoke for him. The Priest
lifted his hand over his head to bless him, but had
only time to give him the last Absolution. The next
day the news of Lamoricière's death reached Rome by
telegram.

This was fatal news to Mgr. de Mérode. The death
of the General was as a signal for the War Minister's
disgrace. For a long time the blow had been prepared. For many months it had been hinted to the
Pope that Mgr. de Mérode was disagreeable to France,
and that if the French troops were withdrawn, it was

mainly on his account. The Italian papers never
ceased comparing Antonelli to Mérode. They praised
the tact, the ability, the diplomacy of the first, while
they criticized the impetuosity and imprudence of the
second. If the Pope resisted the demands made upon
him, it was Mérode who was the cause. Antonelli, on
the contrary, was a man of progress, and understood
modern times. If Pius IX. were once detached from
his War Minister, he would be more accessible, and
the relations with France would at once become more
satisfactory. Both diplomacy and journalism combined to mislead people's minds, and weaken the
prestige and authority of the War Minister.

Pius IX., pressed to sacrifice him, refused for five
years. At the end of 1864 he explained how matters
stood very openly to Cardinal de Bonnechose. This
Prelate had come to Rome to receive his hat, and his
reception had been one of the most brilliant fêtes of
the year. Welcome to the Emperor, agreeable to the
Pope, of an exquisite politeness and courtesy, which
were remarked not only by the Diplomatic Corps but
by strangers of every nation, his position gave him
the right to hear and to say all that he would. He
used this power discreetly, and as he most highly
esteemed the honesty, disinterestedness and ability of
the War Minister, he praised him warmly to the Pope,
adding a few words upon the criticism of which he
was the object. "What is to be done?" exclaimed
Pius IX. "He has his enemies; but who has not?
He does not flatter, but he serves me faithfully. And
then, how can I forget that it is to him that I owe
the services of Lamoricière, and the whole formation
of my little Army? I know he has defects of manner,
but they are only the excesses of his devotion and

honesty. I cannot think of separating myself from de Mérode."*

After the death of Lamoricière, the Pope was again besieged with reasons for his removal. People represented to him that Mgr. de Mérode had compromised his fortune by buying land and opening fresh streets ; though the reverse was the case. They painted him as absolute, impossible to deal with, violent in his relations with the General and the Ambassador. The Pope was shaken. At this very time a fresh attack of fever compelled the War Minister to keep to his bed for a few days, and the doctors feared a return of the "*perniciosa*" which had put his life in such danger the year before. This last consideration seemed not a pretext but a reason to persuade the Pope to yield to his being placed in retreat for a time. On the 6th of October, 1865, Mgr. de Mérode was sent for to the Vatican, and the Pope announced to him, though not without some embarrassment, that, finding him tired and ill, he had decided to give him a little rest and so relieve him of his functions as War Minister.

These tidings spread rapidly through Europe and caused an immense sensation. The friends of the Church were in despair, its enemies were rejoiced ; but every one was amazed. The Court at Florence could not believe it. La Marmora exclaimed to one of the Secretaries of the French Embassy, " Can you tell me why the Pope has dismissed Mérode ? This news is just come from Rome. We are enchanted, of course, as far as we are concerned. But Pius IX. must have very devoted and very honest Ministers if he thinks he can replace such a Minister as that ! I knew Mgr. de Mérode in Africa, when he was serving in your foreign

* " Journal of Cardinal de Bonnechose," in manuscript.

legion. He may be of an excitable temperament; but never was there a man with a warmer heart or one with greater honesty and disinterestedness!" But the Revolutionary papers did not spare the Prelate who had so long thwarted their designs. They accused both de Mérode and the Pope. The *Journal de Rome* answered them in these terms :—" The hostile press has never ceased to represent in the most sombre colours everything that concerns the Pontifical Government, sparing no class or order of persons, with the malicious object of making them particularly odious and despicable in the eyes of the multitude. Amongst the numberless exalted personages who have been the objects of its calumnies, Mgr. de Mérode figures the first, in spite of his noble character, which would seem to have defied criticism. The press in question has vented all its spite against him at this moment, and overwhelmed him with insults and injuries, on the pretext of his having been removed from his functions as War Minister. If the Holy Father, in his wisdom, has thought it advisable to make this change, it is from peculiar circumstances, and especially from the necessity laid upon this illustrious Prelate to look that his health, which was failing. The fact remains after the Pope has lost none of his affection or esteem for one who has always rendered himself so worthy of both."

While causing this note to be inserted in the official organ, Pius IX. added some words which made this testimony even more precious to Mgr. de Mérode. He showed the greatest concern for his health and had public prayers offered up for his recovery. " Let him take care of himself," he said, " for the Church and for me ! "

The War Minister bore the weight of his disgrace with the greatest dignity; but his heart bled, and he allowed his intimates to see how much he felt it. Cardinal Antonelli omitted nothing to assure him that he was a stranger to what had taken place. He spoke with marked interest of his health, went constantly to see him, and showed him the most affectionate interest. His greatest consolation, however, after God, was from the visit of his brother, Comte Werner de Mérode, who came to pass a month with him, and left him with the impression of that something being added to his great virtues which misfortune alone can bring.

Mgr. de Mérode's correspondence during these critical circumstances was full of the noblest sentiments. At the first moment, he thought of leaving Rome. "I think of leaving on Wednesday by Civita Vecchia, to come and have a good rest in France and Belgium, which I sorely need. How right Theresa is in saying, '*Martha! Martha! sollicita es et turbario erga plurima.*' We should be much wiser in quietly saying our beads, than worrying ourselves to death to produce nothing!'" * A few days later, however, his health improved and he gave up his intended journey. "Here I am," he writes, "having just left my office at the Pilota, where I have been winding up everything for the last two hours, and am returned to the Vatican, to resume my life as it was six years ago. What is very annoying are the commentaries of the Italian press and the private conversations in Rome. My dismissal is attributed to a thousand causes, one more absurd than the other. The real truth is, that it is simply an act of the Holy Father's will. I would not

* Letter of the 12th October, 1865, to Comte Werner de Mérode.

willingly have abandoned my post. So then I was sent into retreat 'for reasons of health'; while one hundred scudi a month are assigned to me 'till the day when I am to receive a fresh appointment.'" *

Still further to console his relations, he wrote a few days later to his sister-in-law, the Comtesse Werner de Mérode, as follows :—

"The reading of your letter was a real balm to my poor heart, in the midst of all its bitternesses and worries. Happily the storm which suddenly burst upon me only carried clouds. Nothing on earth gave rise to it. I am in perfect peace, both as to what regards me personally, and as to the different administrations which have passed through my hands. There is perfect order in each one of them, and not a penny of deficit. Not one of the people employed by me has committed the smallest act of malversation. Certain people had fancied they should find quite a different state of things! But all good wishes are not granted."

The caricatures of the day did not spare him, but no one laughed at them more heartily than himself, and he sent them to his own people to amuse them. We will only add to this account some of his comments on the newspaper versions of the affair :—"The *Débats*, I see, attributes my departure to altercations with Cardinal Antonelli. This is a complete mistake; for never have I been on better terms than lately with His Eminence. I receive on all sides marks of sympathy which are very capable of consoling me for the absurd rumours current in the public press. According to one, I had taken to flight; according to another, I was put in prison! Yesterday the vine-

* Letter of the 21st October, 1865.

dresser at the Villa Altieri met me for the first time
since I had ceased to be War Minister. He told me
how hurt and annoyed he had been at all that had
been said about me in the Piazza Navona. I have
gone back to the Vatican, and to my service as Cameriere. I own I should have preferred my liberty and
to remain simply a Canon of St. Peter's. But how
can one quarrel with Pius IX. ? "

We will quote a few words, in conclusion, from a
beautiful letter addressed to his sister, Mde. de Montalembert :—

" I will not say much about my change of position.
The newspapers have said enough to prevent one's
talking of it any more. I do not know what will
happen in the future. God alone is the Disposer of
all things, and all that remains to us is to allow ourselves to be led by His grace in the path which He has
pointed out, of justice, truth and honour. That is all
that I wish for in this world."

Mgr. de Mérode left his office at the moment that
Lamoricière left this earth. After the death of the
General, he had remained alone in the breach,
struggling against diplomacy and hostile opinions
from without and against routine from within, to
give the Pope a fine Army and real credit, and to
place his finances in good order. He succeeded
thoroughly. Veuillot said of him : "He deserves
either the prison of St. Angelo or the purple. I vote
for the purple ! "

Innocent as he was, no one could imprison him ;
though they hesitated in awarding to him the honours
he deserved. But he remained, whether his enemies
would or no, the greatest friend of the Pope, and his
most faithful and devoted servant. Veuillot might

well say in his praise, "No one knew him so well as Pius IX., and no one loved him so much!"

After having spent five years in forming an Army, in embellishing Rome, in making his name terrible to the enemies of the Church, and in forcing them to hesitate in their plans and draw back in their enterprises, he was about to pass the following five years in seeing the Pope enjoying the fruit of his labours, the Emperor compelled to renounce for a time the execution of the Convention of September, the Zouaves increase in number and valour, the battle of Mentana avenge Castelfidardo and Ancona, and the little State, consolidated by his hand, holding its ground in the midst of empires which were crumbling around it. Mérode helped to retard the fall of the temporal power from 1860 to 1870, feeling that that question was the key of the arch of all European monarchies. His name, placed by history side by side with that of Lamoricière, will be hailed from age to age, among the heroes of that crusade which lasted for ten years, and which will have its place in the annals of the glories of the Church of God.

CHAPTER VIII.

From 1865 to 1870.

Mgr. de Mérode Archbishop of Melitene and Almoner of
Pius IX.—His wonderful Ministry of Faith and Charity
—The charitable Establishments which he created and
restored—The *Zoccolette*—The Sisters of the Precious
Blood—The *Vigna Pia*—The Trappists of the "Three
Fountains"—Recruiting of the Zouaves and the forma-
tion of the Legion of Antibes—The Fêtes of the Centenary
—The Battle of Mentana—The Vatican Council—The
entry of the Piedmontese into the City of Rome.

ON leaving the War Office, Mgr. de Mérode published
the following Order of the Day :—

"His Holiness, out of an anxious desire for my
health, has deigned to relieve me of my office as War
Minister.

"Before separating myself finally from the Pontifical
Army, I wish to express to the men who compose it
my deep gratitude for their services; for the pleasant
relations we have always had together, and for the
ready help they have given me under all circumstances. During the six years we have passed together
we have gone through many vicissitudes and had
trials which were very hard to bear. The recollection
of these will, however, be dear to us through our
whole lives, for it is a recollection of self-abnegation, of loyalty, and of fidelity to conscience and to
duty.

" I am confident that the Holy Father will ever find in you soldiers full of honour and courage, worthy of the illustrious chief whom you have just lost by death, and of the great cause which you have undertaken to defend."

This recollection of self-abnegation and sacrifice, so worthily expressed, was, for some months, the only recompense of the War Minister. Reduced to a pension of 100 scudi a month, he, perhaps, might have been embarrassed to meet his obligations had not his brother generously opened to him both his purse and his heart. He thanked him in his own fashion, saying, " I have read, these last few days, St. Francis Xavier's letters. The first is addressed to his brother at Obanos and pleads for money from him. It is true that it was not a question of streets or new quarters ; but St. Francis did not reckon more fully than I have done on the abundant dew of fraternal liberality."*

The example of the Saints, meditation and the reading of Holy Scripture consoled and strengthened him. He went to see many convents and monasteries, which he always delighted in ; and when he found any inscription or text which answered to his thoughts, he applied it to himself and quoted it in his correspondence. One day he stopped before the monastery of Sta. Sabina, where there were some paintings by P. Besson. This Dominican, who was one of the first disciples of P. Lacordaire, had just died at Mossoul, with the reputation of being not only a great painter but a great Saint. Mgr. de Mérode remembered his merits when reading the inscription which he wrote at the entrance of the cloister : " *In silentio et spe erit fortitudo vestra.*" " Those words," he ex-

* Letter of the 11th December, 1865.

claimed, "were written long ago in the Book of Wisdom. But the recommendation suits me to-day better than any one. My strength must henceforth lie in silence and hope. I shall try and take that text as my motto."*

"Do not pity me more than I deserve," he writes a little later. But the love of his brother, who came to spend three months with him, touched him beyond words. He writes to his sister-in-law in terms of the most affectionate gratitude for so generously consenting to separate herself from her husband for his sake. He writes :—

"The Psalmist, to express his sorrow, exclaims, 'The waters of tribulation have entered into my soul.' That was a little bit my case, but we have so shaken and exhausted them, Werner and I, in our interminable conversations, that it has produced on me the same effect as the drainage which Werner appreciates so highly in his meadows when they are yellow and impoverished by the stagnant water in the soil. I feel nothing any longer in my heart which does not flow freely. The great point now is to find out how one can make use of all this in the right way for the good of one's soul. If one really loves God, everything should turn to one's profit. Pray for me and ask Him to help me to profit by it all."†

It was in these beautiful dispositions that he prepared himself for the Episcopate. The Sovereign Pontiff had chosen him for his Almoner, the post being vacant by the promotion of Mgr. de Hohenlohe to the Cardinalate. But there was some delay in his ap-

* Letter of the 11th December, 1865.

† Letter of the 13th March, 1866, to Comtesse Werner de Mérode.

pointment. Named Archbishop of Melitene *in partibus infidelium* in the Consistory of the 22nd of June, 1866, Mgr. de Mérode was consecrated on the 1st of July in the Church of St. Peter. For many reasons he chose this Basilica where he had been for a long while one of the Canons.

Beloved by his brethren, kind and helpful to every one about the church, his consecration was a real fête to them and a joy to the whole town. The Consecrator was Cardinal Patrizi, assisted by Mgr. Berardi, Under-Secretary of State, and Mgr. Pie, Bishop of Poitiers. Mgr. Pie had specially asked leave to take part in the consecration, wanting to give his friend a striking proof of the high esteem and devoted affection he had always felt for him. A few days later Mgr. de Mérode was appointed Almoner to His Holiness. In that way he gave up his duties as Cameriere and the weary waiting in the ante-chamber. But the Pope's affection for him remained unabated, and he always claimed him as the privileged companion of his daily walks or drives.

One of Mgr. de Mérode's best friends, who was also a devoted admirer of Pius IX., has very ably explained how this affection, which arose at the time of the Pope's first interview with the Abbé de Mérode, grew stronger and stronger since he had attached him to his person, and notably since what the world called his "disgrace."

"This affection," writes Mgr. de Ségur, "rests on the entire union of their sentiments, and is not in the least impaired by the divergence in their characters. Pius IX. loved Mgr. de Mérode's ardent faith, his grandeur of soul, and his absolute devotion to the Church; in all of which qualities the faithful servant resembled his master. He admired also immensely his natural pride; the way he despised all secondary things and the material wants and comforts of life; his contempt for the petty intrigues of diplomacy and the little meannesses of human nature; and in this also they were alike.

"As to his ardent temperament and his liberty of speech, which, with his combative spirit, often brought him into trouble, Pius IX., though he might not always approve, secretly enjoyed it, and very often was excessively amused at his sallies. He profited by them also; and the frankness and independence of spirit shown by Mgr. de Mérode in conversation taught the Pope many things and many details about persons and events of which otherwise he would have remained ignorant. He did not accept all his verdicts, or always appreciate people in the same way. But it is everything for a Sovereign, even he be a Pope and a Saint, to have about him a man of such largeness of mind and such a great heart; one who said out loud exactly what he thought, even if his speech were not always conformable to the strictest prudence and impartiality."*

We might quote a thousand anecdotes to confirm this judgment of the happy and intimate relations which existed between Mgr. de Mérode and the Pope. One day, when Pius IX. had listened for some time to what Mgr. de Mérode was telling him, and smiling at the sound but severe judgments he was passing on people and things, he stopped him, all of a sudden, and cried out, "Mérode, you talk too much. I am going to shut your mouth!" Mérode replied, laugh-

* "A Winter at Rome: Portraits and Recollections," by the Marquis de Ségur, pp. 139, 140.

ing, "I am quite willing; only you must, at the same time, shut my ears."

Mgr. de Mérode was quite ready to allow the occasional intemperance of his frankness; but how could the Holy Father be offended at being contradicted by a man who loved him so well and who served him so devotedly? The Prelate judged himself without mercy, and his apparent rudeness towards others was nothing in comparison to what he dealt out to himself.

One day he met with an accident which filled the whole Vatican with consternation. He had fallen from a scaffolding which had been put up in one of the chapels of the Palace for the repair of a picture, and in his fall he had broken his leg. When it had been set he heard that the Pope was coming directly to see him. It was during the Vatican Council. "His Holiness is really much too good to me!" he exclaimed. "I do not deserve such attention." Then, with a shrewd smile, he added, "I am sure the Pope would much rather I had broken my tongue instead of my leg!" One of his friends came to see him, and exclaimed, "I do admire your patience. I never should have expected it of you!" "Ah!" he replied; "but I am doing penance. If I fell, it was because I did not hold myself firm enough to the corner-stone of the Church: *Non satis firmatus supra petram.*"

The duties of Papal Almoner were eminently fitted to satisfy his zeal; as those of War Minister were to delight his boldness. There, as in the midst of camps and soldiers, the measure of his devotedness was to devote himself without measure. To pray, to give; to pray always, to give more and more, and to know no obstacle, no truce, no rest in the exercise of his charity; such was his life during the whole of his

Episcopate. The Pope's Almoner has not only the distribution of the Pontifical alms, but the superintendence of all charitable and educational establishments. But his personal piety, as well as custom, imposed another duty upon him—that of confirming little children in danger of death. In these three functions he was henceforth to spend his life.

Mgr. de Mérode had two classes of alms to distribute. One class is regulated by old usage and distributed on the occasion of certain Feasts. The other varies according to circumstances. These alms have a secret character; and, as the Pope receives petitions from all parts of the earth in favour of the poor and needy, his private budget of charity is very much in excess of the public one. In spite of the immense sums Pius IX. annually received from all nations, his prodigious generosity often left him in a deficit. He never reckoned what he gave; nor did his Almoner. But when, after Mgr. de Mérode's death, the accounts had to be overhauled, it was found that the Prelate had advanced sixty thousand francs to the Pope. The first thought of his brother, who was his heir, was to give this advance to the Holy Father. He could not have better interpreted the thought of one who would have ruined himself a hundred times over in the Pope's service, if God had not specially blessed the speculations in which he had risked his fortune and braved human wisdom in order to give more to the poor of Jesus Christ.

Alongside of this glorious service we must place another, of which faith alone can estimate the beauty and grandeur. This was the confirmation of children in danger of death. Pius IX., when recommending to him this work of charity, related an anecdote in his own life, which was as instructive as it was edifying. When he was Archbishop of Spoleto, they came one evening and knocked at the door of the Palace to ask him to confirm a dying child. It was very late at night, and the Archbishop proposed to put it off till the next day. But the mother exclaimed, " My child may die to-night ! " " If such a misfortune were to happen," replied the Archbishop, " you know that you may feel quite happy about him, and that his salvation is sure, as he has been baptized." " I know," she replied ; " but he will not have such a fine place in Paradise, and it will be all your fault ! '" At these words the Archbishop felt he could resist no longer, and went at once to confirm the child. Pius IX., while telling this story, admired the faith of the mother, and wished that his Almoner should never deserve such a reproach.

The anxiety and zeal shown by Mgr. de Mérode in fulfilling this ministry lasted to the end of his life. No matter how late at night the call came, off he would start, often on foot, to the most distant quarters of the town ; going into the poorest houses, and giving the holy oil to the dying children with a faith, a piety, and a tender charity which nothing ever slackened. What rendered his visits even more precious was the interest he took in the poor families of the children, never leaving them without some marks of his generosity and sympathy ; and their gratitude was expressed in the warmest manner. One poor mother exclaimed : " Now I feel that my boy may go to Heaven. I shall see him one day, thanks to you, with two rays of glory, that of his baptism and of his confirmation." With his zeal for the salvation of little children, we can imagine with what care he watched over the schools entrusted to his superintendence as the Pope's Almoner. In the transtiberian (or *Trastevere*) quarter there are two popular schools, one kept by the disciples of the venerable La Salle, the other by the Belgian brothers, called "Providence"; a recent foundation, but one which resembles the admirable French Community both in their dress and their devotion to poor children. The Archbishop of Melitene protected the one, founded the other, and filled both with his own generous ardour. Hundreds of children have passed through their hands. Their manners, their progress, and the perfection of their education astonish strangers. Rome has nothing to envy, either in Paris or Brussels, as far as regards the primary education of little boys.

The education of the girls was more difficult. Among the establishments under the direction of Mgr. de Mérode we must first mention what are called the "*Maestre Pie*," of whom he became, as it were, the second founder. Their origin dated from the seventeenth century. Two ladies of Viterbo opened two schools in that town, one for rich and one for poor children. Cardinal Barbarigo gave them the rules for their Institute, of which Clement XIII. approved. The town of Rome obtained the establishment of similar schools in the eighteenth century, and when Mgr. de Mérode became Protector of the Institute it numbered eight schools, with a central House situated near the place of Sta. Lucia. The Pope gave each mistress five scudi a month. The Almoner soon perceived that it was high time to enlarge the house in which they and their pupils were huddled together, and, above all, to improve its sanitary arrangements. He enlarged the halls, renewed the pavement and staircases, and took special care of the holy women who thus devoted themselves to the instruction of the common people. It was necessary that they should pass creditable examinations in order to obtain their certificates. Mgr. de Mérode gave them masters, and encouraged them in every way; while, to increase their faith and make them enter more fully into the spirit of their Institute, he drew up a life of their holy foundresses—a book which is full of instruction and edification.

The reform of the Institution called "*Delle Zoccolette*" gave him infinitely more trouble. It is a curious page in modern Roman history, of which we will give a brief outline.

At the approach of the Jubilee of 1700, Pope Innocent XII. ordered his Almoner, Jerome Berti, to collect any young destitute girls whom he might find begging in the town, and to place them in a building situated near the church of St. Eloi, commonly called "*The Blacksmith's*" Church. Clement XI. developed the Institution, and transferred it to a house near the Ponte Sisto, originally founded by Sixtus V. The Roman people nicknamed it "*Delle Zoccolette*," alluding to the shoes worn by the poor women in that quarter. They remained here till 1811, when they were dispersed under some pretext by the French Government, who had usurped the Holy City. But no sooner had Pius VII. returned than he replaced the poor women in their Home, confiding the care of them to his Almoner, according to the spirit of the foundation.

However beautiful the idea may have been, it was singularly ill carried out. The House was governed by a regent, or mistress, chosen by election every five years. Every sort of intrigue was resorted to to obtain this post, and, still more, to keep it. Influential families protected the different candidates, and hence the direction of the Charity fell into bad hands. No rules or discipline were observed. There was neither order, nor cleanliness, nor economy; while the poor women for whom it was intended were in need of everything, and their mistresses lived upon the patrimony of the poor.

Mgr. de Mérode found out these flagrant abuses at once, and determined to put a stop to them. His charitable zeal was also excited by the sight of the population of that quarter, which is the poorest in Rome. The men are employed from morning to night in the tanneries; the women in the tobacco factory; while their children ran wild in the streets, without care or schooling, and rapidly fell into every kind of vice and mischief. The *Zoccolette*, to be really useful, ought, therefore, to be largely increased; and, instead of only housing a few destitute women, ought to become, to the children, the sick, and the workmen of that neighbourhood, a real help and Providence. Evidently lay-women, however good and devoted, were unequal to such a task, and Mgr. de Mérode felt that the only Order which would really meet the need was that of St. Vincent of Paul, whose admirable Sisters he had already employed in the Military Hospital. He could not have made a better choice, but it went against the routine, the prejudices, and, above all, the pretended rights of a multitude of people, and terrible was the storm which arose in consequence.

When, on the 22nd of November, 1866, the Sisters of Charity came to take possession of the House, the revolution broke out. The mistresses, who were furious at losing their authority and their money, burst into tears and angry recriminations. Outside, the fury was even greater. People declared that so arbitrary and unjust a proceeding was worthy of Mgr. de Mérode : that it was one of those enormities of which he only was capable : that he did not understand the Roman character : and that to subject these ladies to French domination was either to drive them out of the house, or to be the cause of their death. An incredible number of persons of every rank took up the quarrel, and went to the Pope himself for redress. Even the more moderate amongst them implored him to revoke a measure which they characterized as brusque and intemperate, and in which the want of tact and temper of the Belgian Prelate was clearly shown. But the Pope, who had himself approved of the whole thing beforehand, and was determined to put an end to the previous abuses, was neither moved nor disconcerted by the popular clamour, and desired Mgr. de Mérode to carry out his plans without heeding the opposition.

Mgr. de Mérode had no intention of drawing back. He found in his clever originality a way of attacking the evil by the roots, and reducing the calumniators to silence. He knew very well that even the Italian religious communities were among his opponents, and one day went into one of their principal convents, summoned the members of the community together, and announced to them the arrival of the Sisters of St. Vincent, together with the noble works they were about to undertake. Then changing all of a sudden his voice and manner, he fixed his penetrating look upon them and said : "I have told you what they are, and yet you detest them !" At these words, which showed that he had seen into the depths of their hearts, they remained silent and colouring, though the Superior feebly tried to deny the feeling. Mgr. de Mérode got up, would not listen to their excuses, and only said as

Q

he left the room : " My daughters! I must beg of you to show a little more charity towards your French sisters. They, like you, have the strongest love for God and their neighbour. Like you, they devote themselves to the service of the poor, and, more than all others, they have a right to your respect and affection."

This brusque visit had excellent results. At first the nuns were angry ; then they calmed down ; their confusion changed into regrets, and the cause of the Sisters of Charity was finally won in all the communities of Rome. By this clever manœuvre Mgr. de Mérode had deprived the adversaries of the reform of their most powerful auxiliaries. He next proposed to the old *Zoccolette* to leave the institution and accept a pension of five scudi a month. The younger ones joyfully accepted the proposal—the more aged preferred to remain ; every sort of care was taken of them, and by assigning to them a separate part of the house, they could follow their own rules, and be more or less independent of the Sisters.

The new *régime* was promptly established. Mgr. de Mérode increased the buildings, added several of the neighbouring houses to the Home, and organized every department necessary for the service of the poor. It became a real blessing to the whole quarter. A *Salle d'Asile* was opened for children of both sexes. The poor mothers, who were obliged to go out to work, brought their little ones with the greatest joy to the good Sisters' tender care during their absence. By the side of the crêche beautiful schools were opened, where the number of children increased daily. Then the Sisters began an orphanage, where between two and three hundred little girls were clothed, fed, and taught with an intelligence and a tender care which speedily silenced the critics, and filled every visitor with feelings of gratitude and admiration. Alongside of the schools was a room for a consulting doctor, who came every morning to inspect the sick people of the district: a large dispensary adjoined it, where medicines were distributed gratuitously. A little further on a bakehouse and an economic kitchen were opened, where the poorest and most destitute came to receive their daily meal. A spacious chapel completed the building. Mgr. de Mérode supplied the altars, sacred vases, vestments, and pictures; but its greatest ornament was the holy Prelate himself, who came constantly to offer the Holy Sacrifice and bless his dear Sisters, of whom he had been the Father, the protector, and the friend. As long as he lived the embellishment and perfection of this Home was ever dear to his heart. In a visit he paid to Paris in 1869 he visited all the analogous institutions in that city, questioning the Sisters of St. Vincent de Paul, taking notes upon any little improvement they suggested, and determining to imitate at Rome in their minutest details the marvels of order, cleanliness, activity, and devotion which Paris has carried to an ideal perfection in her charitable institutions. His last wish had been to add a larger crêche to this establishment, but death prevented him. We feel confident, however, that God, who had counted all his great merits and holy desires, has transported him from the spot he had made an earthly Paradise to that Heaven where he sees the clear vision of God, and sings with the angels of those little children whom he cared for so tenderly on earth.

Another important educational work which he took in hand was that of St. Aloysius de Gonzagua, situated in the Via Porta Leone. The Sisters of the Precious Blood, who keep this school, were founded by St. John Baptist de Rossi, Canon of St. Maria in Cosmedin, and lately numbered among the saints. This great servant of God opened a hospital there in 1731, and he, with the help of B. Gaspard del Buffalo, founded the congregation of the Precious Blood to serve the sick, and governed it till his death. The rules were approved by Pius IX. in 1854, and Mgr. de Mérode obtained that same year the addition of a school to the hospital. All the authorities were against him; but the Pope cut short the discussion and ordered the opening of the school. Mgr. de Mérode built large schoolrooms, bought gardens for playgrounds, and did everything to make them bright and pretty. The children were enchanted, and very soon the schools became too small for the teeming population. Mgr. de Mérode at once bought an adjoining building, turned it into class rooms, and thus doubled the number of children. But there was not a single district in Rome where his presence did not make itself felt. He enlarged the schools in the Corso near the Piazza del Popolo, and founded others in the Via dell Arco di Gennasi. All the necessary school furniture, maps, books, and pictures were supplied by him, at his own cost, in every educational establishment. He could not be generous by halves, and by thus putting education within the reach of the youngest and poorest of the people, not only without any expense to themselves, but with every material advantage, he left no plea for the workmen to refuse their children so great a benefit, while his enemies could find none for hostile criticism.

The daily exercise of this ministry of faith and charity tried Mgr. de Mérode's health a good deal.

The doctors strongly urged him to leave Rome during the hottest summer months, and to pass a little time in France or Belgium. He followed their advice, and came to rest among his own people and to breathe once more his native air. But this time it was vitiated by the cholera, which laid waste all the country about Rixensart and its neighbourhood. He was staying there in a house which belonged to his father, and which he shared with Mde. de Montalembert. The inhabitants honoured him as he deserved, and were too happy to have such an Archbishop in their midst. He preached at Rixensart, to the great satisfaction of his audience, ordained at the Abbey of Fougerloo* during Ember Week, and, yielding to the entreaties of the Marquise de Meüs, consecrated the new Church of Argenteuil. The King of the Belgians sent for him, received him at Ostend, and overwhelmed him with marks of esteem and consideration. But the most living remembrance he left of this journey in the hearts of the people was his devotion to the care of the cholera patients at Rixensart, whom he nursed while living and buried when dead. He and the Curé had often to carry the victims to the cemetery and to dig their graves, the sextons having taken to flight. On one occasion, the Curé having been sent for to administer to a dying man, the Archbishop himself carried the coffin to the burial ground. His extraordinary charity and courage on this occasion are registered in the archives of the parish, dated the 28th of September, 1866.

Hardly had he got back to Rome than another sick bed claimed his care and his wonderful power of sooth-

---

* Fougerloo was the principal Belgian Abbey of the Canons Regular of St. Norbert, called Premonstratensians.

ing the last hours of a man on his passage to eternity.
We will give an extract from his letter to his brother
on this occasion :—

"My dear Werner,—The good Dr. Alertz gave up
his pure soul to God this morning at nine o'clock. I
had obtained from the Holy Father the permission to
say Mass in his room. There I gave him Holy Communion, as viaticum and extreme unction. He had
paralysis of the throat at last, which prevented his
swallowing anything. He used to come and see me
constantly in the Vatican, and one day the conversation fell on the way in which sick people were abandoned by the doctors. He told me that up to the
last moment a doctor might diminish the sufferings of
the dying. That that was what the ancients called
euthanasia—i.e., an easy death, a death without pain.
The last time that I was by his bedside he could hardly
speak, and yet he turned towards me, and, pointing
to the doctors around him, said with a smile in a
low voice, '*Euthanasia.* There is nothing but that
left !' The death of this old friend, whom I found in
1845 so full of your journeys together, of those of
Montalembert, and of the affairs of the Archbishop of
Cologne, Mgr. de Doste, &c., is for me like a tomb
closing a whole epoch. The poor old man was alone,
isolated, forgotten by the world. He showed me
always the greatest affection, and I returned it
heartily."

The September convention had been carried out and
the French flag had left Rome on the 6th of December,
1866, leaving the Eternal City and the patrimony of
St. Peter to the sole care of the little army which had
been formed by Mgr. de Mérode. At first the departure of the French troops had no apparently bad con-

sequences. The enemies of the Temporal Power wished to take their time before making a final assault. The French Government had authorized, under the title of a Roman Legion, the recruiting of a new body of men to strengthen the Pontifical Army, under the command of Colonel D'Argy. Cardinal Mathieu, Archbishop of Besançon, who had known this brave officer in his Episcopal city, had persuaded both the Emperor and the Pope to consent to his being the chief of this new Legion. D'Argy passed two years at Antibes in forming and disciplining these troops. It needed all his vigilance and his paternal care to prevent desertion, for the Revolutionists, anxious at this recruiting, tried to counteract it in the most deceitful and outrageous manner. But D'Argy succeeded even beyond his hopes. Tall, with a martial air, and a proved bravery which had been tried by forty years of service and active campaigns, he attracted a multitude of young officers, fresh from college, who esteemed it an honour and a joy to serve the Holy Father under such a commander. The soldiers were not less ready. Many were volunteers, but others were still under military law, trained men and capable of any amount of devotedness, for their courage was animated and sustained by faith.

Whilst the Antibes Legion thus prepared itself for the Pope's service, the veterans of Castelfidardo and Ancona came back to Rome from all sides to resume their glorious service. Mgr. de Mérode, it is true, was no longer War Minister; but General Kanzler, who had succeeded him, carefully kept to his traditions; and the Prelate neglected nothing which would make their residence in Rome useful and agreeable to the young crusaders. Their behaviour was admirable;

many bore illustrious names; and all were honoured
by the friendship and kindness of one whom they had
so long looked upon as their chief, and whom they had
never ceased to revere for his bravery and personal
holiness. The people in Rome treated the Papal
troops with a marked respect, which made them easily
forget that the Revolutionary papers dubbed them the
" mercenaries " of the Pope. *" Signor Soldato "* was
the way they were addressed in the streets, which
plainly shows the consideration in which they were
held.

The budget of the little army was no more in Mgr.
de Mérode's hands, but the regularity he had established went on the same. Supplies also did not fail.
Many Belgian dioceses, as well as German and French,
had undertaken to pay for a certain number of Zouaves.
Each man cost 500 francs. Artisans, servants, poor
factory girls, all came forward with their little savings
to help in the annual maintenance of these Papal
soldiers. The subscription called " Peter's Pence,"
which was spread and consolidated in every country,
assured millions to a King in that most exceptional of
positions; a King living, that is to say, upon alms;
and yet able, with this sole resource, to maintain his
army, his court, and his missioners throughout the
whole Christian world. M. de Corcelles for the last
ten years had helped in the administration of the Papal
finances, and the tabular statement he drew up showed
ever-increasing resources. Cardinal Antonelli displayed admirable talents in this administration, to
which Mgr. de Mérode rendered full justice.

The year 1867 may be reckoned among the most
glorious and consoling in the life of Mgr. de Mérode,
for during that period his devotion to the Holy See,

bore great and striking fruit. First came the centenary of St. Peter. The Prelate, who had seen 200 bishops gathered together for the definition of the Dogma of the Immaculate Conception, and who, eight years later, had done the honours of the Pontifical Army to the prelates of both worlds assembled for the canonization of the Japanese martyrs, found himself, in 1867, among the 512 pontiffs who surrounded the throne of the successor of St. Peter to celebrate the eighteenth century of the first Pope. When these glorious festivities were over he went on a short holiday to France, to escape from the burning heats which had already so severely tried his health.

During this holiday he accepted, at the entreaty of Mgr. Angebault, Bishop of Angers, the task of consecrating the new church of Loroux-Béconnais, to which the remembrance of Lamoricière was closely united. The General had contributed largely to the building of this church. His friend wept for joy while praying for him, and blessing the place where everything brought his piety and generosity to remembrance. The Bishop of Angers and the Abbé de Solesmes were present, and the Abbé Sauvé, Canon of Laval, preached. No one could have been more happily chosen to speak of Lamoricière, who was his intimate friend, as well as Mgr. de Mérode's. Before leaving Angers Mgr. de Mérode went to see a nun who had inhabited Imola while Pius IX. was Bishop of that town, and who was now in the Convent of the Good Shepherd. He brought her the special blessing of the Holy Father, and heard from her a multitude of touching incidents of the Bishop's charity before he became so great a Pope. From Angers Mgr. de Mérode went on to Solesmes, where Dom Guéranger received him with the greatest respect. He honoured in him not only the Pope's Almoner, but the son of his illustrious friend Comte Felix de Mérode and the brother-in-law of Comte de Montalembert, who had so favoured and encouraged the restoration of the Benedictines in France, and the renewal of those great labours which are the honour of learned humanity. That day, in the refectory, a notice in Latin was read upon the Comte de Montalembert, as one of the noted benefactors of the abbey, and this delicate praise was received by Mgr. de Mérode with much pleasure and gratitude.

When the Pope's Almoner returned to Rome he found the Peninsula again troubled by a fresh revolutionary enterprise directed against the Papal States. Garibaldi's brigand hordes attacked Acquapendente, Ischia, Valentano and Canino. At the news of these fresh aggressions Catholics throughout the world asked themselves if the soldiers of the Pope would be numerous enough to hold their ground without the help of France. Napoleon, as usual, hesitated ; gave orders for the embarkation of an expeditionary corps ; then revoked them ; then renewed them, and the army corps commanded by General de Failly luckily had embarked, and was well on its way before a fresh counter-order reached Marseilles, which, fortunately, came too late, and would have indefinitely adjourned the departure of the French.

This corps landed at Civita Vecchia on the 29th of October. It was only just in time. On the 26th the little town of Monte Rotondo, five leagues from Rome, had been attacked by Garibaldi, at the head of 5,000 men. The Antibes Legion, who formed the garrison, numbered only 350. This handful of brave soldiers defended themselves for two days, repulsed five assaults, and left Garibaldi so exhausted as to be unable to march on Rome. The Pope was half-saved; General Kanzler completed the victory by leaving the city on the 3rd of November with 3,000 Pontifical troops. "Come," he exclaimed to Dr. Ozanam and several other Frenchmen, who were organizing the Ambulance service, "come, and you will see a really fine battle." He marched straight to the enemy, and met him at Mentana. It was he who led the attack. "Come on, my Zouaves!" exclaimed de Charette, "go at them with the bayonet, and remember that Frenchmen are looking on." The French, in fact, had actually arrived on the battle-field to insure the victory of Mentana, which was, however, won by the Pontifical troops. The Zouaves performed prodigies of valour, driving back Garibaldi into the fort, and braving the murderous fire from the walls without flinching for a moment. "Bravo! Bravo! Zouaves!" cried the French spectators of their courage and enthusiasm. General de Polhés then ordered an advance of his troops, the noise of the rifles mingled with the roar of the cannon, Garibaldi took to flight, and the Pontifical Army, mistress of the battle-field, re-entered Rome with the French troops, glad to share with them the laurels of the day.

The martyrs of that fight will have their place in history. Belgium and France, Holland and England, bought with their blood the victory which for three years arrested the sacrilegious invasion of Piedmont. The order of the day made honourable mention of the Quélens, the Quatrebarbes, the Guérins, the Dufournels, the Wyatt-Edgells, and many others, whose bravery was the talk of the whole world, and whose graves are still visited by pilgrims to the Eternal City.

The Dufournels were two brothers, whom God did not separate either in life or death. Emmanuel fell in the fight at Farnese, Adéodat under the walls of Rome. Adéodat survived his mortal injuries for six days, and said: "I am going to rejoin my brother, and shall be as happy as he is." While he was on his bed of suffering Mgr. de Mérode hastened to pay him a visit, and expressed a hope that God, content with his brother's sacrifice, would preserve him for his Father, for France, and the Papacy. "Ah! Monseigneur!" replied the young martyr, "do not wish that. Rather pray that God may accept to-day the sacrifice of my life, for the world is full of dangers, and I am very weak."

The sacrifice of the Dufournels stirred up the whole province of Franche-Comté to its very depths. In one month the diocese of Besançon sent upwards of 300 volunteers as Pontifical recruits. They came from the mountains of Doubs, some for the Antibes Legion, which Cardinal Mathieu protected with princely generosity; others to join the Zouaves or dragoons. A good number came from the Maîche property, belonging to the Mérodes, and went, like the Belgians, to knock at the door of the Vatican, and to see the Prelate who had organized the Papal Army. Mgr. de Mérode received them with a kindness and benevolence which often melted them to tears. He never forgot that he was a native of Franche-Comté as well as of Belgium; and these two nations, of which he represented so well the independent character and the religious devotedness, were equally proud of his services, so great in the sight of God, so misunderstood and little recognized by men, but at last absolved by public opinion, now that those services had been crowned with success and victory.

This feeling spread even amongst the Italian aristocracy, which, until now, had been so distrustful of strangers, and full of prejudices against the Pontifical Zouaves. Pius IX. himself was reassured. He then resolved to convoke an Ecumenical Council at Rome, hoping to be allowed to see after the spiritual needs of the Universal Church in peace, whilst the Revolution, crushed at Mentana, seemed for a moment to forget Rome and abandon her prey. Opened on the 8th of December, 1869, the Vatican Council brought public attention again to bear upon Mgr. de Mérode. They sought for him in the ceremonies, and pointed him out behind the Sovereign Pontiff, with his modest look, his rapid step, which could hardly be controlled by the slow march of the procession, and his manner, which was at once sacerdotal and military. In spite of his height he always tried to hide himself from observation, and to baffle those who sought to guess his thoughts. His life was just as fully occupied and as austere as before, and he neglected none of his charitable works. Every one knew that his table was more than frugal, and he hardly dared risk inviting his friends. But his brother, Count Werner de Mérode, came to pass the month of January with him. " I am going to take advantage of your presence," Mgr. de Mérode said to him, " to put my house in order. You shall order the dinners, and we will each of us invite our friends."

When the guests arrived, however, it was almost always found that the table was too small. Every one laughed ; but the interest of the conversation made them forget the awkwardness. Mgr. Pie, Mgr. de

Dreux-Brézé, Mgr. de Falloux, Mgr. de Latour d'Auvergne, Mgr. Dupanloup, Mgr. Bastide, Mgr. Sauvé, the Viscount de Meaux, M. Victor de Broglie, and many other remarkable men met round this hospitable table, where every one admired in the Prelate his noble tone, which no amount of familiarity could make anything but aristocratic, his wit and pleasantry, and, above all, his personal mortification, which could not escape any one's observation.

But after the dinner Mgr. de Mérode generally proposed a walk, and took all his company outside the walls to see some of his pet establishments or some archæological discovery. The author and translator of this book had both the pleasure of taking part in these excursions, and from the notes of the former we will extract a few passages:—

"One of Mgr. de Mérode's dearest creations is the '*Vigna Pia*,' where 130 children, mostly orphans, are gathered together in a fine house surrounded by a vast enclosure. This property belonged personally to Pius IX., who had given it his name, and had charged Mgr. de Mérode with the duty of founding an Agricultural School there, in which useful trades should likewise be taught. Carpenters', shoemakers', and tailors' workshops occupy the boys indoors; while outside they cultivate the garden and fields. The Archbishop of Mélitene first took his guests to the terrace, from whence the eye embraces the whole Roman Campagna, the lazy course of the Tiber, the town, and the ribands of white smoke which pointed out the line of the new railroad. Then directing our attention to the population thinly scattered over the vast Campagna, he would talk feelingly of the miserable condition of the poor labourers.

" ' Those who come from the Provinces,' he said, ' come hoping to find work in the vast desert called the Campagna. The roads of communication are few and far between; the small inhabited centres are widely apart; the marshes exhale pestilential miasmas; and the temperature gives them a pernicious fever which carries them off in a few hours. The only food of those poor people consists in a coarse kind of bread, water which is almost undrinkable, and for a treat on Sundays, now and then, some salt meat. Those ruined huts which you see is their only shelter at night; but the insects drive them out of them, and they generally sleep in the open air. When the fever takes them, if a cart passes they throw the poor fellow on the faggots or casks with which it is loaded, and bring him into the town. Others try to make their way on foot. They almost always knock at the door of the Lateran or St. Spirito Hospital, which receives them as beggars. Very often death surprises them in the midst of the Campagna, where they are utterly abandoned. In that case, the congregation of the " Good Death " receives notice, and goes and fetches the corpse and buries it; but it is a most melancholy state of things.' "

Then he showed us his little colony of young agriculturists, strong, healthy boys, well clothed and well fed. He took us all over the garden and fields, hoping that the " *Vigna Pia* " would become a model for all future agricultural schools. He thought it would be the surest way of fertilizing the Roman Campagna.

The colony is under the care of the Brothers of St. Joseph of the Congregation of the Holy Cross at Mans. The Superior said to us, " This may be called the

eldest daughter of Monseigneur the Archbishop. For
the last fifteen years he has taken the most charitable
care of us. For many years he would come here
on foot at six o'clock in the morning on Sundays
and feast days to say Mass for us. We had no priest
in the house. The distance from Rome, the fear of the
bad air and the poverty of the institution, did not allow
us to think of a chaplain. It was the Pope's Almoner
who served us in this capacity! He used to catechize
the boys after Mass, help and direct us in all our works,
and show himself a real father to us all. Our house,
then, was situated on some very low, unhealthy ground.
He moved it up to the top of the hill, and he has never
ceased improving and enlarging it. After having spent
30,000 francs of his own in this way, he put the administration into the hands of a Commission chosen
by the Holy Father. But he has kept the spiritual direction of the work, and that is why it flourishes, under a
protection at once so powerful, so generous and so
secure.''

On leaving the " *Vigna Pia* " the Archbishop promised us another day a visit to the Convents of the
" *Three Fountains*," of which he had been the restorer
and benefactor. After he had made us visit the
Basilica of *St. Paolo fuore le Mure*, where we had the
happiness of meeting the Cavaliere de Rossi and hearing from his mouth an explanation of all the antiquities which had been collected by this illustrious
archæologist in the corridors of the cloister, Mgr. de
Mérode invited him to accompany us to the " *Tre
Fontane*," so that we might enjoy his science and
erudition a little longer. The abbey, which had been
confided to the Trappists, had only, at that time, twelve
acres under cultivation. But it was the beginning of

a great work, which will extend itself eventually far
into the Campagna, and do much to purify and dis-
infect that marshy ground. The monks are almost
all French ; some are from Staoueli, near Algiers ;
they have intelligence, zeal and courage ; if needful,
they would have a martyr's bravery. The ruined state
of their cloister does not discourage them ; for the
three churches which they serve by their holy recollections serve to revive their faith and confidence.
Here is the church where St. Paul received his death-
blow, and where, according to tradition, his head falling three times on the soil, three famous fountains
sprang up, the temperature of which is essentially
different in each. Nearer the entrance gate is the
church dedicated to St. Anastatius, where St. Bernard,
when saying Mass, was happy enough, by the merit
of the Holy Sacrifice, to release a soul from purgatory.
A monk with the accent of a native of Franche-Comté
came up and congratulated us on being in Mgr. de
Mérode's company. He said, " The Archbishop is
the most signal benefactor to our monastery. It is
only through his advice and with his money that we
have been able to struggle on against the climate,
the fever and despair. The interest he has taken in
our work gives us a real strength. Formerly the
soil round the Abbey Church had been raised under
the idea that it would make it more healthy. The
very reverse was the fact. The damp invaded the
walls, and what you see now is nothing to what it was
before. By Mgr. de Mérode's orders the whole ground
near the building has been lowered, and the earth has
been carried away by the convicts, who have also drained
all the fields ready for cultivation. The eucalyptus
has been planted everywhere, and wo make from it

R

a kind of liqueur, which is excellent for preventing
fever." Our Trappist made us taste this and then
took us all over the monastery, showing us the ventilation which Mgr. de Mérode had carried out, the
windows he had opened, and the drains he had
made to carry off the stagnant water. By his generosity and care the monastery has thus been made
habitable. The Trappists never think of leaving it
now save in the very height of the fever season;
and, when they return, the fever which used to deci-
mate them has disappeared, and left them to labour in
peace.

Whilst we had been listening to these explana-
tions the monks had recognized de Rossi, and hastened to show him a stone which had been lately
dug up near the abbey, and on which were inscribed
some unknown characters. At the first sight M. de
Rossi declared the inscription was Armenian, and the
date that of the twelfth century. "This is very
precious," he exclaimed, "for it is only the second we
have found in Rome in this language. It only shows
how cosmopolitan this city was in all times. All the
people of the earth have passed through it, and their
passage is proved by the different languages they have
left behind them."

I looked now at the group gathered round the inscription. What a strange company! Three French
Religious of the family of St. Bernard; Mgr. the
Archbishop of Mélitene, their protector and friend, who,
more than any one else, encourages and carries out the
reforms and useful works which the country demands.
By their side Comte Charles de Mérode Westerloo
and Comte Werner de Mérode, a Belgian Jesuit, Father
de Buck, noted among the New Hollandists; the young

Prince Victor de Broglie ; the Bishop of Loretto ; and, above all, the Archbishop of Quito ; three languages, seven nations, two worlds, assembled with the great Roman Archæologist on four feet of ground, to verify a recollection of the twelfth century, close to the altar where St. Bernard worked miracles, and near the church dedicated to St. Anastatius and to the spot which witnessed the martyrdom of St. Paul !

When, on returning from these excursions, the sight of some military fête attracted the Fathers of the Council to the Villa Borghese, it was not Mgr. de Mérode who did the honours of the review. But looking at these 14,000 men, the Zouaves, the Antibes Legion, the artillery, the dragoons, the cavalry, the National Guards of the Campagna, all, Pontifical or strangers, with a martial air and a fine presence, manœuvring with precision, mounting guard with pride, ready at a moment's notice to fight to the death, one could not help remembering the just and true words of Lamoricière to the Prelate who engaged him in the Papal service : " *We two will make the hole ; and after us these brave fellows·will rush in and enlarge it.*" Mgr. de Mérode had seen without jealousy this camp, this barrack, this army, which he alone had created, pass under the command of another ; but all the spectators and the strangers gathered together in the Holy City did not fail to recognize that it was to him that the Pope owed his present forces ; and that to him was due the credit of having rehabilitated in public opinion the formerly despised title of "Papal soldier." Even up to 1870 he contrived to enroll many of his young relations, or friends of his family, either in the Zouaves or the Antibes Legion ; and when they arrived he looked after them with

paternal care ; put them at their ease by his frank and
hearty manner, and looked after their souls as well as
their bodies, with that ardent faith which burst out in
all his speeches and was reflected in all his works.

The Council had its days of mourning as well as its
feasts. Such was that caused by the death of Col.
d'Argy, the Commander of the Antibes Legion, in which
was enrolled one of Mgr. de Mérode's nephews, M. Alof
de Vignacourt. An adjutant at the taking of Algiers, and
a Colonel at Mentana, d'Argy had won his first epaulette
in Africa, and left his last in Rome, while defending the
Pope and civilization. He died on the 27th of January,
1870, and, two days after, his funeral obsequies were celebrated in the Church of St. Louis. More than a hundred
bishops of every nation and of all rites were gathered
round that altar mingling in the same hearty regrets.
The Pope's Almoner was at the head of the mourners.
He had hastened to the bedside of the dying man to
bring him the benediction of the Holy Father, and the
Colonel said to his Major, who was also present :
" To-morrow you will mention this blessing in the
order of the day." The officers wept bitterly over the
loss of their Colonel, saying to de Mérode, " He
was the best of comrades ! " and the Archbishop consoled them by answering, " And the best of Christians."

The news of Montalembert's death, which came as
a surprise upon every one six weeks later, was to
Mgr. de Mérode the greatest possible sorrow. For a
long time he had felt deeply for the sufferings which
nailed this champion of the holiest cause to a sick bed.
He had gone to see him at Roche-en-Brény, and had
fortified his great soul in the struggle with mortal
sickness. With all the help which religion and family

affection could give, his beloved sister now lost her glorious husband; he himself the dearest of friends and brothers; the Catholic Church a defender and a mainstay whose irreparable loss has only made itself felt more cruelly every day during the last fifteen years. He loved as much as he admired him, and if any little difference arose on any question, he would gently say, " Don't forget that you are the cause that I am an ecclesiastic, and that I am at Rome!" or else, alluding to the polemic between the *Univers* and the *Correspondant,* " I remember all that you said to me about the Church and the Legitimists; and, without entering into the quarrel, I will only say that if one only be with the Church, one is monarchical and liberal enough!" This great servant of the Church had had time, in spite of the suddenness of his death, to cry, " *Pardon! My God! Pardon!*" sublime words of faith and humility. The Pope ordered a special service for him in the Church of Sta. Maria, in Trastevere, and insisted on attending it himself, alone, and without his Court. Mgr. de Mérode went to thank him, both in his own name and in that of his family. The faith, eloquence, and patriotism of the man; all the great causes for which this magnificent orator pleaded in our Chambers, especially on the Education Question; the historian of the monks, the beautiful writer—all tended alike to make this premature death a cause of universal mourning throughout Europe. No one now, however blinded by prejudice, can be ignorant of the fact that he had declared solemnly that if the Infallibility were defined by the Council he should submit to it at once, with the docility of a son who feels that his Father has a right to command his obedience. " The Pope is our Father," he said, " as well as our guide. We must both love and obey him; and that without hesitation."

It cost still less to Mgr. de Mérode to make an act of complete adhesion to the Papal Infallibility. But he waited for the day when it became a dogma to accept what Peter spoke in the name of Jesus Christ. He was not a theologian, and he took no active part in the discussions at the Council, though he willingly listened to the opinions of his friends on the points which came before them for deliberation. In truth, the definition of the Infallibility was contrary to his feelings. He was afraid it might deter Protestants from entering the Church and might cause a schism in Germany—a view strongly held by Mgr. Ketteler, Bishop of Mayence. This motive induced him to range himself with the minority of the Council. People were very much astonished, and some ventured to speak of it to Pius IX., complaining that he had in his service an Almoner who disapproved, not certainly of the Infallibility of the Vicar of Jesus Christ, but of the opportuneness of the definition. The Pope, however, was neither surprised nor offended. He knew Mgr. de Mérode well, and knew also that his frankness would not allow him to feign a feeling which he did not possess.*

Others have quoted the conduct of Mgr. de Mérode as an authentic proof of the liberty of the Council. If some people would have preferred to see him (as on every other occasion of his life) follow at once the Pope's lead, we must allow that his vote was a proof of his sincerity. He gave it in the General Congregation when the definition of the Infallibility was resolved upon, and

* In the Appendix is given an account of what passed at that time, taken from his own lips.

abstained from appearing in the last solemn sitting
when it was proclaimed. But that very evening he
was at the Pope's feet, and adhering—the very first—
to the new dogma. The fears of the greater part of
the German Bishops were not justified. It was the
State, and not the Church, which tried to make a
schism in Germany, and failed. The Church set an
example of fidelity, courage, and faith, which, for
the last fifteen years, has called forth the admiration
of the whole world. Rome having spoken, the question
is settled. The obedience has been unanimous and
complete. Not a single Bishop hesitated. Many had
doubted as to the opportuneness of the definition, fear-
ing the consequences which might ensue. This was
the preoccupation of human wisdom; but human
wisdom is often at fault. Mgr. de Mérode owned it
without difficulty, and rested more fully than ever on
that sacred and fundamental stone which alone re-.
mains immovable in the midst of the vicissitudes and
revolutions of the world.

The Revolution which followed was well calculated
to enlighten the blind, to speak to the deaf, and to
make the whole universe attentive to the judgments of
God. This Revolution was the consequence of the war
which broke out, the day after the definition, between
France and Germany. The definition was on the
18th of July. On the 19th à Cabinet courier carried
to Berlin the declaration of war. The French Government instantly recalled the 6,000 men who, at Civita
Vecchia, were guarding over the safety of the Holy
Father. They pretended to need them for the defence
of the country. But that very same day the Emperor
lost 6,000 men at Wissembourg, as if God would take
from him just as many soldiers as he had taken away

from the Pope. Dates, in this case, are as eloquent as figures. It was on the 4th of August that the French flag left Civita Vecchia. It was on the 4th of August that the Emperor, at Wissembourg, felt the humiliation of his first defeat.

There was nothing left at Rome but the Pontifical Army, which had been increased, but was still, numerically, very small. But officers and soldiers had but one heart and one soul for the cause of Pius IX., and the preservation of the patrimony of St. Peter. Hardly six weeks were allowed them, however, to prepare their defence against Piedmont, which invaded the Papal States on all sides, so that the Pontifical troops received orders to retire and concentrate themselves on Rome. There the only hope was in prayer. On the 19th of September the Pope went out from the Vatican, for the last time, with his faithful Almoner, and went to pray at St. John Lateran's, afterwards mounting on his knees, in spite of his seventy-eight years, the twenty-seven steps of the staircase which our Blessed Lord is said to have ascended when He was brought before Pilate.

On the 20th began the bombardment of the walls of Rome under the orders of General Cadorna. The enemy's artillery made a breach in the gates of San Giovanni, San Sebastiano, Porta Pia, and the Pincio. Their entrance being thus made easy, the Sovereign Pontiff gave orders for capitulation. Addressing himself to the representatives of the Catholic Powers who had gathered round him at this critical moment, he said : "It would be impossible to continue the struggle without causing the shedding of much blood and the loss of many valuable lives. It is not for myself that I grieve, but for those brave sons of mine who have come from so many different countries to defend me as their Father. I release my soldiers from their oath of fidelity, and disband my army."

General Kanzler signed the capitulation. Charette obeyed with the resignation of a Christian, but the despair of a soldier. Mgr. de Mérode flew to visit the wounded in the Hospital of Santo Spirito. He said to Count de Mortillet, who accompanied him on this visit, and who had been his old Aide-de-Camp: "Let us thank God that this noble cause did not perish under our hands. I feel I never should have survived it!" He gathered together his faithful Belgians, embraced and helped them, and sent them back to their own country with every mark of his paternal affection. All was consummated!

CHAPTER IX.

From 1870 to 1874.

Pius IX. a voluntary Prisoner in the Vatican—Exemplary fidelity of Mgr. de Mérode—He defends his charitable Establishments against the Conquerors of the 20th of September—New Embassy of M. de Corcelles to the Holy See—The Services he renders to Mgr. de Mérode—The Illness of Mlle. Albertine de Mérode—Her Brother comes twice from Rome to assist her—Her Edifying Death—Relations of the Prelate with Cavaliere de Rossi—He acquires the Domain of *Tor-Marancio* — Excavations carried on at his expense—Discovery of the Catacomb of Domitilla and the Basilica of St. Petronilla—Fête given in this Basilica on the 14th of June, 1874, to the American Pilgrims—Speech of Mgr. de Mérode—Presentiment of his approaching end.

PIUS IX. resolved not to leave Rome, and to live in the Vatican as a voluntary captive to duty. This resolution, which he announced in the month of September, 1870, was confirmed two years later in an interview with Cardinal de Bonnechose, Archbishop of Rouen. This Prelate had come with offers from the French Government to propose that he should leave Rome and fix his residence in France. " Come back and see me in a few days," replied the Pope, " and I will give you an answer." This answer was a little ivory plaque, with a gold rim, on which was represented, with exquisite art, the " *Domine, quo vadis.*" Giving the

medallion to the Cardinal, the Pope said to him:
" St. Peter was stopped at the gates of Rome when he
was fleeing from the city to escape persecution, by Our
Lord Himself, bearing His Cross. 'Where are you
going, O! my Lord?' exclaimed St. Peter. 'I am
going to Rome to be crucified afresh,' was the
Saviour's answer. The Apostle understood, retraced
his steps, and died, like His Master, by the torment of
the Cross. Well, Cardinal, I do not wish to be exposed to the same reproach."

Mgr. de Mérode remained at the foot of the Cross of
Pius IX. with as much firmness and attachment as
Pius IX. himself at the feet of the Cross of St. Peter.
He would have followed him to the end of the world,
and would have said to him, like St. Laurence to St.
Sixtus on his way to martyrdom : "Where are you
going, Lord, without your Deacon?" He had been
his War Minister and the ornament of his Court.
There was no longer either army or Court; but there
were still rights to defend, alms to distribute, powerful
enemies to brave, iniquities to expose, and, above all,
the poor, the sick, little children and nuns to protect,
and save from injustice and wrong. That was enough
to occupy Mgr. de Mérode's great heart, and to make
him devote to the Pope the last years of a life which
had been consumed before the time and entirely worn
out in his service.

In the days which followed the Revolution of the
20th of September his eyes and his heart were often
turned towards France, which had become the theatre
of war and the victim of German occupation. He followed his dear Zouaves in their glorious campaign.
He saw both the East and the North invaded by
the stranger; Franche-Comté at bay; Villersexel, the

home of his childhood, in flames; all the villages
in the neighbourhood pillaged and destroyed by the
enemy. His brother wrote to him on the 16th of
November as follows :—

"If you are badly off at Rome we are not much
better at Trélon. We are expecting our enemies every
day; they already occupy Haute-Soane and le Doubs.
But the Prussians are playing a bold game. The
Army of the Loire and that of Paris may well inflict
some check; it is always dangerous to push one's
advantage to excess. In the material order as in the
moral, one must beware of turns of fortune. The
Beatitude of the Gospel only promises the earth to the
meek : ' *Beati miter, quoniam ipsi possidebunt terram.*'

"How can one help saying that with a little fore-
sight and energy, with the employment of any of the
distinguished men who abound in France, all these
miseries might have been averted ? If only our
Statesmen had been ably supported—Thiers, Montalembert, de Falloux and the rest, the Emperor would
have been brought to reason, and the two unities of
Germany and Italy, which have overturned Europe,
would never have been effected, to the detriment of
Rome and France."

At the news of the battle of Patay, Werner de Mérode
cannot help sharing his joy with his brother. "I
think things are looking better. God seems to be
looking upon France with eyes of pity. How you
must rejoice in the success of your Pontifical Zouaves !
What a wonderful thing it is to see this Army Corps,
so ill-used by the Ministers, Ambassadors and Generals
of the Second Empire, standing now in the very first
rank as the defenders of France ! Every one now is
quoting and admiring them, as, in old times, they did

the Zouaves in Africa. To-day it is the army of
Pius IX., of Lamoricière, of de Mérode, of Charette,
who are at the top of the tree! What glory for the
Pope! What a consolation for his old War Minister!
You now see, my dearest brother, a justification of all
your labours and the accomplishment of all your
provisions."—(*25th of November*, 1870.)

But then came the sad news of the defeat of Bour-
baki, and the Doubs mountains were furrowed by
flying soldiers hotly pursued by the victorious
Germans. Mgr. de Mérode, hearing all that they were
suffering at Villersexel, sent at once 5,000 francs to his
brother, who had given the like sum, to relieve the imme-
diate sufferings of the district. During that time Mde.
de Montalembert begged in both worlds, and her great
name, the recollection of her husband, and the account
she gave of the French misery, touched all hearts in
England, in Holland, in Belgium, in Canada, in New
York—everywhere, in fact. A large portion was distributed by her in Franche-Comté; 50,000 francs in
the Doubs and Haute-Soane alone; so that the names
of de Mérode and Montalembert were once more
blessed by the grateful sufferers. Comte Werner de
Mérode, who had been elected a member of the
National Assembly in the Doubs and the North, kept
his brother informed of the feelings of his colleagues;
of their anxious desire to come to the rescue of
the Pope, and of the steps they had taken with the
new Government. M. Thiers addressed a circular note
to the Great Powers on the abnormal condition of
Rome since the Italian occupation. This state of
things troubled the conscience of all good Catholics;
it was a direct attack on the rights of sovereigns and
the peace of Europe, and the maintenance of the Holy

See was a duty incumbent on all Governments. If France could not at that moment spare her children for the defence of the Vicar of Jesus Christ, at least she could be the first to lift up her voice in his favour. A Congress seemed necessary to solve the question. Bavaria, Austria and Belgium promised their adhesion. A petition signed by 100,000 Belgians, and which contained all the most illustrious names in the country, was sent by M. Werner de Mérode to M. Thiers and M. Jules Favre, to demand the intervention of France in favour of the Holy See. The Episcopate of France, acting on the initiative of Cardinals Mathieu, Donnet and Bonnechose, took the same step and sent in petitions signed by innumerable persons in each Diocese. The immense majority of the Constituent Assembly voted in favour of the measure ; but it was all in vain. What France had done in 1848 she would not renew in 1870. The Pope, touched by these demonstrations, showed his gratitude to M. de Belcastel by a Brief, and to M. W. de Mérode by an Autograph Letter, in which he charged him to express to his colleagues of the National Assembly the warm gratitude of the Holy Father and his abundant Benedictions.

M. de Behaine had remained at Rome in the capacity of Chargé d'Affaires to the Holy See. There his attitude was that of a true Christian, to Pius IX.'s great relief. But no sooner was the French Government re-established than they sent an Ambassador to the dethroned Sovereign, whom they were unable to restore by force of arms. First it was M. de Harcourt, a name agreeable to the Holy See, and which recalled the services rendered to Pius IX. in 1848. In 1872 M. de Corcelles succeeded him, and this choice did

great honour to the tact and good taste of M. Thiers.
M. de Corcelles was the man who of all other French
diplomatists Pius IX. loved the best. On undertaking
for the third time this post, unique in the world, and
in which greater delicacy than ever was required, M. de
Corcelles was rejoiced to see once more his dear Xavier,
and to be able to give him fresh proofs of esteem and
affection. The Archbishop very soon needed all his
help to preserve the grave interests for which he was
responsible. The conquerors of Rome disputed the
Pretorian Camp with him, of which he was the sole proprietor; they drove from the prisons of St. Balbina the
Belgian Brothers who guarded the young prisoners;
they threatened the convents and monasteries; in fact,
fear, sorrow, and mourning were felt in every direction.

Mgr. de Mérode, however, was not a man to be easily
disconcerted. Strengthened by the French Embassy,
he made the Belgian Legation interfere at the right
moment, consoled the Religious in their distress, and
forced the Government, for a time, at any rate, to
respect the schools and convents. Thus the Sisters of
Providence were left in peace in charge of the House of
Correction, which he had transferred from the Termini
to the Villa Altieri, which he had bought with his own
money, and on which he had expended more than one
hundred and twenty thousand francs. The Italian
Government soon found that they would have to reckon
with a man who, though deprived of his former authority,
continued to visit the sick, the poor, and the prisoners
in the Institutions he had founded, and the prestige of
whose high character was felt by every one. He made
no secret of his feelings towards the usurpers; but his
very frankness was terrible to them. They dreaded his
criticisms, his sarcasms, and his sharp speeches, more

dangerous to the conquerors than the sword ; for, once masters of the Eternal City, they tried to reign more by half measures than by violence. The municipality, therefore, were anxious to conciliate him, and though they changed the name of the " Via Mérode " into " Via Nationale," they entered into negotiations with his man of business in order to purchase the property which belonged to him.

It was far otherwise with the Government. For four years he was at open war with them through his lawyers, for their unjust appropriation of the Pretorian Camp. To their obstinacy he could only oppose justice and right, and the decision of the Law Courts, who gave it in his favour.

"Ah, Monseigneur!" said an august personage to him one day, "you don't know the Piedmontese. Remember that it is they, in all countries, who work underground. They are cunning and crafty ; and they are an obstinate race, who never give up what they have once got."*

This lawsuit was not finished when Mgr. de Mérode died. At last the Pretorian Camp was sold by his heirs to the Government, but at half its value ; the usurpers having invoked a pretended law which conferred certain rights upon them as regarded public buildings.

Notwithstanding all this ill-will, however, the great works of Mgr. de Mérode in embellishing Rome were fully appreciated. M. de Resie relates that he once passed a very interesting evening with the Comte de Behaine in company with Mgr. de Mérode and Baron Haussman. A great plan of Rome was laid on the table ; and while Mgr. de Mérode was astonished at the quick eye of M. Haussman, who, after only spending

* "Mgr. de Mérode," by Henri d'Idéville, 1874.

eight days in Rome, had already seized all the points of improvement which were possible, the Prefect of the Seine was equally struck with the wisdom shown by the Prelate in his recent improvements, and ended by assuring him that he could not have done better had he been himself charged with the embellishment of the town.

After the invasion, the ground purchased by Mgr. de Mérode rose immensely in value. The square metre in 1868 was only worth eighteen francs; one or two houses were built, and the price rose to twenty-five francs; but after the 20th of September it increased in a fabulous manner. But it was not only by the square near the railway station, and the opening out of the new streets of Turin, Florence, Naples, and Modena that the genius of Mgr. de Mérode showed itself; but by his purchase of a large space on the right bank of the Tiber, not far from the Castle of St. Angelo, and opposite the Ripetta. He traced the plans for new streets on a spot called *Prati di Castello,* which have already become popular, and the prosperity of which is not doubtful, as it is close to the busiest quarter of Rome. A bridge which he projected has been thrown over the river at this point; and the new quarter promises to realize all the hopes of its founder. Even before his death he foresaw its success. In the month of April, 1874, he came to lunch with an old friend, and, rubbing his hands and laughing with that hearty, frank laugh which communicated gaiety to every one, he exclaimed, while sitting down by the mistress of the house : " Do you know, Duchess, that I have begun the day very well. I have just sold the first villa built on the *Prati di Castello* for two hundred thousand francs. I can't help laughing still at the

s

amazed look with which one of my clerks heard me announce the excellent bargain I had made to my engineer. I had hardly turned my back than I heard him muttering to his companion : ' *Eh ! il matto non è già tanto matto.*' ('The madman is not so mad after all.')"

"But, of whom was he speaking, Monseigneur ? " inquired the Duchess.

"But of me, Madame," replied Mgr. de Mérode, laughing. "Don't you know that all the Romans call me ' Il Matto ' ?"

Before the fall of the temporal power he had said : "I know that the Revolution is bent on our ruin. It will be a struggle between the sects and the Catholic religion ; and as we are the weakest, we shall be beaten for a time. But what I want is, that in the eyes of Europe, even if we fall, it will not be because we have not known how to govern." After the 20th of September he said, "Let us everywhere face the enemy. No discouragement. No vain lamentations. Acts and not words. It isn't the newspapers which will save us, but good institutions and great sacrifices. Sooner or later we shall regain what we have lost. We must pray, teach, build and work."

That is why he bought the "*Alt-temps*" Palace, and appropriated it to higher studies, both in letters and sciences. The Government had turned the Jesuits out of the Roman College. It was one of the first duties, therefore, to create new houses to receive the youth whom the Italian Revolution wished to corrupt. Mgr. de Mérode gave to the new College a rich physical cabinet, the latest and best mathematical instruments, and a chemical laboratory. It is still reckoned one of the most flourishing in Rome.

The Prelate's heart, however full of good works, was

about to be cruelly tried by the illness and death of his young sister, of whom we have already spoken.

Mlle. Albertine de Mérode, who had completed her years of probation at the Convent of the Trinità dei Monti, had been for some time in failing health. She made her first vows, however, and the Pope wished to bless her before her departure for France, which the doctors had advised. On the 6th of August, 1871, she was received by Pius IX. with Mde. la Marquise de Wignacourt, who, after spending a month with Mgr. de Mérode, had decided to accompany her sister on her journey. A peculiar circumstance marked this audience. The nuns of the Sacred Heart, who had accompanied their young companion, drew back discreetly when Mde. de Wignacourt came up to the Holy Father, and Mlle. Albertine made a movement to join them. But the Pope stopped her, smiling and saying: "I understand that the links of family are stronger there than here," pointing to the group of nuns, and thus characterizing the supernatural spirit with which the young Religious was actuated ; and then added, as she knelt by his side and he blessed her—"I see that she wishes to go to Paradise ; but she cannot go without the permission of the Pope !"

Hardly had she arrived in France, however, than she became worse, and it was necessary to hasten matters, so that she might pronounce her last vows. Père de Pontlevoy received them at Paris, in the Convent of the Rue de Varennes, and the next day she started for Bordeaux, where the doctors gave still some hopes of cure. The care with which she was surrounded did not leave her any illusions as to her state ; but she was still able to superintend the studies or the recreations of the pupils, and flattered herself that she could still be of

s 2

some use. But by degrees even these light duties had to
be given up. She was grieved, and said of her illness :
"It is a hard cross, even if one bears it going and
coming." The air of Montpellier was not more favourable to her than that of Bordeaux, and it was finally
decided to bring her back to Paris. She returned in a
state which made every one foresee a speedy end ; and
silently made all her last preparations. One day, her
niece, Mlle. Thérèse de Montalembert, was walking
with her in the garden of the Rue de Varennes, and
Mde. Albertine said, " We are going to make a novena
to Notre Dame de Lourdes. Sometimes one obtains
the reverse of what one asks, for God judges this to be
better for us. If we could only get Him to let me go
home ! " And then, on her niece remonstrating, she
added : " It would not be sad, dear child, for surely it
is not sad to go to heaven ! " The next day, however,
she said : " I hope I did not give pain to Thérèse ;
but we must accustom ourselves to the idea of separation."

Mgr. de Mérode, who could not be under any illusion
as to her state, asked leave of the Pope to make a short
stay in France and Belgium. His visits were the
greatest charm and consolation to Albertine. The
sisters, who were frequent witnesses of their meetings,
talked of the "holy joy" with which he always
filled her. But he did not feel that he had the
courage to announce their final separation, and went
away without wishing her good-bye. The sick nun
understood him, and also made her sacrifice in silence.
But another family duty called him to the Château de
Marchais, to see his cousin, the Prince of Monaco.
After having spent some days with him, he started for
Strasbourg and Baden, accompanied by his chaplain.

Don Marcello. He was expected at Baden by the Duchess of Hamilton, whose daughter had married the Prince of Monaco. The Archbishop went to endeavour to prevent an imminent rupture between the husband and wife. But the negotiations failed, and he returned to Rome. Pius IX. had regretted his long absence, yet deigned to approve of it, on account of the grave reasons which had lengthened his stay. But hardly had he resumed his service with the Holy Father than the news of his sister became more alarming. He communicated them at once to the Pope, in the following terms: "Most Holy Father! you told my sister that she must not die without the Pope's permission. She obeyed you; but I think God is now calling her, and she only waits for this permission to leave the world." The Pope smiled sadly, with tears in his eyes. "Is it so? Then, my dear son, take it to her yourself and return to her at once, bearing all my blessings." The Archbishop flew back to his dying sister, according to this gracious permission. The day after his arrival in Paris he wrote the following lines:—"Albertine is nearing the gate of eternity every hour. Her poor body is torn to pieces by her cough; but, as for her soul, it is always filled with a holy joy. As soon as she had received Extreme Unction she wrote to her nephews to tell them the consolation and happiness she had felt at receiving this Sacrament. This morning, she had on her bed Aloff's* answer, our old officer in the Roman Legion, whom his aunt's letter had found in the Atlas mountains near Médéah. This brave young fellow, who in these last years has so often braved death, answered in a timid note the words of

* M. Aloff de Wignacourt.

one who is meeting her last hour with such faith and hope. Death for Albertine is not, as for the soldier, a matter of bad luck; it is the road to eternal life. I have said Mass in her room this morning, and to-morrow, please God! I shall do the same, and will give her Holy Communion."

From that moment the Holy Sacrifice, which gives strength and life to all other sacrifices, was offered each day by Albertine's dying bed. After Mass, during which she received Holy Communion as Viaticum, the Archbishop said his prayers and thanksgivings in her room, and often out-loud. Then they would have a little pious talk sometimes, even a gay one, mingled with recollections of Rome, liturgical prayers, and family news. The ladies of the Sacred Heart flattered themselves, now and then, that the danger was lessened. When they tried to make Albertine share in this hope she would say, smiling: "The end will be whenever God wills. I am ready." "Yes," answered Mgr. de Mérode, "I remember at Rome your pupils used to call you 'the ever-ready mistress,' because you were always pleased to go to them." " Well, let me go towards the angels who are waiting for me, I shall be more pleased still!"

Another day she asked news of Pietro, the old cowman, of the Trinità dei Monti. "Ah!" exclaimed the Prelate, "that was an old friend of yours, and you made him believe that in your childhood you had had the care of the cows." Upon this he told the community that one day she was teaching Catechism to the servants, and that to interest them she explained to them very graphically how Jacob led his flocks to Laban. Pietro, struck with the natural way in which she described the difficulties of the march, said

gravely to her : *"Ma, Signora Madre! dite me un poco, se avete trattato, pure Voi, este bestioline? Ne parlate tanto bene, parc che avete fatto il mestiere!"* *
Mde. Albertine smiled at this recollection and specially recommended Pietro and the other servants at the Trinità dei Monti to her brother's kindness. It was pleasant to her to remember in these last days how she had loved the humble and the poor, and the naïf astonishment she had often caused among them by her sympathy and kindness. She frequently said she was sure she would find many of these poor humble souls in Paradise, whose society on this earth had been such a real pleasure to her.

On the 20th of October, the oppression and difficulty of breathing increased, and every one thought her last moment was at hand. It was the Feast of *Mater Admirabilis*, a day so dear to the Mothers of the Sacred Heart. She rallied a little later in the day and talked to the Superior about the poor people she had known at Trélon, Villersexel, Rome and Rixensart, begging that she would send them some little pictures in remembrance of her, especially those which had the Sacred Heart and the Crucifixion for subjects.

Mgr. de Mérode came very early the next morning to his "dear little sister," as he often called her, bringing with him the very ritual which the priest had made use of at the death of her mother, out of which he recited the appropriate Psalms and prayers for the dying, and then gave her the Apostolic Benediction. When she had received it she asked for her Crucifix, kissing the feet with inexpressible tenderness.

---

* "But, Rev. Mother! tell me if you have never yourself had to deal with beasts like that? You describe it so well that one feels you must have learned the trade!"

One of the mothers supported her head. Her niece, Mlle. Catherine de Montalembert, who was kneeling at her right, kissed her already cold hand; while at the foot of the bed the Archbishop of Mélitene said the prayers for the agonizing.   Thus she who had so generously broken all earthly ties to devote herself to God and His poor found herself, on leaving this world, surrounded by all those who were so dear to her.   De Mérodes, Montalemberts, Wignacourts, all were there, either in person or by letter.   Her Superior drew near, and asked her if she would like to renew her Vows of Religion.   " Oh, yes ! " answered the dying nun, in a firm voice.   They were her last words.   She passed out of this world under the care of the Archbishop, who had been to her more than a brother, and who carried away with him, on returning to Rome, the consolation of feeling that he had received the last breath of that beautiful soul at the very moment when she had exchanged earth for heaven.

He stopped at Florence to say Mass for her on the Altar of the Annunziata, giving large alms in his sister's name, and having Masses said in all the poorest convents to obtain as soon as possible the release of that pure soul, should any earthly imperfection have retarded her happiness.   He found a heap of business awaiting his return to Rome, which having concluded, he went to make a retreat of eight days in the Passionist Monastery of San Giovanni e Paolo, from whence he wrote the following beautiful letter to his sister-in-law :—

" ROME, 30th *March,* 1873.
" SAN GIOVANNI E PAOLO.

. . . .

" It is a long time since I have written to you, and I will not leave this place, where I have been making an eight days' retreat, which ends to-morrow, without giving you some news of myself, being very sure that when once I get back to my work I shall fall back into my bad habits of neglecting my correspondence.

" You have not forgotten, I dare say, a certain conversation in which you said several things to me which I felt were profoundly true. I thanked you on condition that every time we met you should talk to me again in the same sense. This conversation has often come back to my mind during this retreat, which has been, perhaps, rather long, but where I have not found myself weary for one moment.

" In old times, I don't know why, the Passionists made a disagreeable impression upon me. How unjust I was to these excellent Religious! I have been reading the life of their holy founder, St. Paul of the Cross. He lived only in the last century. Born the same year as Voltaire, he died three years before him, *i.e.* in 1775, at eighty-one years old. He was the emulator, or rather the continuer, of St. Francis of Sales. He worked wonderful miracles; but was especially distinguished by a passionate love for our Lord Jesus Christ in His sufferings, and for the salvation of souls.

" There were thirty Ecclesiastics in the retreat, of whom five were Canons of St. Peter. Two Fathers preached to us four sermons a day. Besides this, we have had two meditations given us under the direction of an old monk, who told us all we could theologically know of Heaven, of the transformation of souls in God by sanctifying grace, and of the resurrection of the body. I regret very much that you were not here to hear all the beautiful things he said, which you would have retained far better than I.

" Well, to-morrow I am going back to the Vatican, and begin anew my busy life. This business increases every day in a frightful way; my time is spent in conversations about lawsuits, citations, forced expropriations, and the like; I begin to be overwhelmed with it all. I forgot to tell you that I have become the successor of Sta. Lucina, who gathered together the bones of the martyrs and buried them in her garden. I am on the point of entering into the heritage of St. Domitilla, niece of the Emperor Domitian. The Cavaliere has put the same life into this which he does into everything."

We see by the end of this letter that the Archbishop of Mélitene meditated a great undertaking in the interest of Christian antiquities. From his first arrival in Rome he had taken the greatest interest in these matters. The Abbé Gerbet had initiated him, both by his conversations and his books, into this great subject. Abbé Gerbet was the best friend of his father : he had blessed the marriage of his sister at Trélon with the Comte de Montalembert; he had taught at Juilly ; and no one knew Xavier better than he did. He received him then with great joy when he first came to Rome, where the Abbé had studied for ten years, from whence he had, twenty times over, been on the point of returning to Belgium, but where he stayed on for ever, because he always found something fresh to learn and admire. The first volume of his *Sketch of Christian Rome* had just appeared. Abbé Gerbet made Xavier read it, and thus fired his enthusiasm for the Eternal City, and especially for the Catacombs, where so many wonders were daily discovered. This was the first impression Xavier received at Rome, and which remained profoundly engraved in his mind.

Twenty years later we find him with Cavaliere de Rossi, listening to his lessons at the Lateran, introducing him to all his most distinguished guests, praising his discoveries, and penetrating with his curious spirit more and more into all the details of this Subterranean Rome, with its tombs and cemeteries and ancient inscriptions. Mgr. do Mérode treated Cavaliere de Rossi with marked distinction, and took every occasion to show the affection he entertained for his person and the admiration he felt for his discoveries. As long as the Papal Government lasted, subventions to carry out these great works were easily obtained ; but after 1870 the resources failed, and the new Government, knowing his attachment to the Holy See, showed him nothing but ill-will. What the Pope no longer could, and the King of Italy would not, do, Mgr. de Mérode undertook, with his usual princely generosity. It was his last work.

In 1854 Cavaliere de Rossi had discovered a Catacomb on the Ostian Way in a private property which bore the name of *Tor-Marancio*. His very first excavations revealed to him that here was the ancient Catacomb of Domitilla, so famous in early Christian tradition. Flavia Domitilla, the niece of Domitian, had been converted to Christianity, and had had a catacomb excavated in her property to receive the relics of the martyrs, and among the rest those of St. Petronilla, and the bodies of Nereus and Achilles, officers of Domitian's Court, who had been put to death for the name of Jesus Christ. It was also known that alongside of the cemetery had been built a Basilica in the fourth century, which was dedicated to St. Petronilla ; that Gregory the Great had preached many of his homilies from the steps of this altar ; that during the course of the seventh century this Basilica was frequented by pilgrims of all nations ; and that the Pope Gregory III. (in 731–41), after having established a station there, had enriched this church with many precious ornaments. But in 755 the Lombards, who besieged Rome under the conduct of King Astolphus, devastated all the cemeteries and Basilicas situated outside the town. Pope Paul I. transferred to a safer place the relics of the illustrious martyrs ; and the first and most solemn translation was that of the body of St. Petronilla, with its sarcophagus, to the Mausoleum which had been erected in the Vatican. Both the Basilica and the cemetery were closed in the eighth century under the Pontificate of Leo III. The cemetery, which was situated in low and marshy ground, was submerged by the rains, and the bodies of St. Nereus and Achilles were transferred to Rome, to the Urban Basilica which bears their names.

Cavaliere de Rossi had already arrived at the second stage of the cemetery, where epitaphs, columns, and sarcophaguses were daily discovered, when the proprietor of the soil intervened ; a contest arose as to the nature and value of the discoveries, and finally de Rossi had to abandon the work for the time, only taking care to cover up the columns with earth. The works were consequently stopped for twenty years, when Mgr. de Mérode became the proprietor of the Tor-Marancio, and the neighbouring vineyard, in which was the public entrance to the cemetery. Hardly had he got possession than he put the whole ground at the disposal of M. de Rossi, and the excavations were resumed. "This work is really worthy of the great heart which was its sole author and adviser," wrote

the great archæologist.* It was in November, 1873,
that the cemetery was reopened. They hunted in vain
for the sarcophagus and the four columns which had
been discovered in 1854. In 1870 they had been
clandestinely removed. But the bases of the columns
were exposed, and very soon a perfect Basilica was
discovered, with its apse and its three aisles, of about
the same size and extent as the Constantine Basilica of
St. Lorenzo in *Agro Verano.*

Each day M. de Rossi found fresh proofs of the
authenticity of his discovery. First, the tombs of the
Martyrs, with the inscription which had been composed
in their honour by Pope Damasus, the letters and
words of which were distinctly recognizable; then
another inscription on a walled-up tomb, attesting the
date of sepulture of two other saints in 395. Mgr.
de Mérode was wild with joy. In the winter he
braved the cold and wet; in the summer the heats of
July, forgetting himself in his anxiety about his
beloved Basilica. As the Marquis de Ségur justly
said, it was his last passion, and it absorbed him
altogether. He associated his brother, his sisters, and
all his friends in his joy, and Rome never had greater
charms for him.

But M. de Rossi was not yet satisfied. On the
23rd of December, 1874, after having had the rubbish
removed behind the apse, he discovered an *arcocilium,*
in front of which was a tomb. In the niche thus
opened out was a painting of a veiled matron, dressed
in a kind of dalmatic, and in an attitude of prayer. An
inscription in red letters above her head announced
that this lady's name was *Veneranda.* Her left arm
is extended on the breast of a young girl, who seems

* Bulletin d'Archéologie Chrétienne, 1873–75.

to be welcoming the deceased. At the feet of this girl is a case full of books ; near her head an open book, like the Gospels seen in the catacombs at Naples ; and to the right and left of her face is seen the inscription : "*Petronilla Martyr*." Evidently the mortal remains of Veneranda rested close to the body of the martyr ; and this painting, which dated from the end of the fourth century, was a complete justification of M. de Rossi's hopes. Nothing now was wanting ; but at the date of this discovery, crowning all the rest, Mgr. de Mérode had passed away to a better world. The long visits he paid to the excavations on that unwholesome soil, and at an epoch when the air of the Campagna was so bad that they had been obliged to send away the workmen, were the real cause of his premature death. He brought back from the Campagna the germs of death, and his strong constitution, already weakened by fever, ended by breaking down, before he was himself aware of his danger.

Full of this work, he spoke of it throughout the year 1874 with the enthusiasm of a poet and the eloquence of a priest. "One evening," writes an intimate friend of his to the *Univers*, "I had the honour of accompanying him to his dear Basilica. He spoke to me with enthusiasm of the discoveries they had made, and of his determination to preserve the Christian cemeteries from official profanations. The weather was glorious. We were walking in fields, enamelled with wild flowers, which all turned their heads to the setting sun. The Archbishop stopped and cried out : 'See how they follow the movements of the being which gives them life! Ah, if we only knew how to live as the flowers do ! If we could only continually turn our souls towards God!' Upon which he began speaking, with an eloquence which was inexpressibly charming, of the delights of meditation, praying our Lord, out loud, to hasten the moment when he might, as a humble flower, fix his soul for ever in eternal contemplation."

Another day he went to fetch his friend Mgr. Bastide to walk with him to his dear Basilica. On the way he began to talk to him about their careers in life. "We are getting old, my dear friend," he said, "and who knows whether God will not call us very soon to Himself? On what little things does the fate of a man hang! You ought to have been Curé in the Diocese of Besançon, and I had dreamt of nothing but the humbler post of Vicar in that of Malines. In the Doub Mountains you would have taught Catechism admirably, as do the Curés of the country, especially the one at Maîche, who used to delight Montalembert. I should have preached, sometimes in French, sometimes in Flemish, visited the sick, founded schools and the like. Well, God disposed of our lives in a totally different way, and transported our pulpits to Rome. Not that we preach much, either you or I, in the ordinary sense of the word; and perhaps the directors of the Besançon Seminary and those of the College at Malines would not have found us either great theologians or wonderful orators. But still we preach after our fashion, you at the Vatican in the Loggias of Raphael, and I in the Catacomb of Domitilla. Rossi preaches too, though a layman, and he preaches admirably; for his discoveries explain Christian antiquity, and prove that the same articles of Faith were believed then as now, and the same seven Sacraments; and that paintings and

relics were held in old times in equal honour and
veneration."

Thus talking, they arrived at the catacomb, and
Mgr. de Mérode spoke with effusion of St. Domitilla,
of St. Petronilla, and of the Holy Martyrs—Nereus
and Achilles. "What a discovery!" he exclaimed, at
last. "Allow that de Rossi has not his equal!" Mgr.
de Bastide interrupted him here by saying: "Well,
you must own that he was very lucky to find you to
help him!" "Don't talk of that," replied de Mérode.
"That is the way I revenge myself on these Piedmontese who have usurped Rome. They would willingly
have shut up both the catacombs and the cemeteries.
That is why I buy them, and have thus got possession
of the Tor-Marancio and the Vineyard Sacripanti.
Wherever the catacombs are menaced I shall go on
buying them up. And what is the most amusing is,
that I pay ready money for them, with the gold which
Piedmont gives me to get possession of the streets and
ground which I was so reproached a year or two ago
for having bought!" Upon which he rubbed his
hands with a malicious smile, and looking at his
workmen and the excavations, added: "Listen to me,
Bastide. I am meditating here a great Fête, in which
you must help me. You know we are expecting a
great Pilgrimage of North Americans. They have
been visiting the principal sanctuaries in the North,
and are then coming to receive the blessing of Pius IX.
You shall preach to them, with your usual eloquence,
in Raphael's Loggia, and explain to them the dispute
of the Blessed Sacrament. But I don't mean them to
leave Rome without paying a visit to my Basilica. I
will give them a breakfast here and propose a toast at
dessert, which shall not be as long as your sermons."

The Fête he had thus announced came off on the 14th of June, 1874. The American Pilgrims accepted it with joy and gratitude. They had covered over the half-excavated ruins with planks and red carpeting; put up the Altar, and, at the end of the Apse, the chair from which St. Gregory the Great pronounced his famous homilies. The walls were covered with ever-greens and flowers. Round the Apse was the beautiful inscription : " *Corpora Sanctorum Martyrum in pace sepulta sunt et vivent nomina eorum in Æternum.*" The verses composed by Pope Damasus in the fourth century, to adorn the tomb of St. Nereus and Achilles, were on the side walls.* One might have fancied oneself in old times. Nothing was wanting. Even the lamps had been borrowed from the catacombs, and the alabaster basin where the lights swam in oil —symbols of that Faith which is fed by grace.

Cardinal Franchi celebrated the Mass and distri-buted Holy Communion to the Pilgrims. After the service was over Mgr. de Mérode took his guests into a vast barn, which he had transformed into a banquet-ing-hall, and had decorated with as much elegance as simplicity. The breakfast he gave them was enlivened by sallies of wit and most agreeable conversation, mingled with warm praises of their host. At dessert he got up and recited, as a toast, the little sermon he had spoken of to Mgr. Bastide. Alluding to the

---

* Militiæ nomen dederant sævumque gerebant
  Officium, pariter spectantes jussa tyranni,
  Præceptis, pulsante metu, servire parati.
  Mira fides, rerum subito posuere furorem.
  Conversi fugiunt, ducis impia castra relinquunt;
  Projiciunt clypeos, faleras telaque cruenta.
  Confessi gaudent Christi portari triumphos,
  Credite per Damasum possit quid gloria Christi.

T

presence of Mde. de Corcelles, the French Ambassa-
dress, he began by thanking Divine Providence which
permitted the nephew of La Fayette, assisted by the
grand-daughter of the General, to receive the American Pilgrims on the spot which had been the patrimony
of St. Flavia Domitilla, and which had remained so
long celebrated, from the pilgrimages of the first
Christians to the tombs of the early martyrs. He
then spoke of General La Fayette, of his courage, his
bravery, his popularity : adding, however, that though
his great heart was adorned with all human virtues, it
left much to be desired in the way of religious faith.
" The tenets of Divine mercy are impenetrable," he
added. " What we see around us at this moment
proves that the great country which M. de La Fayette
served with such fidelity, devotion and honour, con-
tains the admirable elements of which you are yourselves the representatives. That is one of the sweetest
consolations of the Church of Jesus Christ, to whose
Divinity you have borne witness as clearly as those
recorded in past history. So much so, that after
having read the words inscribed by St. Damasus on
the tombs of St. Nereus and Achilles : ' *Credite per
Damasum possit quid gloria Christi*,' we can say,
while admiring your fidelity to Pius IX. : ' *Credite
per Pium possit quid gloria Christi.*' "

These were the last words ever spoken in public by
this great Prelate. Already he felt in his soul a presentiment of his approaching end, and for the last year
he had made no mystery of it among his intimate
friends. The oppression of his chest, and the hoarse-
ness of his voice struck them all. Only on the eve of
the Fête he had given to the Americans one of them
said to him : " Do take care of yourself, Monseigneur !

You seem to me to be tempting death ! " " Must we not all die ? " replied Mgr. de Mérode, gaily. " My grandmother used to say to me : ' The manner of one's death is only a detail : the age at which one dies is another : but neither one nor the other deserve consideration. The only important thing is to be always ·ready.' "

One day he said to one of his devoted servants, " Poor Luzzi ! What work I do give you ! In a short time it will be much worse, for you will have all the bother of my funeral. But after that you will have a long rest . . . . and I too ! " With this presentiment he loved to sing in his room the " Requiem," the " Libera," and the verses and responses in the office for the dead. " That is," he would exclaim, " what they will soon be singing at St. Peter's at my burial : but they will sing it much better than I, for I don't understand much about it ! " He thus mingled gaiety with the most serious thoughts, and was softly going heavenwards under the protection of the holy martyrs whose Basilica he had discovered, and whose glory he had recalled to the memory of the whole Christian world.

CHAPTER X.

A Portrait of Mgr. de Mérode—The Unity of his Life—The character of his services and the object of all his undertakings—His feelings as regarded the Church, his Country, and his Family—His friendships and social relations.

"NOTHING was more difficult to seize," writes the Comte de Carné, "than the original features and character of Mgr. de Mérode. They were so made up of contrasts, and varied so in his conversation, that one must have lived with him for a long while to be able to understand both his physiognomy and the harmonious accord of his great soul, which, living always under the eye and in the presence of God, cared little or nothing for the judgments of men. To the habits of a cenobite he united the pride of a nobly born knight of old; and though his heart literally overflowed with charity, he did not spare his enemies either rude sallies or spicy epigrams. Representing all the glories of an illustrious past, he yet had a passion for modern innovations; and, solidly seated on the rock of Christ's Church, in his administrative proceedings he was bold even to temerity, and drew back before no obstacle or resistance to accomplish a desirable reform or effect an improvement."

This description is perfectly correct. Mgr. de Mérode was a mixture of a man of the past and a man of the present day; and contrasts which in others would have jarred, with him formed a grand and consistent character, which religion had brought to a high degree of perfection.

The triumph of the Church was the great object of his life. It was the country of his soul. He wanted to see her strong, honoured, and glorious; but he could not have served her more faithfully in the hour of triumph than he did in that of adversity. He had a passion for any great cause which, humanly speaking, seemed lost. In the middle ages he would have been the first, like his ancestors, to join the Crusaders at Jerusalem to deliver the Tomb of Jesus Christ. In this nineteenth century he attempted another crusade—the deliverance of the Pope and the preservation of Rome. This last crusade failed, like that of Godfrey de Bouillon and St. Louis. But neither Rome nor Jerusalem will remain for ever captive. The new kingdom of Italy will never be consolidated while it retains Rome as its capital. Whether the question be solved by the pen or the sword, its solution is none the less inevitable in the future. The hour approaches when, so far from being the prisoner, the Pope will become the arbiter of Kings, and his reconquered throne will be the centre of wisdom and a model to all nations.

It was with this view, and in the sole interest of the Papacy, that Mgr. de Mérode made himself the minister of reform and progress. Roads, streets, aqueducts, railroads, telegraphs, barracks, prisons, schools, convents, agricultural establishments, hospitals of every kind—all were transformed, created or renewed. At Bologna, in 1858, during the Pope's triumphant progress through his States, Mgr. de Mérode asked to see the prisons. Fearful of inspection, and consequent reforms, the authorities replied that the keys could not be found. Instantly he sent for two masons, made a breach in the walls, and marched into the prison by the breach he had made.

At Rome he carried on by night the works at the Termini which he had been forbidden to do by day. This came to the ears of the Pope, together with an unfavourable report from the Commissioner of Works. But Mgr. de Mérode implored the Pope to come and judge the question with his own eyes. Pius IX. went. It was on the Monday after Easter, 1866. After having carefully examined the works and questioned the engineers, he did not hesitate to express his entire approval of the plans, and the satisfaction he felt was visible to every one. This visit put a stop to all opposition, and the works were at once completed.

Mgr. de Mérode's boldness was backed up by thorough knowledge of his subject. All the newest physical, chemical, and mechanical discoveries had been studied by him, as well as architecture and political economy. By turns engineer, architect, and builder, he did not hesitate to alter any plans which he thought were wanting in stability or grandeur. If the expense was the obstacle he set it aside at once. All he considered was the interest of the Church, the glory of Pius IX., and, above all, the good of the people. We must say a few words also of his extreme anxiety for education, and of the number of schools founded, increased, and restored by him. "Those who see danger to the Church from the better instruction of the people are blind!" he would exclaim. In fact, Mgr. de Mérode did more in Rome in twenty years to overcome this prejudice than had been done for the last century; and in that sense he may indeed be looked upon as the greatest benefactor to the rising generation and the true friend of real progress.

" *Ubi bene, ibi patria,*" he would say. " I accept this adage, but in the Catholic and not egotistical sense. One's country, in my eyes, is wherever one can do most good. That is the way I understand the *Ubi bene.* Let us stop at Rome as long as we have the hope of being useful there, of doing good, and rendering service to the Church. That is the idea the early Fathers had of their country when they declared that exile could not touch them, for all the earth was the Lord's. This grand and large idea is not understood in these days. People like to live where they are comfortable, and not where they can do most good, in spite of contradictions and worries. It was not thus that Count Rossi argued when he was Minister to Pius IX. Italian, he became a naturalized Frenchman, to be more free. As a Frenchman he was again naturalized as an Italian to serve the Pope and the Church. He had noble views, generous sentiments, and a great heart."

In fact, the more active was the Revolutionary Propaganda, the more Mgr. de Mérode struggled for truth, justice, and liberty. Always ready, ever on the watch, as agreeable to God as he was dreaded by evil men, appropriating every invention, every improvement, and every discovery for the good of the people, he could afford to say to them, " This is the work of the Church. She is not your enemy, but your benefactress and your mother ! "

After the Church he loved Belgium, his earthly country, with a really touching anxiety for her interests. He loved her not only because she was the cradle of his family, but because she had always held a glorious

place in the history of the Church. He remembered
with pride the title of Daughter of the Roman Church,
given to the church at Liège ; the struggle made by
the doctors of Louvain against Luther's heresy; the
way in which Gallicanism had been defeated when it
tried to invade Belgium ; the glory of the martyrs of
Gorcum, who confessed amidst torments their inviolable fidelity to the Holy See; their resistance to the
Josephite laws, and the courage with which his grandfather, Senator in the First Empire, had opposed the
incorporation of the Roman States under the First
Napoleon.

But the part which his father had played in the
events which had brought about the independence of
Belgium was dearer to him still. This revolution, to
the honour of the faith, the language, and the commercial and political interests of his fellow-citizens,
had given Belgium a place among European nations.
This place they have worthily guarded, and the wisdom of King Leopold increased it. This Prince, who
had received such signal services from Comte Felix de
Mérode, felt for his whole family the esteem and affection with which he had regarded the great Liberator of
his people. The Queen of the Belgians had greatly
praised the ecclesiastical vocation of Mgr. de Mérode,
and when she died, in the prime of life, Mgr. de Mérode
celebrated a funeral service on her grave. Ever since
he had been asked to Court, and never paid a visit to
Belgium that the King did not invite and wish to have
him near him. The contrast of their characters only
showed, in a stronger light, their mutual esteem for
one another. The King loved frankness, and greatly
admired his loyalty and devotion to the Holy See.
Although himself a Protestant, he knew how to recog-

nize and esteem the great merits of a prelate who did such honour to his kingdom.

It was impossible not to hold the country of Mgr. de Mérode in great consideration at the Vatican. Belgium had been the first to re-establish Peter's Pence, and was one of the most faithful in her payments. She gave not only her money, but the blood of her children. Mgr. de Mérode, who was so devoted to his Zouaves, was not less proud of having amongst them so many of his countrymen; and nothing made him happier than when these poor people came to him to ask, in the Flemish language, to be presented to the Pope and to get a blessing from him, and a Rosary for their old mother.

People have accused Mgr. de Mérode of not loving France. It would be more just to say that he did not love the Second Empire, which, surely, was excusable. But he loved Franche-Comté, and delighted in the fact that that province of France had been, under Philip II., united with Belgium. He loved the beautiful mountains of Le Doubs, for the Pope was loved there too, and he had found there, as in Belgium, both money and men to help in his defence.

The relations of Mgr. de Mérode with his own family were a perfect model of what a priest's should be. He put the service of the Church above all the rest, and when it was a question of labouring for or defending her, he put everything else aside to accomplish this duty. His correspondence with his own people was therefore very irregular. He writes: "You know I am, above all, an ecclesiastic, so you must not be surprised at my long silence, and be content to know that I never forget you before God." But when any spiritual work was to be done he was always ready. First

Communions, marriages, sickness, death, found him full of eagerness to be of use or consolation. He took the greatest interest in the religious instruction given to the children, and in their progress in the Catechism, and cared far more for that than for the success of their studies. We find the name of Herman de Mérode, his brother's eldest son, continually recurring in his letters, and to him he sent his first archiepiscopal benediction. One of his nephews, as we have said, had joined the Roman Legion, and his tender affection for him is constantly revealed.

" I only see Aloff once a week," he writes, " and he is always very busy. His functions of sergeant, which he fills with great conscientiousness, absorb a great part of his time. He passes the rest with Mgr. de Bastide and at the Rospigliosi Palace, where he dines once a week. He is developing rapidly, has a charming manner and appearance, and every one finds him extremely agreeable. I only wish Théodoline were here to enjoy the success of her son." *

During the time he was War Minister Mgr. de Mérode could rarely write to or visit his family; but when he became more free his heart turned yearningly to his old home, and towards those so dear to him. The Duchesse d'Aosta, who was for a short time Queen of Spain, was his cousin. As a Queen he asked nothing of her; but when she became ill he looked after her, and multiplied Masses and prayers both for her and her children. Queens, in these days, have more anxieties than pearls, and few know the bitter tears they often have to shed! Mgr. de Mérode, who had so often witnessed the Pope's sorrows, could feel for misfortunes to crowned heads more than most people,

* Letter to the Comte de Mérode, 25th Jan., 1868.

and all the more when such miseries are hidden from the public eye.

During the last years of his life his brother or one of his sisters came to Rome continually to pass a few weeks with him. They came back each time more full of admiration for his great virtues. His holidays also were more frequent and longer, and he spoke of them on his return to Rome with the greatest pleasure.

" What a happy time we had together at Trélon ! " he wrote to his sister-in-law. " I do not know how to thank you enough for your welcome and all your goodness towards me—may God guard and bless you ! " Then he speaks of the deep peace he had felt with his sister, Mde. de Montalembert, at Roche-en-Brény, and thanks God for the admirable way in which she orders her home, for the charities she gives, and for the dignity with which she maintains the honour of her birth and the great memory of her husband.

The answers he received from his family are sometimes mingled with joking criticisms upon his dress. Thus his brother writes : " All the ladies of the family have been enchanted with your visits to Belgium, and edified by your virtues. But they implore me to say something to you about the deficiencies in your toilet. They are hoping you may find a careful servant to mend your cassocks, and wish you to imitate the Bishop of Namur, who is always so well-dressed. I hate bothering you with these tiresome remarks ; but people have talked about it so much that I think you ought to know it. I hope you have read the good and pious speech of the Archbishop of Bourges, at Limoges, on what a Bishop ought to be. If he be clothed in silk and gold, it is to show how straight he must walk in the paths of wisdom and piety. He ought to live alone in the midst of his books, with the fathers, doctors, and saints, so as to make the honey which should fall from his lips for the nourishment of his Christian flock. How I should have liked to have read this speech with you!"

After his Episcopal consecration, Comte Werner de Mérode makes some comments on the fresh obligations now laid upon him :—

"You say every day to the people when you turn round to them, *'Pax Vobis.'* Give yourself a little of this peace by taking time to breathe between your many great undertakings ! . . . . You admired the pacific manners of the Oriental Bishops at your Vatican Council. Try and resemble them a little, and fancy you are an Eastern Bishop too ! . . . . But, forgive me ! I feel I am like Grosjean who lectures his Curé ! "

When the anniversaries in his family came round, the feasts and birthdays, or the sad *"mementos,"* Mgr. de Mérode never forgot them at the altar, though he seldom wrote. On one occasion he excused himself in this fashion :—

"My dearest Sister Theresa,—I don't know how I have let slip the 15th of October without giving you a sign of life. It is very certain that I did not forget you before God on that day, the Feast of your holy Patroness. I read very carefully on that occasion her famous meditation on the *'Pater.'* It seemed to me that I enjoyed it more than I had ever done before. What wonderful considerations on our dignity as children of God, and as destined to become part of His Kingdom ! But, as you know, I would much rather read than write. I therefore kept your feast by reading St. Theresa. You often attack me for not doing things like other people. This is a case in point. The important thing is that the work should be done; the manner of it only the accessory!"*

The choice Mgr. de Mérode made of his friends through his whole life shows, not only his warm heart, but his clear perceptions and his wise judgment. Whether in garrison, in his campaigns, or at Rome, he had the most agreeable relations with all his comrades or companions; but in selecting his friends he chose only those who were real Christians, and for whom he felt an esteem and affection which lasted through life.

His first friend in Rome was the Abbé Bastide, and their affection for each other continued for twenty-five years without a break in their intimacy. Mgr. de Mérode, who loved to contradict people, even the Pope, willingly let himself be contradicted by Mgr. Bastide. The cordial gaiety and amiable pleasantries of this true friend made him accept all his observations without a demur. When he wanted to tell the Archbishop a home truth, he put it in verse, and pretended that the song was popular in the streets of Rome. The destinies of the two Prelates seemed to be linked with one another. Bastide died only eight months after Mérode, after a long illness. In the last days of his life he often turned his eyes heavenwards, as if he saw some supernatural vision. "Come, Mérode! come!" he cried when he was dying, opening his arms.

The intimacy between them became still closer after the arrival of Mgr. de Ségur. This young Prelate, who had left the world like the others, and was related to Mgr. de Mérode, attached himself to him from the very first with that instinct common to chosen souls. Abbé Bastide was their inferior in birth; but his wit,

* Letter to Mde. W. de Mérode.

his piety, and his devotedness made him their equal. Never were three men more unlike each other ; and yet who loved one another more truly. Mérode was a soldier, Bastide an artist, Ségur an apostle. Their courage, poetry, zeal, and love of souls gave to their joint works an energy and strength hitherto unknown in Rome. Mérode brought his bold initiative, Ségur his ardent zeal, Bastide the sweetness and persuasiveness which were in his character, and all three devoted to God, the Church and the poor their youth, their life, their strength, and the gaiety which was in their nature.

Mgr. de Ségur had been named Auditor of the Rota. He had stayed first with his cousin on arriving at Rome, and though very mortified in his private life, he soon perceived that Mérode was more mortified still. He passed three days with him before he was installed in his own apartment, and said laughingly afterwards : " Never was I more edified than during those three days ; but never was I worse fed ! "

The three friends combined to evangelize the soldiers, children, and poor, each according to his ability. Bastide preached to the soldiers ; Ségur heard their confessions ; Mérode obtained for them no end of privileges and graces, presented them to the Pope, and thus attached them to the cause of the Church.

Their Sundays were specially edifying. They began in the midst of the children, and ended in the middle of the soldiers at St. Luigi dei Francesi. At five o'clock in the morning Mgr. Bastide beat up the men in the barracks, and the church was always crowded. Mgr. de Ségur gave the instruction. Mgr. Bastide began in his sonorous voice the fine hymns known to the soldiers : and after the Benediction in the evening Mgr. de Ségur received every one who wished to speak to him, or to go to confession in the sacristy. This often lasted till eight or half-past eight o'clock, to the despair of the cook, which was increased when Monseigneur de Ségur brought four or five unexpected guests with him to dinner. His table was extremely simple : sometimes Mgr. Bastide and Mgr. Lacroix would laughingly grumble : Mgr. de Mérode generally joined them at supper. He had spent his day at the " *Vigna Pia* " with his orphans ; and then with his Belgian brothers and sisters in the prisons saying Mass, teaching, preaching, or confessing ; and as he had left the Vatican at five o'clock in the morning he had often forgotten to breakfast or dine. When he came in to supper he would eat some soup in haste, in which he poured a quantity of water, and then take a piece of cold meat and some lettuce leaves. But if the *menu* was poor what gaiety and brilliant *repartees* seasoned these repasts !

Mgr. de Ségur only stayed four years in Rome. Struck with blindness, and forced to give up his official duties, he went back to his own country, deprived of the light of the eyes, it is true, but more filled than ever with the supernatural light of the soul. His Apostolate began under the eyes of the Holy Father, went on, with his benediction, in France, and was spread through the whole world by his beautiful writings. His little treatises on Catholic doctrine are known wherever the French language is spoken, and have been translated into all modern languages. Mgr. de Mérode and Mgr. Bastide wept at his departure but he himself had to weep for their deaths. Pius IX., who had survived the two first, was mourned in his turn by the third ; but he soon followed him to the grave. The tears and regrets of these Christian heroes form to-day the flowers of their heavenly crown.

The successors of Mgr. de Ségur, as Auditors of the Rota, continued the same charming relations with Mgr. de Mérode, though they could not replace his friend. After Mgr. de la Tour d'Auvergne, who finished his career in the See of Bourges, and Mgr. Lavigerie, who is so gloriously continuing it in the Sees of Algiers and Carthage, it would have been difficult to choose one more agreeable to Mgr. de Mérode than Abbé Place, who is now Archbishop of Rennes. M. Place, whom his family had destined for the Bar, left it to enter the Church. He had made his theological studies at Rome, and was closely united with Mgr. de Mérode. In the "Notes of a Diplomat" we find this description of him : "The new Auditor of the Rota is just arrived. He is a man of the highest merit, extremely well read, and very agreeable in conversation ; but, with it all, most modest and unassuming."

In the following year a young Breton Priest, the Abbé du Cosquer, came to replace to Mgr. de Mérode the void which death had made among his intimate friends. He was very like him in character : witty and agreeable—rather a *frondeur*, but profoundly attached to duty, and capable of any sacrifice to serve the interests of the Church. Sent by the Propaganda to conclude a Concordat with the Government of Haiti, he succeeded so well that he was made Archbishop of Port-au-Prince. But unexpected difficulties arose, and at the end of three years he returned to Rome for help and direction. A cruel illness came to add to his trials. He died in the arms of Mgr. de Mérode, who gave him, to the last, every consolation which friendship and religion could afford. But it was not only in France and Belgium that he found devoted friends, but equally in England and America, where his name is ever held in affectionate veneration.   He had a marked sympathy for England, and watched with the keenest interest the progress of the Faith in the former Island of the Saints." Cardinal Wiseman was a special object of his admiration.   When he was summoned to Rome, in 1854, to take part in the definition of the Immaculate Conception, he begged to see the works of charity which Mgr. de Mérode had established.   His visit to the Prison of Sta. Balbina determined him to choose those same Brothers for the care of the schools of Brook Green, and North Hyde, near London.   Cardinal Manning, in his visits to Rome, never omitted thanking Mgr. de Mérode for the help which he had given his illustrious predecessor in this matter.   Two other Englishmen of noble birth, Mgr. Talbot and Cardinal Howard, had daily relations of the most agreeable kind with the Pope's Almoner, and the only regret of the latter was that he did not live long enough to sit by his side in the College of Cardinals.

Another intimate friend of Mgr. de Mérode's was Mgr. Sauvé, formerly Rector of the Angers University, who inhabited Rome on several occasions ; first, as Chaplain at St. Luigi, and then as theologian to the Pope during the preliminary work for the Council.   One day Mgr. de Mérode proposed to Mgr. Sauvé to go with him to see the old city of Toscanella. " We arrived at night," writes M. Sauvé, " and it was with some difficulty that they received us.   The Archbishop of Mélitène had to declare his title as Pope's Almoner to induce them to open the gates of the town ; and we had the same difficulty about an hotel.   But hardly had we got into a poor little apartment than

U

we heard a bell which rang furiously and woke the whole town. It was two o'clock in the morning. "What on earth can that be for?" exclaimed Mgr. de Mérode. He called the landlord and asked what it meant.

"Why," replied the astonished innkeeper, "it is for the people who are going to gather in the harvest." "But why do they wake them so early in the morning?" "Why? Oh! to hear Mass." "But it isn't Sunday, or a Feast Day?" "No matter, your Excellency. This Mass is said every morning during harvest-time. It was founded by a Cardinal many years ago for the poor people who have to go and work in the harvest-field at dawn of day."

"What a lesson for us!" exclaimed Mgr. de Mérode. "Look at these poor people, who have such hard work in this great heat, and during these long days! They get up hours before the sun rises to hear Mass, and it is a Cardinal who founded this service, at such an early hour, all the days of the week! And this pious custom continues! The Mass is said, and all the people go to hear it still! What a lesson for us, my dear Sauvé! Let us resolve to go off this very morning and say our Mass, however fatigued we may be, and never to omit it again!"

Mgr. Sauvé relates another edifying anecdote of Mgr. de Mérode, when he became seriously ill in 1855. The doctors discovered that he had an interior abscess, and the symptoms were so dangerous that his brother was summoned to Rome. Pius IX. came to see him, and finding him as usual on a straw mattress, only covered with an old bit of green carpet, he sent him a comfortable bed, with a positive order to make use of it. One evening, M. de Sauvé was by his bedside and found him unusually sad. "Bastide has been to see me," he said, "but he gave me but poor consolation. Come and read to me something more strengthening. Read me the homily of Pope Gregory the Great in the "Common of a Confessor not a Bishop." Abbé Sauvé took his breviary and began the Gospel: "*Sint lumbi vestri præcinti et lucerna ardentes in manibus vestris.*" Then follows the commentary of St. Gregory: "*Duo sunt qua jubéntur; et lumbos restringere et lucernas tenére.*" "Let us have faith and chastity," added the Prelate, underlining the words—"*Nec cástitas ergo magna est sine bono ópere: Nec opus bonum est áliquod sine castitáte.*" "Nothing! nothing!" interrupted Mérode again, repeating the Latin and underlining it; and then clasping his hands and turning his eyes up to Heaven, he added: "*Restat, ut quisquis ille est, spe ad supérnam pátriam tendat.*" The reader finished the Homily with as much emotion as the sick man: "*Venit quippe Dominus.*" (He knocks, when in the midst of the anxieties of life, He announces to us by the pains of sickness the approach of death.) "*Pulsat vero, cum jam per ægritudinis moléstias esse mortem vicinem designat.*" Here the attention of the sick man was redoubled, and the reader went slower so as to share in the consoling words. St. Gregory continues: "*Aperire enim judici pulsánti non vult, qui exire de corpore trepidat; et videre eum, quem contempsisse se méminit judicem formidat. Qui autem de sua spe et operatione securus est, pulsánti conféstim áperit, quia lætus judicem sustinet. Et cum tempus propinquæ mortis advénerit, de gloria retributionis hilarescit.*" This joy, this smile, lighted up the features of Mgr. de Mérode. His friend read on with a voice choked with emotion; but

declared he had been more edified by him than he had
ever been before in his life.

Thus Mgr. de Mérode prepared himself for death in
the flower of his youth. But God, Who had His designs for him, raised him up again and preserved him
for a few years longer to give more striking proofs of
his faith and charity. The interior abscess burst; the
sick man was saved ; and, three days after, he went
back to his poor prisoners at Sta. Balbina !

The Pope, who was more delighted than any one to
have kept his beloved *Cameriere,* invited him to dinner
one day with his brother at the Convent of " *St. Agnese
fuori delle Mure.*" It was on the 12th April, 1855.
The company gathered round Pius IX. consisted of
Cardinals, Ambassadors, and French and Italian
officers. After dinner, the floor of the room where
the Pope and his guests were sitting gave way, and
the whole company were precipitated from the first
story to the ground-floor, amidst a frightful mass of
falling beams, rubbish, and dust. But no one was
badly hurt. Pius IX. clung to a beam which had not
given way and was the only one who did not fall into
the room below. At the moment of the accident,
Mgr. de Mérode had gone with his brother and Mgr.
Talbot to look at the Baptistery of St. Constance, a
charming little chapel, of which the roof is ornamented
with mosaics of great antiquity. At the noise of the
fall of the floor, they flew back to extricate the Pope
from his perilous position. Mgr. de Mérode took him
back to the Vatican, nursed him with the tenderest
care, put him to bed and spent the whole night by his
bedside, with true filial affection. He began, with his
strong faith, by thanking God, Who had preserved His
Vicar ; and said his beads several times as an act of

thanksgiving. The gaiety and wit of this faithful watcher completed the Pope's recovery. He told him all sorts of comic incidents connected with the accident—the terror of one, the exclamations of another, and the fright of the Generals, who were more ready to brave the enemy's cannon than the fall of the floor on which they stood. The next day the Pope declared himself quite well; and Mgr. de Mérode could take his brother back to Florence. Abbé Sauvé, who was with them, relates that on passing by Orvieto, Mgr. de Mérode, who was then full of the reform of the penitentiary system, insisted on stopping at Monterozi to visit the prison. A prisoner put out his hand through the bars of a cell on the first floor and asked for an alms. "Put out your hand, then," answered Mgr. de Mérode. "Wait a minute," replied the prisoner, "I will come down and open the gates for you." The stupefaction of the Prelate and his companion may be imagined. The prisoner comes down with the keys in his hand, begs them to excuse the fact that the jailer is ill and himself does the honours of the prison. "That's what I call a prisoner on parole!" exclaimed Mgr. de Mérode, laughing. "I don't think you could find such another out of the States of the Pope."

It is not necessary to say how much Mgr. de Mérode was sought for in society, nor what an honour it was considered to receive him. He went out rarely, but when he did, it was with his usual frank simplicity; without any fuss or ceremony, neither attempting to hide his feelings, nor to alter his exterior, nor to pretend to opinions which he did not feel. Although he was not himself aware of it, his noble personality made him appear quite apart from and superior to other men. His efforts to maintain the Pontifical Government, the ·wonderful improvements he had carried out, the buildings and reforms he had inaugurated struck public opinion. Whether strangers or Romans, every one wanted to see him. In the salons of the Embassy, or in the Palaces of the Roman Princes, there was a marked sensation whenever he appeared. "*Eccolo !*" they would say, "Here he is!" At the Court of the Tuileries as at that of Florence, he was looked upon as their most formidable enemy, and the principal obstacle to their dark designs and (unavowed) covetous proceedings. Hence, even there, there was the same eager curiosity to see him and the same wish to hear his opinions.

The Marquis de Ségur gave a most accurate description of him in society. "He was in constant movement, and his person spoke as much as his lips. But this movement did not exclude distinction or dignity. Everything in and about him showed his high birth. The brusque manner in which he sometimes indulged did not prevent him, when he wished, from showing the most charming amiability and the most exquisite politeness., No one knew better than he how to pay the most graceful compliment ; but, on the other hand, he would lay a man's conscience bare with a single word. One evening we had dined together with Comte Armand, then Secretary of the Embassy at Rome, who was to play so decisive and courageous a part, a few years later, after Mentana. Among the guests was Listz, the wonderful pianist, who had not yet donned his cassock, but who must have ordered it, for he appeared in it a few days later. He was a very agreeable man, speaking wonderfully well on a host of subjects, and very distinguished both in manners and appearance. After dinner we had a long talk with him, and when Mgr. de Mérode rose to go, he said, with exquisite politeness, ' Monsieur Listz, you are delightful to listen to . . . . even at the piano ! ' This was less an epigram than a trait of his patience and courtesy. Listz lodged at the Vatican with Mgr. Hohenlohe, whose apartment was next to that of Mgr. de Mérode. Our Prelate disliked music, and especially the piano. It was a real act of self-denial on his part to bear with such a neighbour, and the *nuance* of criticism, mingled with his compliment, was the most softened expression he could find of the annoyance he felt at having to listen to him daily in that manner."*

The independence of his character prevented his sacrificing either his duty or his opinions to please the world, in which his public position necessarily threw him. But the dominant feature in his character was his love for the Church. His undertakings, his friendships, his letters, his conversations, his daily life, in fact, all bore the same stamp of sincerity and religion. A diplomat, on whom had been bestowed for himself and his heirs a patent of nobility, received in the following terms Mgr. de Mérode's congratulations : —" The title which the Pope has just granted to you, and especially the circumstances under which you have received it, will, I am sure, make it very precious to you. As for me, you know that I very much prefer the gifts of Pius IX. to those of the Emperor. Believe me, people in the world will have long ago forgotten the legends and chronicles of the Napoleons, while the Popes will still reign in the Vatican ! "† .

* Mgr. de Ségur, p. 157.
† " Journal of a Diplomat in Italy," p. 367.

This is a reflection of that immortality with which future history will signalize the services of Mgr. de Mérode; and after having related how he redeemed the honour of the Church, even in the midst of defeat, we may repeat what M. de Bach, the old Austrian Ambassador at Rome, said to Comte de Mortillet, who had been the Aide-de-Camp and Chief Secretary of the War Minister, "Monseigneur de Mérode is a great Minister of a small State!"

CHAPTER XI.

Mgr. de Mérode's private Life—His little defects and his
great virtues—His Spirit of Faith, Piety and Humility—
His Mortification and Self-Sacrifice—His extraordinary
Charity.

THE holy Prelate who was thus preparing himself
for death had filled a great place for twenty years in
the Catholic world. In diplomatic circles he had been
hardly judged, for diplomacy cannot stand frankness.
He spoke the truth to the Pope, expressed himself
freely on the conduct of the King of Piedmont and the
Emperor of the French, joined no political party or
coterie, and never borrowed his opinions from others.
This noble independence made the originality of his
life and the grandeur of his character. Mgr. de
Mérode paid court to no one, and only made war upon
abuses. Intriguers, men who were double-dealers and
capable of doubtful money-transactions, found no
favour in his eyes. He loved all men of proved honesty
and capability, brought them forward, took their advice,
and willingly followed it. If he inspired jealousy, he
never himself knew what that odious vice meant. He
was accused of being brusque and impetuous. His
brusquerie did not prevent his goodness and kindness ;
and his impetuosity fell before the silence of those who
witnessed it. People used to reproach him for his
" *bon-mots* " and witty speeches in the midst of his

functions. We will quote one or two. One day he announced the visit of some English people to the Pope. "Holy Father!" he exclaimed, "the people I am going to present to you to-day will not exhaust your treasury of Indulgences, for they are all heretics!" Another day, seeing a certain number of Spanish Bishops coming in with their big hats, of which the turned-up wings give the appearance of a bark in full sail, he exclaimed, "Here comes the Spanish Fleet! Here is the invincible Armada!" Now no one esteemed the Spanish Episcopacy more than he did, and no one ever dreamt of taking offence at what was only a harmless pleasantry. All we can say is, as M. de Corcelles did, that Mgr. de Mérode had too much wit and fun in him, especially with men who had none!

Such was Mgr. de Mérode, with his little defects and his great virtues. He hid the latter with as much care as other people take to show them off. His private life reveals him as he was. The old saying that "No one is a hero to his valet" was certainly contradicted in his case. His old servant said once to the translator of these lines: "*To know what a Saint Monseigneur is, one must live with him!*" The ancients said that the house of the wise man should be made of glass, in which all could look. Let us cast a glance at Mgr. de Mérode's and we shall see the real man, with his faith, mortification and charity. Faith, with the de Mérodes as with the Grammonts, is a family inheritance. In the long genealogy of their House one finds many Saints and Blessed; but not one who had to blush for his religion. Faith is transmitted in the blood, by good example and by habit; but it is only hereditary on condition that it is cultivated and kept up. God keeps it in the hearts of those who ask; He only restores it, when lost, to those who humbly implore it. It was granted to Xavier de Mérode not only to continue but to increase the spiritual patrimony left to him by his ancestors. It is a great honour to have a priest in one's family; but then the priest must, by his virtues, enhance the respect and esteem in which his priesthood is held. Xavier had the happiness to do this, for he had all the qualities which God demands of one wholly devoted to His service. He sanctified his own Family by sanctifying himself.

His spirit of faith showed itself in all the religious acts of his childhood and youth. We have spoken of his First Communion, and how one saw on that day the way he loved God. But when he became a priest, then the feelings of faith, adoration and love which filled his whole being transformed even his face, and inspired the deepest respect in all who saw him. This man, so quick in all his movements, became perfectly calm and measured when celebrating the Holy Sacrifice. His distractions, the rapidity with which he went from one thing to another in ordinary life—the whole man, in fact, had changed, when once he set his foot on the threshold of the sanctuary. It was then only the holy Priest who appeared before the Angels around the Altar, and the faithful who assisted at the office. One felt that at that time he thought but of God, spoke only to God, saw no one but God. Without ever hastening his way of saying Mass or ever retarding it, which he used to condemn as a languor of soul, he observed the smallest rubrics with the most scrupulous attention, for he had entered into the fullest sense of the whole, and the most minute ceremonies had their value in his eyes. Religious, priests, relations, friends,

strangers, all who had the privilege of assisting at his
Mass, if even it were but once, went away penetrated
with the same feelings with which he was himself
filled, and profoundly touched by his look and manner.
Nor was this a mere passing feeling. Whether in the
midst of the most solemn assemblies or in the most
obscure and humble chapel, he was always the same.
His chaplain and servants remarked that after his
thanksgiving, his generous heart became more generous
still. That was the moment to propose a good work
to him. But in general he waited for no petitions from
any one, but, only consulting Jesus Christ, flew to devote
himself to the many and great works of mercy in which
his day was spent, determining to increase, maintain
and extend them as an offering to that God of the
Eucharist Whom he adored with such burning love.

With the same spirit of faith did he perform his
canonical duties in the Basilica of St. Peter. As
War Minister, he might have pleaded his arduous
duties, as Pope's Chamberlain his audiences, as
Almoner his incessant visits to the charitable institutions he had to superintend. But he never made any
one of these things an excuse. Go when you would
he was always in his stall, morning and evening, at
High Mass and Vespers, and always with the same
recollected look and manner. When people could
not find him in his apartment, it was to the Sacristy
at St. Peter's that they went; to fix a moment for
an audience a great number of strangers and foreigners
who had letters of recommendation to him, adopted
this plan. The edification he gave them was as great
as his welcome was easy, agreeable and sympathizing.
During the recitation of the Divine Office, the edification he gave around him was not less. After having

prayed and knelt for some time, he took his breviary, reading it often out loud, so as to articulate the words better, and when the beauty of a particular Psalm or lesson struck him, he would sing or declaim the passage, with an accent which betrayed his deep piety. If an unexpected visitor came to interrupt him while he was saying his office, or if some charitable duty were urgent, he would leave his breviary; only to resume it the moment he was free, and making it a matter of conscience to begin again the interrupted psalm or chapter. "Men," he would say, "have a right to our time and our services; but God's rights are still more sacred, and if His service must be interrupted and hindered, we must begin again with still greater love and fervour."

When he was praying, whether in public or private, his face took an expression of devotion and recollection which struck everybody. People found that he then had a striking resemblance to St. Charles Borromeo, as he is represented when on his knees. It was true that he had some of his features, his height, and his attitude; but it was the light from above illuminating his whole face which made the real likeness to that great Saint. He was the same before the Blessed Sacrament, when he went to visit, as was his constant habit, the church where It was exposed, on his way from his walk; or when he went to this same exercise of piety in St. Peter's. Humility is an offspring of Faith. Those who believe in God, who adore and love Him, know how great He is, and how miserably small they are before Him. Mgr. de Mérode, who was so proud before the powers of earth, annihilated himself before God, especially when he saw Him in the person of His poor. He hunted them out in the most miserable quarters, performed every kind of service for them with his own hands, washed their feet and their wounds in the hospitals, and in fact managed to penetrate everywhere ; partly owing to his position, partly under the penitent's garb which Charity lent him to dissimulate his rank and take the humblest place with the suffering members of Jesus Christ.

" The Confraternities of Penitents which are so common in Rome," writes the Marquis de Ségur, " perform the most wonderful works of charity and self-abnegation. It was as a member of one of these that Mgr. de Mérode gave himself up, without stint or measure, to his love of penance and mortification. Among these confraternities, many of which are almost as old as the Church itself, some are vowed to prayer and expiation, others to the relief of all spiritual or material miseries. The care of the sick, the poor, the abandoned, deaf mutes and blind, the giving marriage portions to poor girls, visits to the condemned and to prisoners, the burying of the dead ; —there is no work which they do not perform. For a Christian, there is no sight more beautiful and no charm greater than that of the ' *Sacconi* ' in Rome.'"*

The Roman nobility and the Princes of the Church all enter into these confraternities, where humility is so well practised. Mgr. de Mérode enrolled himself early amongst them, and was too glad thus to exercise the most secret and meritorious works, happy to hide himself under the mask of penitence and to receive insults while begging for alms. One of the most honourable of these confraternities is the "*Sacconi*," whom we have mentioned, and whose business is to hunt out

* " A Winter at Rome," by the Marquis de Ségur, p. 147.

and relieve the "*pauvres honteux.*" It was the one dearest to Mgr. de Mérode, because it brought upon him more rebuffs and humiliations. The grey habit he wore effectually concealed both his birth and his Episcopal dignity, and he did not mind receiving injuries.

He stopped one day talking with a shopwoman, and excited her wrath by his pious importunity. She seized a stick, threatening to turn him out of doors if he did not instantly leave the house, and as he hesitated, she carried her threat into execution. The Prelate came home quite joyful at having suffered something for Jesus Christ. One of his friends, who had been a witness of the transaction, said afterwards : " When he could no longer fight for the honour and rights of the Holy See, he wished for nothing better than to be beaten for the love of God and His poor. I believe he did his best to obtain this result, and three days of begging, insults and blows, were the revenges which his humility loved to wreak upon himself."*

We have often heard tourists say that the sight of certain disorders in the place where the Catholic Religion has established the seat of her empire, has made them lose, or, at any rate, weakened their faith. They have listened to exaggerated stories, without going to the root of things : they have seen amiss and judged hastily. It was just the reverse with Mgr. de Mérode. An intimate knowledge of the feelings of the people confirmed his faith, and no one had more opportunities of studying the religious sentiment of the Romans than he had. It was not among the nobility that he sought for this, but among the common people, who continually edified him by their faith and simplicity. He used to relate

* Marquis de Ségur, p. 155.

a conversation he had once with a gardener in Rome.
Certain insects were ravaging his garden, and all
human means had been exhausted to destroy them,
but in vain. The man said : "We must have the
garden blessed so as to deliver us from this pest."
"That is very simple," replied Mgr. de Mérode;
"ask the Curé to come and do this service for you."
"Ah!" replied the gardener, "you see, it is not a
simple priest, or one who merely says Mass, that we
want; I shall go and find some holy Religious—a
Passionist, for instance. The prayers of those monks
are always heard and answered." He loved also to
describe the resignation which the peasants showed
amidst the greatest poverty and misery : a picture, a
crucifix, an image of the Madonna, would console them
for everything, from the value they set on holy things.
Mgr. de Mérode never failed to distribute such pious
objects amongst them, at the same time that he
emptied his purse in their hands. He would add a
few words of advice and encouragement, ask their
prayers, and leave them as much edified by his faith
and charity as he was by their resignation.

When he became Archbishop, as we have said, one
of his duties was to give confirmation to dying children.
He had given orders to his servants to receive, at any
hour of the day or night, those who sought him for
this purpose; to wake him if he was asleep, and to be
ready to follow him no matter where. One night a
poor mother of a family knocked at his door at eleven
o'clock at night, saying that one of her children was
dying, and begging the Bishop to come at once to
confirm him. The servant, who wanted to go to sleep,
answered that Monseigneur was gone to bed, and that
he could not be disturbed at that hour. The child

died in the night, and the unhappy mother came back
to the Vatican early the next morning, partly in tears
and partly indignant. The Archbishop was just
going out to look after his works. The moment the
poor woman saw him she stretched out her arm and
cried out, with that accent peculiar to the Romans:
"Ah! it's you, is it, Monseigneur? They said in the
city you were a Bishop, and that you would come at
any hour to confirm children in their agony. Last
night I came to implore you to confirm my child, who
was dying, and your servant turned me from your
door! It's your fault if my poor dear boy is dead
without receiving the Sacrament, and that is why he
will never have so good a place in Paradise!" And
then she began to sob with that despair which Italian
faith alone gives, when it is a question of the soul
and of eternal glory. Mgr. de Mérode, as indignant
as the poor mother that he had not known of this
late summons, turned towards the servants in the
ante-chamber, and said to the woman: "Which is
the servant to whom you spoke, and who sent you
away?" "There he is!" she answered, pointing
with her finger to the valet, who was striving to hide in
a corner. Nathan accusing David with his "*Tu es
ille, vir,*" was not more terrible. Mgr. de Mérode,
who never sent away his servants, even when they
served him ill, was without mercy for this man, and
turning towards him said: "It is you, then, who have
done this great wrong! Well, you are not fit to be
the servant of a Bishop. Go this moment. I will not
keep a day longer in my service a man who makes me
thus neglect my duties." And having at once paid
the servant his wages and dismissed him before the
woman who had borne witness against him, he gave a

x

large alms to the poor mother, saying : "You can now go and tell in the city how I treat all those who send away, without telling me, people who come to summon me to attend the dying."

The respect he had for the Priesthood made him greatly honour those ecclesiastics whose conduct was above suspicion : he sought their company and took their lives as examples. But he detested careless or worldly priests. His name and his social position compelled him to go now and then into society ; but he only remained in the salons long enough to satisfy these demands, and always came home at an hour which was neither too late for prayer nor for study.

As to his chastity, calumny fell of itself before the daily life of such a man. To defend his inviolable purity, he may be said to have had three angels— Faith, Mortification and Charity. His mortification exceeded that of Lacordaire even—another of those unknown heroes of self-sacrifice and abnegation ! To find it out, even in part, it required the anxious and vigilant eye of a sister, who, while he was War Minister, arrived unexpectedly at Rome, went into his room, and obtained certain confidences from his faithful servant, showing the anchorite's life he led amidst the splendours of the Vatican. Let us listen to Mde. de Montalembert :—

"Xavier was not expecting me, as I had made up my mind to surprise him, and chose the hour when I knew he would be at his office. His ante-chamber had only two or three chairs, and a broken-down sofa. I passed into the drawing-room, which was like the parlour of a poor little curé in a country town. I opened the door adjoining, which was his bedroom.

There I found a wretched iron bedstead, with one or two straps across it, and a kind of hammock above, in which was a coarse counterpane. 'Who sleeps here?' I asked his servant. 'Why? Monseigneur!' 'How is that possible? He cannot even stretch himself out upon it!' 'Ah! Madame, I am going to tell you. He had a good bed of the right length; but he sent it to some poor man who was ill, and, since that, he sleeps on that wretched thing.'

"Whilst I was talking my brother arrived. 'Oh, my dearest sister,' he exclaimed, 'what a pleasure it is to see you! And Catherine (his niece), how she has grown! But what on earth are you doing here? come into the drawing-room.' 'I was looking at your bed,' I replied; 'you sleep in a hammock: what an idea!' 'Well, it is the soldier's bed in campaign. I wanted, as War Minister, to see how those poor fellows could sleep in that machine after a long march. Well, I assure you it is excellent. It is raised from the ground, and one is thus away from the damp.' 'Yes, I understand that it is better than sleeping on the ground; but this campaigning-bed is not what the troops have in garrison. How do you manage to keep in it at all after a day of such fatigue at your office, and with those long legs of yours, which are always starting off at daybreak for some convent or other?' 'Oh, I assure you I sleep capitally in it; it suits me to perfection!'

"I saw that it was done on purpose, and I did not dare say any more; his jokes on the subject were only to hide his voluntary mortification. Throughout he showed that same spirit of self-sacrifice, reducing himself to the strictest necessaries, and that more severely than any Trappist or Carthusian. We talked about all sorts of things, and then, whilst Catherine was gossiping with her uncle, I went to say a word to the servant, alluding to that unhappy bed. With an embarrassed manner, and lowering his voice for fear of being heard, he said : ' Madame la Comtesse won't repeat it to Monseigneur ? but I feel convinced, though he does not like any one to know it, that he has made a vow of poverty.' Another day, at the War Office, we went to try and see him for a moment. He came in like a whirlwind, talked of affairs and accounts, and then, stopping for a moment to look at the clock, he said : ' I see it is one o'clock, and I have not yet breakfasted. But I have arranged it all ; they are to bring me a meal from the barrack.' While he was speaking a man came in, bringing him a soldier's portion of soup. He devoured it talking to me all the time. ' What a good soup ! ' he exclaimed, when he had finished it. ' How well the Pope's soldiers are fed ! ' A miserable little bit of bouilli beef and a piece of coarse bread followed this broth. In ten minutes it was all done. ' What an excellent break-fast ! ' he exclaimed. ' I don't believe that in Paris or in Brussels you would get anything like it ! '

" One was obliged to say nothing and to leave him to his penitential régime. But I spoke about it to his ser-vant, and told him that, with such extraordinary fatigues of mind and body, this soldier's ration was not enough ; that a little roast meat, well cooked and fresh, might, from time to time, be substituted for the ' bouilli.' ' Ah ! Madame, it is too true ; but I have tried over and over again and failed. The first time, he sent the roast meat to a poor family ; the second he was very angry and threw it out of the window ! ' "

The fasts and days of abstinence of the Church

were observed by Mgr. de Mérode with real monastic
rigour. He never would listen to the distinctions
between "*magro stretto*" (or a strict fast) and a
milder one, such as is the custom in Rome even in
Lent. He used to say he knew only one fast; such as
he had seen at his grandmother's table at Villersexel.
Like the Marquise de Grammont, he abstained from
taking anything before dinner on any pretext, and his
collation was composed only of salad and dried fruits.
He used to tell a story of the way his grandmother
made her guests observe the fast as strictly as herself.
One day a Bishop was breakfasting with her, to whom
they brought a boiled egg, which his delicate health
authorized his eating. But the Marquise saw it in a
moment and ordered it to be taken away, saying to
the Prelate : " Excuse my servant, he has made a
mistake ; that egg was intended for a sick child."

Mgr. de Mérode abstained on Wednesdays, Fridays,
and Saturdays, adding a third day to the two observed
in Rome. He fasted every Friday in honour of the
Passion of our Lord. When he was alone no one
knew to what lengths his mortification went. During
the last few years of his life his Chaplain, Don
Marcello, breakfasted with him, and the food was more
abundant, though not better prepared. But his own
rigid habits never changed. The author of this book
recalls a breakfast he once was invited to at Mgr. de
Mérode's as one of the pleasantest recollections of his
life. He was so agreeable, so full of delicate attentions, and his conversation was so interesting, that the
table was entirely forgotten. There was neither soup,
nor roast, nor entrée, yet one had well breakfasted with
the Archbishop of Mélitène !

We have only now to speak of his charity. It would

fill many volumes. He practised it with that extraordinary generosity which he showed in everything;
stripping himself of all he possessed, and giving at the
same time his money, his heart—the whole of himself,
in fact, with a magnanimity which admitted of no
return upon himself, and no thought for the morrow.
After the sale of the streets and houses he had built,
his alms were royal in their profusion. " You are, then,
very rich, Monseigneur?" exclaimed a Superior to
whom he had given a large sum. " I am sure I do not
know why God is so good to me," he replied, smiling,
" and lets me have so much money; I never ask Him
for it!" What his humility would not confess, the
poor knew well. God gave him the money, knowing
that the whole would be spent in good works.

A very poor family, with three sick children, sent for
him to give the youngest, who was dying, the Sacrament of Confirmation. At the sight of the extreme
misery of the place, tears came into his eyes. He sent
his servant at once to buy a bed and bedding; and the
man, having executed the commission, returned, saying
he would get a porter to carry the things to the poor
man's house. " That would take too long!" exclaimed
Mgr. de Mérode. " The child is so miserable where he
is!" Saying this, he gets into his carriage, drives to
the shop, puts the bed, mattresses, and counterpane in
and out of the brougham, jumps in after them as well
as he can, and tells his coachman to drive as quickly as
possible back to the hovel. There he arranges the bed
himself, takes the child in his arms, and places
him in it. He finds that the father is owner of a
cab which had broken down, that his horse was dead,
and that this succession of misfortunes had completely
ruined him. Mgr. de Mérode bought him a fresh cab

and a fresh horse, sent the children to school, and thus
was the making of the whole family, who, until his
death, most gratefully remembered his generous protection.

It was not necessary to appeal to his charity; he
would hunt up cases for himself, and find out in a
moment those who were really deserving of help. One
day he met a young man with one arm, upon which he
stopped him and asked him the cause. It seemed that
he had been a victim to a Dutch volunteer, who had
joined the Pontifical Zouaves, and who, in a fit of mad-
ness, on the 22nd of August, 1870, had shot at some
passers-by out of his window, killing some and wound-
ing others. Unable to work, this poor young fellow
had joined some strolling musicians, whereby he gained
a few pence. Touched at the story, Mgr. de Mérode
found out the mother of the young fellow, undertook
his education, and thus enabled him to earn his living
by teaching. The faithful servant who supplied us with
these details spoke also of what he did for poor children
covered with ulcers, for old men who had been abandoned in garrets, above all for *pauvres honteux*—people
who had known better days, and would sooner die than
beg—to whom he perpetually and secretly distributed
alms. But we must listen to what he said of his
master in the public calamities which fell several times
on the city of Rome :—

" The charity of Christ urges us," writes the Apostle.
Monseigneur certainly felt its effects, for he was the
first to fly to the succour of the wounded in the Seristori
Barrack, and arrived before the dust was laid caused by
the falling building. The lamentable cries of the half-
buried victims went to his heart. He called upon the
neighbours to help him, and himself set the example of

removing the rubbish and releasing the half-buried men whilst the public were still hesitating. Thus he saved eleven soldiers who, without his energy, would have shared the fate of their sixteen comrades, whose bodies were found under the ruins. This accident happened on the 22nd October, 1867.

"On the 28th December, 1870, when the Piedmontese inundation was hardly calmed, another, that of the Tiber, came to add to the calamities of Rome. The deluge only lasted twenty-four hours, but it invaded all the houses in that quarter, drove out hundreds of poor families, and left them without bread, without shelter, and without clothes. Mgr. de Mérode flew to the rescue, and organized relief works throughout the town. He improvised kitchens, and distributed upwards of five hundred thousand rations of soup and bread. But this was not enough, for the homes of these poor families were still under water, their furniture had been carried away in the flood, and the few who had saved certain articles were afraid to use them in their wet and broken state. The servant who described the distress to us added: "Monseigneur distributed coal twice a week during the month of January among the sufferers. He opened a carpenter's workshop to repair the bits of furniture which had been saved from the wreck and to make others. Under these circumstances I had the honour of serving him in the office of comptroller, accountant, shopman, cook, and general manager, in all of which offices he himself shared. In that way I won not only his kindness but his friendship. It was the reflection of his charity to the poor which fell on me when he saw that I served them faithfully."

·This deep and wide-spread compassion for the poor

was not a mere human feeling in Mgr. de Mérode, but arose from his supernatural Christian charity. Hence he preferred hidden works, and such as men cared little for. He used often to say that nothing had been done when so much remained to do; and that his Divine Master was not sufficiently served and honoured in the person of the poor. Thus, when he began the reform of the prisons, no sooner had he placed Sisters in care of the condemned, than he occupied himself with those who were awaiting their trial, and placed them in a separate house with other nuns. Then, the house being too small, he bought a larger one; a chapel was wanting, and he built that. The prisoners needed air during recreation, so he added a terrace, where they could walk. The cells were too narrow, he had them enlarged. Two parlours were needed, one to receive the authorities, the other to enable the prisoners to see their relations: they were promptly built; so that this prison excited the admiration of all visitors. The people confined in it were the poor; that was enough for Mgr. de Mérode. He did not look at the faults of the inmates; or, rather, he regarded them as redeemed by the Blood of Christ.

To record his private acts of charity as well as his public ones would be to describe every day of his life. One day, as he was walking through an obscure street, he heard cries of distress from one of the houses, and saw a crowd gathered round it. He stopped at once to inquire into the cause. It was the case of a poor widow who could not pay her rent. They had seized all her goods, which had been brought down into the street, and the sale was about to begin. The Prelate asked the amount of her debt. "Sixty-five francs," answered the public crier. Mgr. de Mérode paid it at once, and turning to the woman said, "Put back your

things in their places, and come and see me to-morrow."
She looked at him as if he had been an angel from
Heaven. He was recognized by some one in the crowd,
and had to fly to escape from the demonstrations of
popular admiration. The next day he stopped the first
words of gratitude on the lips of the poor woman by
asking her for an account of her circumstances, and
for the price of her poor room, &c.; and then, giving
her the rent for six months in advance, said: "Go and
find your landlord, and thus re-establish your credit.
If he asks you how you have become so rich all of a
sudden, tell him it is God's secret and yours."

It was impossible for him always, however, to escape
the demonstrations of gratitude shown him by the
people. One of the prisoners at the Termini, whom
he had converted, and who had been set at liberty, was
washing at a public fountain in company with some
other women. Mgr. de Mérode passed, she caught sight
of him, and flew to kiss his hand and to pour out her
thanks and blessings on his head. The others heard
her words, surrounded and cheered him. One of
them, however, cried out, " We have not yet broken
our fast to-day ! " " Well, then, go and make a fine
breakfast ! " he exclaimed, laughing, emptying his
purse among them, and so escaped all further demonstrations of gratitude. This expression of public feeling was even more frequent in the country, especially
when he went to the poor people in the Campagna to
give them the Sacrament of Confirmation. In the
transports of their gratitude, profoundly touched at the
sight of so much love, humility, and charity in the
person of so great an Archbishop, penetrated especially
by the fervent piety with which he recited the prayers
of the Liturgy, the poor mothers would kneel all along

the road as he passed crying out, " *O, Monsignore buono ! Beato lei Patre e beata la Madre che l'ha fatto !* "* He could not stop these demonstrations which his tender charity had evoked. But when he had got back to his carriage he speedily earned fresh gratitude. If he met an old man going back to the city, or a workman who was late, he would stop, take them up and leave them at their own houses before returning to the Vatican. Or, perhaps, he found some sick person whom the fever had seized on the road, and who, breathless and exhausted, could go no further. Then he would stop, get out of the carriage, place the sick man or woman in it, and telling the coachman to drive to the hospital, would himself return on foot.

In his consideration for the poor and sick, and for people in an inferior position, he showed the greatest delicacy on every occasion. All charity is not bread. Such and such an act, or expression of care and thought, attest far more than material alms the charity of a Priest. A mark of esteem, a bow kindly returned, a little bit of loving advice, distinguish true charity from vulgar benevolence or deceiving philanthropy. A Bishop, a Priest, or a Superior ought not always to reproach those under them, for it is not by humbling one's inferiors that one corrects them efficaciously. Mgr. de Mérode, on one occasion, gave a striking example of this kind of charity, which only great hearts know. On a certain Sunday in winter, when the weather was very bad, he went to say Mass at a Convent, and waited a whole hour at the door in the bitter cold for the porteress to open it. His patience might well have been exhausted, and he might perfectly have

* " O ! good Monseigneur ! Blessed be the father and mother who gave you birth ! "

gone and said his Mass elsewhere, as the nuns were
sure of another later.   But no ; he reflected that it
might retard their Communion, and therefore waited
patiently until the door was opened.   The delay was
owing to the porteress having overslept herself, and it
was her business to ring the bell which called the nuns
in the morning.   The whole Community was covered
with confusion.   The Superior came to make her
excuses and brought with her the poor porteress, asking for a penance.   The Prelate, looking at the Sister
weeping at his feet, exclaimed, " A penance for you,
my good little Sister, who sacrifice yourself every day
for the good of the house !   God forbid that I should
dream of such a thing !"   Then smiling, he added,
" Well, I am going to give you one !" and turning to
the Superior, he said, " To-morrow morning you will
be good enough to let her sleep two hours longer than
the rest of the Community !"

On another occasion he had passed the night by the
bedside of a Sister in danger of death, to whom he had
given all the last Sacraments, and had made the recommendations for the departing soul.   As he was
leaving her, at four o'clock in the morning, he turned
to her and asked her " if she had not a special devotion to some particular Saint ? "   " Yes," she replied,
" I have the greatest confidence in the Madonna at
St. Mary Major's."   " Well !" exclaimed Mgr. de
Mérode, " I am going straight to that church, and
there I will offer up the Holy Sacrifice for you."

When he went to visit the prisoners, if he found that
any of their families were in debt and difficulties from
their detention, he would pay them and thus relieve
their minds.   If they had brothers or sisters without
any education, he would place them in different schools.

Or if, again, he found a boy with happy dispositions, whom, with a little help, one could raise in life, he would make every sacrifice to meet the wishes or hopes of the parents. If they asked a small sum of him he always gave more. He bore with no delay or explanation, declaring that by putting off giving one lost all the merit of one's alms. "*Bis dat qui cito dat*" was his motto. We will conclude with one of his last acts at *Tor-Marancio*.

A small but honest farmer in the neighbourhood of Rome lost all his fortune, and found himself reduced to work for his daily bread. A spade was his only resource. He came into the town, hoping to find work more easily. But he was old, his health was weak, and he very much feared that no one would employ him. The Sunday called Sexagesima is the day on which the Gospel is read about the labourers in the vineyard; and it is the custom on that day, from allusion to the sacred text, for the workmen in the Roman Campagna to come, with their tools in their hands, and offer themselves in the public squares of Rome to work by the day. The poor farmer stood there all Sunday with his spade in his hand, at the disposal of those who wished for labourers; but every one thought him too old and no one hired him. The poor fellow retired, with despair in his heart, and wrote a petition to the Pope to explain his sad position. He signed it "Rossi," which was his name; but he had forgotten to add where he lodged. Pius IX. gave the petition to Mgr. de Mérode. "Here is a man for you. Have him sought for and try and find him some work." Such a desire was an order. It was six o'clock in the evening; but he would not put it off till the next day, and sent for his man of business. "Marchesce!" he exclaimed, "you must go and find this farmer who asks the Pope for work. He is old, he is sick, he has a spade in his hand, and he is called Rossi." "But, Monseigneur, how on earth shall I find this man at this time of night?" "Where you will! in the street—in the square where workmen are hired—in the public-houses near. Go and inquire, but find me the man!" Marchesce went, very doubtful as to the result. His search that night was vain; but the next morning at daybreak he went to the square and looked in all the corners. At last he perceived an old man, miserably dressed, who was standing with a spade in his hand, in an obscure angle of a side-street. He recognized the description and asked him his name. "I am called Rossi, and I am waiting to be hired; but no one will have anything to say to me because I am too old. Ah! if the Pope had only received my letter!" Marchesce was perfectly satisfied, carried him into a shop, gave him an excellent breakfast, and then told him to go that very day at a certain hour to Tor-Marancio, where he would find work and a protector.

Marchesce then went in hot haste back to the Vatican, to announce the good news to the Archbishop. Mgr. de Mérode was so delighted that he burst into tears of joy, while he thanked him with his whole heart. One would have fancied that he had received some signal favour. That very day he went to Tor-Marancio, where Marchesce presented the poor old man to him. Mgr. de Mérode blessed and consoled him; and then gave orders that he should be well lodged and well fed, and that only such light work should be given to him as was proportioned to his age and strength.

The gratitude of Rossi was extraordinary. The Pre-late never came once to Tor-Marancio that the old man did not throw himself on his knees to thank and bless him. A few months later his "Protector," as he always called him, ceased to come as usual. Then the rumour of his dangerous illness spread through the yard. Rossi was inconsolable. The day that the news of the Archbishop's death reached him he threw down his spade and took to his bed. Two days later he had followed him to the tomb.

CHAPTER XII.

1874.

MGR. DE MÉRODE was only fifty-four years old, and he
was about to be promoted to the Sacred College. Pius
IX. had settled that he should be made a Cardinal
at the next Consistory. But death sometimes antici-
pates the intentions of men. In vain had the purple
been prepared for him. It was not yet ready when the
Archbishop of Mélitène breathed his last.

Towards the end of the month of June, 1874, he
still visited his favourite excavations at Tor-Marancio ;
but his step was slower, and the change in his appearance struck every one most sadly. Nevertheless his
energy and his heart were always the same. He wished
that the Religious Communities should share the joy of
his discovery. The Sisters of the Congregation of the
Precious Blood were invited by him to come to the
Catacomb with their pupils and those who frequented
the schools. He met them at a given hour, gave them
a breakfast, and then took them over all the excavations.
There, after having related the history of St. Domitilla,
St. Petronilla, and St. Nereus and Achilles, he spoke

of the fidelity of the first Christians and the heroism
of the martyrs. Children and nuns all hung upon his
words, but they little thought they were hearing him
for the last time. But the hour for Vespers at St.
Peter's was at hand. He started, wet through with
perspiration, to obey the bell which marked the hour
for this duty. But the last summons, that of God,
was soon to make itself heard. It was the beginning
of July. The first five days he said his Mass as usual
in his chapel, went out in the afternoon in his carriage,
and looked after his usual works. But on the sixth his
illness became very serious, though it was unexpected
by all save those who had watched him narrowly. But
in reality he carried death in his face. Though the
heat was overwhelming, he ordered his carriage and
tried to take his usual drive at four o'clock. But his
legs failing him on trying to go downstairs, he gave it
up and consented to go to bed and send for the doctor.

From the first moment the danger was evident. He
had acute pneumonia, together with a return of the
fever called "*perniciosa.*" The doctor compelled his
patient to leave the cell, and the wretched couch on
which he had slept for twenty-four years, and to be
moved into the drawing-room on a bed which had been
hastily put up, and the first of which he had consented to make use—it was only, after all, the one on
which he was to die. This room adjoined his chapel.
The doctor told him he could thus hear Mass without
difficulty, and he made no further objections.

During the seventh the fever increased. There was a
consultation of doctors, and notice of his danger was
sent to the Holy Father, to the Chapter, and to his
intimate friends, while telegrams were despatched to
his family. All Rome, alarmed at the bad tidings,

Y

joined in prayer. Many Religious Communities had
the Exposition of the Quarant' Ore with this intention.
Surprise, emotion, grief, gratitude, every feeling which
was aroused by the terror of losing him, burst out
amongst the clergy and the faithful. The poor flew in
masses to the churches; from every quarter men
flocked to hear the news and to read the bulletins : in
the Sacristy of St. Peter's, at the gates of the Vatican,
with the officers on guard, the inquirers never ceased.
Sometimes a sign of discouragement and despair was
the only answer. The doctors had forbidden any one
to go into his room, even his most intimate friends.
Nothing was heard in the passages but mourning,
lamentation and woe.

At seven o'clock in the evening the Pope came to
see him. This visit filled the dying Prelate with joy.
He tried to rise from his couch, and after having
thanked the Holy Father for his paternal anxiety, he
congratulated him on his look of health and youth,
saying how gladly he would offer the sacrifice of his
life for him. " You will bury us all ! " he added,
trying to smile. He then began to pray, imploring
God to shorten his own days and prolong those of
His Vicar in his stead. The Pope sat by his bedside
for more than half an hour, talking to him of affairs of
the Church and of spiritual things. When he left
him, the Pope's eyes were full of tears, and he could
not recover from his sadness. He spoke of the Archbishop's piety, courage, charity, and munificence, and
left him loaded with graces and benedictions. The
effect of his visit was to give Mgr. de Mérode a good
night, and the next day, the eighth, he was decidedly
better. He heard Mass, received Holy Communion,
and saw one or two friends. They found him not

only resigned to die, but full of joy, and in answer to
their condolences he said : "I am quite content ; for
I am going from this miserable life into eternity."
Some one was pitying him for dying so young. "Do
not pity me," he said, "I am going to see my God,
and if I obtain mercy, what are all the finest positions
in this world, compared to the poorest little corner in
Paradise !"

In the evening Mde. de Montalembert, his sister,
arrived. Only the year before she had been in Rome,
and had spent two months with the Archbishop to rest
from all the fatigues she had gone through in begging
for the victims of the Franco-German War. Now she
had come, day and night, at the first telegram, to
soften to her beloved brother the terrors of the last
dread passage. Her courage was equal to any call of
duty. She had attended her husband's death-bed, and
knew all the devoted affection he felt for her dear
Xavier. While assisting her brother, she might have
fancied herself again by the death-bed of Montalembert.
Thursday, the 9th of July, was the last day of his
life. An eye-witness has described the scene in these
terms :—"I cannot tell you what an agonizing and
yet edifying sight this death-bed was. He felt very
much leaving this world, thinking of all the poor, the
destitute, the weak, the little children whom he would
leave behind him. But he was too humble to think
himself necessary, and he drove back this first feeling
with Christian energy, and with a faith in, and a love
of God which dominated all other thoughts in less
time than it takes me to write these lines. He had
asked to see the medical bulletin. Don Marcello would
not give it to him, but he tore it out of his hand,
saying: 'You would like to read it differently from

what it is,' and putting on his spectacles, he read out loud : '*Grave danger, the fever is increasing.*' For an instant his lips trembled, his eyes were troubled, the solemn impression of approaching death passed with a look of agony over his face. Then he became calm, and said to Don Marcello with a quiet and steady voice, while he gave him back the bulletin : ' That is well. Go and bring me my confessor.' After making a general confession, the first word he let fall was one of satisfaction. They brought him Holy Viaticum. At the sight of It, his look brightened, he raised himself in his bed, stretching out his arms to meet It. One saw that, to receive his God, he strove not only to give his whole soul but the last remnant of his strength, and every possible expression of respect. It was admirable !—A little later in the morning, feeling himself worse, he asked for the Prayers for the Agonizing. His Chaplain answered, ' But your Grace is not yet come to that ? ' ' Yes, I am happily come to that,' he replied. ' My ideas are confused in my head, and I want holy words to fix them. Read, read ! ' During this reading his features became lit up, his voice recovered its usual strength, he repeated the Prayers of the Church, and even said them before his Chaplain. In fact, his firmness and courage seemed to increase the nearer he approached to death. One heard him saying several times, with the most lively faith and hope : ' *Accetto, accetto di morire, Dio mio, perchè lo volete ; e lo voglio io, in causa dei miei peccati.*'* These acts of resignation and penitence were made in Italian, and not in his own language—so completely Roman had he become. Thus this last day passed.

---

* I accept death. my God, because Thou willest it, and I will it too, in expiation for my sins.

As there was no longer any hope, the doctors had taken off the prohibition to enter his room, and a number of people could thus profit by the edifying sight he presented. A succession of young men, priests and laity, came to kneel at the foot of his bed and implore his blessing, with many tears. He wished them 'Good-bye,' with a few strong words expressing the faith and love in his own soul with which he had always tried to inspire them. 'Be wise, with the only true wisdom. Above all be faithful. One day you will be, like me, on your death-beds. Happy then he who will die in the Lord!' Then he blessed and dismissed them with the words, 'Do not forget what I have just said to you.' His servants and his men of business came in in their turn. To all he gave a few words of loving counsel, and told them that he had provided for their future. He gave them orders to transmit certain alms and pious intentions to convents, congregations and schools, of which he had been the founder or benefactor. All left him sobbing, with streaming eyes and the deepest sorrow.

"Night now was come, and he remained alone with his noble sister, the broken-hearted witness of this beautiful agony. He spoke to her of her children and grandchildren; of her husband, whose memory was always so dear to him; of her own perfection and of her works of charity, which made her so dear to the Church. They were adieux such as only a great soul can make and a great soul hear. They were mingled with prayers and those recommendations which can never be forgotten, for it is the hour when the soul which is on the eve of leaving the world sees the truth as at no other time, and does not shrink from speaking it.

" When he felt his end drawing near, the Archbishop,

being in the fullest possession of his faculties, asked
them to bring him a folded paper which contained his
will and tore it up.   He dictated a fresh one to his
lawyer, which was very short, and signed it with his
own hand.   He made his brother his sole heir, leaving
a legacy to Mde. de Montalembert and Mde. de Wignacourt, and committing to his brother the care of continuing and providing for his many works of faith and
charity.

  " Having done this, he began again to pray aloud, and
never ceased praying to the end.   Towards midnight
his voice stopped, his eyes were obscured, and at ten
minutes after midnight, on Friday, the 10th July, 1874,
he breathed his last sigh."

  The eye-witness who had thus described his agony
speaks as follows of the appearance of his body after
death :—

  "I never saw anything more extraordinary than
his face after death.   It was not only the sleep of the
just, of which Holy Scripture speaks ; but a kind of
supernatural spiritual joy which was spread over all
his features.   He seemed like one still alive, who had
the happiest thoughts, which seemed to light up his
whole face with pleasure.   His colour was not in the
least changed.   It was not the rigidity of death, but
a look of life and joy which was most striking, and quite
different from the ordinary expression of a man after
death.   Every one remarked it and felt quite consoled
by looking at him.   One was inclined to say, 'What
did he see during those last moments ?'   The reflection
of a happiness not of this world seemed to illumine his
countenance.   I shall live for years and never forget
the sight of his face, so embellished, I might almost
say glorified, as it was by death, and infinitely more

joyous than I had ever seen it in life, although he was often very gay, as are pure souls who are living in God and for God."

On the 13th of July, 1874, at ten o'clock in the morning, a long file of children came from the schools in the Borgo, escorted by the Brothers of Our Lady of Mercy. The procession went close to the houses on account of the excessive heat, till they reached the collonnade on the square of St. Peter's. The children were silent and sad ; and the touching words spoken to them before starting still found an echo in their hearts. At the head of the band marched a young fellow, with only one arm, holding by the hand a little child of nine years old, who was only just out of hospital. The child asked him " Why he was crying so bitterly ? " " Poor little fellow !" he replied, " don't you know that I have lost the only hope of my remaining arm ? And you, thank God that, in your illness, you were known and cared for by one who never heard of a misfortune or a sorrow without alleviating or healing it. We have lost not only a benefactor but a father in Mgr. de Mérode, and we are going to his funeral ! "

The children had all some such tale to tell, and all entered sorrowfully the huge Basilica where the mortal remains of the Archbishop had been placed in the left aisle. An enormous crowd filled the building. Every class of society was represented. Roman Princes, Ambassadors, Cardinals and Bishops were in the front ranks ; but the poor, the little children, those whom the world ignored, were equally numerously represented. Their tears flowed freely, and sobs were frequently heard from the respectful crowd. Respect, love and gratitude were shadowed in every face and found expression in fervent prayers. From the highest to the lowest person present, there was but one heart and one voice to weep, and praise and pray for the great and holy Prelate who had gone to his reward. Another feeling was that of indomitable hope, amounting to certainty, of his eternal bliss. "It is not," as one of his old and faithful servants said, "to obtain the corporal resurrection of Monseigneur that we pray, but to hasten his reception into the eternal joys of Paradise, where so glorious a welcome will await that great soul."

After the funeral ceremonies, his mortal remains were carried to the Flemish Cemetery behind the Vatican. The stone which covers them is simple and plain. The only thing which distinguishes it from the neighbouring tombs is a bas relief in white marble, which is a striking likeness of the Prelate, who is represented kneeling at the feet of our Lord Jesus Christ. But the flowers which decorate it are renewed daily by the piety of the poor. It was a real consolation to the writer of this book to be able, eight years after his death, to gather a fresh flower on this much-loved tomb. In this great Prelate Rome lost one of her most powerful protectors. But on the day when she will regain her liberty, they will go and seek for his remains in that humble cemetery, to place them either in St. Mary Major's or St. Peter's. His name will be inscribed in the Capitol, with that of Lamoricière, among the brave and noble men who have defended to the death the Papacy, the Church, and the City of Rome.

Thirteen years have passed over his tomb, but he has not lost his place in the grateful memory of men. We could quote endless passages from articles pub-

-lished in Italy, France, and Belgium doing the fullest justice to his great and noble heart. The *Journal de Florence*, after praising his devotion and self-abnegation in the service of the Church, concludes with the words: "One glory will remain to him which no other can eclipse. The name of Mgr. de Mérode is associated with all the great acts of the Pontificate of Pius IX. It is he who raised that great movement which the Revolutionists look upon as a defeat, but which we consider a pledge of resurrection and of the future Royalty of the Vicar of Jesus Christ."

Louis Veuillot even, in the *Univers*, speaking of his early death, writes : "Mgr. de Mérode was a man of the highest and most admirable qualities. To-day we can only remember his great heart, his disinterestedness, his sincerity, his charity, which was so ardent and generous. He has done great works; given an impulse to many salutary reforms ; and done much for the Church. Nothing could equal his energy in the struggle against the Piedmontese. It is he who created the Papal Army, who persuaded Lamoricière to come and put himself at its head, while his great soul was not discouraged by the disaster of Castelfidardo. . . . . Until the last day, his name will be honoured by all who knew him. . . . . No one knew him better than Pius IX., and no one loved him more."

The news of his death spread rapidly throughout Italy, and caused universal sorrow. In the thoughts of all, Mgr. de Mérode typified devotion to the Holy Father; and his loss in the prime of life was looked upon as a fresh trial for the Sovereign Pontiff, and a new suffering added to the many bitternesses around him. But the general emotion did not limit itself to tears and regrets. The editor of the *Unità Cattolica*, the Abbé Margotti, conceived the project of having a universal and solemn manifestation of sorrow by services throughout Italy for the repose of his soul.   Sixty Archbishops and Bishops hastened to offer the Holy Sacrifice at their respective altars.   Their cathedrals were hung with black, catafalques with his Episcopal arms were dressed in the sanctuaries, the tribunes echoed to funeral chants—all was done to give these ceremonies the greatest beauty and solemnity possible. A concert of prayers was raised throughout the peninsula, from Ancona to Ravenna, in the Valley of Aosta as in the depths of the Tyrol; in Umbria and Piedmont, in Naples and Sicily, in Rome and its neighbourhood, and even to the Islands of Malta and Scio. Every Bishop took the opportunity to say some touching words in his praise, or to express his own deep sorrow at his loss.   One revealed a touching act of ingenious charity of which he had been witness; another talked of the courageous way in which he had accepted death and cried out with the Apostle : " *Eamus et nos, et moriamur cum illo.*"   They proclaimed him as " the faithful and good servant," " the valiant soldier fighting for Pontifical independence," one who " justly deserved the entire confidence of his Master," the " Elias of modern times," " the father of the poor, the orphan, and the sick."   They congratulated him " on having deserved the hatred of all the enemies of the Church while compelling their respect"; they " deplored his sudden death as an irreparable public calamity." Thus each diocese brought a tribute of veneration and love to the memory of Xavier de Mérode.

The example of the Bishops was quickly followed by the clergy, both regular and secular; and there also the unanimity of their feelings of admiration for Mgr.

de Mérode burst forth in their sermons and addresses;
so that he who had been so generous and magnificent
towards the poor, received, in his turn, the alms so
earnestly desired by the greatest Saints—alms which
expiate, purify, relieve and console. More than 3,000
Masses were said, in a few days, for his intention
in Italy alone, and we only speak of those registered
by the *Unità Cattolica*. The Monastic Orders did
not show less generosity; and day and night the grave
voices of the monks recited the Divine Office for the
deceased Prelate, conjuring Divine mercy on behalf of
a soul so dear to the Church militant. Then came.
the turn of the Confraternities and the pious associa-
tions, who eagerly joined in the same pious demonstrations. We will only mention the congregations of
St. Vincent of Paul, of the Christian Mothers, of the
Perpetual Adoration, of the Catholic Workmen, of
Notre Dame du Paradis, of the Sacred Heart, of the
Sisters of Charity, and countless other Religious
Communities. Even literary societies, grateful for his
protection, had solemn Masses said in his honour.
The Academy of the " Arcades " met on this occasion
at the Church of St. Anicet, and one of its members
sent Mde. de Montalembert the following lines :—

> " Donna! se del fratel, che amasti tanto,
> Piu non vedrai nel mondo il dolce aspetto,
> Pensa che giusto e il visse e benedetto;
> Moriva al Padre dei fedeli accanto ;
> Che degno ei fu del pastorale amanto,
> E come di fede e caritade el petto.
> Che al par di Madre su figliuol diletto,
> Roma il feretro suo bagna di pianto."

It is impossible to enumerate the edifying acts and
holy practices by which the faithful, both men and

women, signalized their piety and grateful affection for the holy Prelate. Assistance at Mass, fervent Communions, extraordinary acts of penance and mortification, recitation of the Rosary, the Way of the Cross—nothing was omitted which could ensure to Mgr. de Mérode, as speedily as possible, in the beautiful language of Holy Church, "refreshment, light, and peace."

It entered into the designs of Providence not to permit that his noble devotedness should receive, on this earth, the reward it had deserved; but it was given him after his death, by the unprecedented crowd of the faithful who flocked, for his sake, to the foot of the altar. A great Pope said : "I have loved justice and hated iniquity, therefore I die in exile." If Xavier de Mérode could have foreseen the obsequies which Italy had prepared for him, he would have said in his turn : "I have loved justice and fought against iniquity, therefore my name will be blessed." After the pompous funeral of the Prince de Condé, Mde. de Sévigné wrote: "It was the most magnificent and triumphant sight which has ever been seen since there were mortals." But to this pomp we prefer the prayers and sacrifices which for sixty days honoured the memory of Mgr. de Mérode ; and if Bossuet were not there to add his eloquence to the funeral, the praises which fell from the lips of such a multitude of venerable bishops, priests, and monks, and the supplications of such thousands of faithful souls, formed a triumph more striking and lasting than the splendours accumulated by Louis XIV. on the tomb of the Prince de Condé. We have seen the album in which M. Margotti has collected all these sermons on the homage rendered by Italy to Mgr. de Mérode. To be thus honoured and thus beloved, one must live as he lived— love the good and the right as he did—have the same determination to carry it out, even to the sacrifice of one's life—the same self-devotion—the same burning charity for the poor, the suffering, and the oppressed. Such is the lesson which speaks to us from every page of M. Margotti's touching selection. As a frontis piece to this collection, the celebrated publisher engraved a beautiful inscription, concise and energetic, such as those of which Italy has not yet lost the secret. We reproduce it at the end of this volume, for it sums up better than anything else the many titles Mgr. de Mérode had to the admiration of pos terity.

May those who read this Biography understand its true teaching, and take away with them the wholesome impression which a character like that of Mgr. de Mérode must make on every honest mind. May they profit by the study of a life, human in some ways, as was only natural, but wherein were combined—which is so rare in these days—the highest intelligence, the strongest zeal for good, the noblest of characters, and the greatest and warmest of hearts !

EULOGIUM.

XAVERIS DE MÉRODE.

CLARO . genere . natvs . apvd . Belgas . Idibvs . Martiis .
Anno . Hvivs . Secvli . vicesimo . patrem . habvit . Philippvm .
Comitem . qvi . in . Rebvs . Publicis . Gerendis . Svmma .
cvm . lavde . est . Versatvs.

Vbi . Primvm . Ætas . belli . patiens . fvit . in . Castra .
Profectvs . dvo . Stipendia . in . Africa . Mervit . vbi . inter .
Eqvites . Adlectvs . est . Legionis . Honoratorvm.

An . in . DCCC . XLVII . altiora . Spectans . impetrata . Militeæ .
Vacatione . Romam . Petiit . ibi . Sacerdotio . iniatvs .
Canonicvs . Vaticanvs . Archiepiscopvs . Melitinensis . ob .
eximiam . virtvtem . in . ore . omnivm . esse . cœpit . exinde .
Pio . IX . P . M . vnice . dilectvs . inter . intimos . eivs .
cvbicvlarios . est . relatvs . Rei . Bellicæ . Universæ . præ-
fectvs . et . Magister . dictvs . Largitionvm.

Tantis . Pontificiæ . volvntatis . significationibvs . lætvs .
noster . se . svaqve . omnia . pro . illivs . incolvmitate .
devovit . in . quem . tanqvam . in . exemplvm . pietatis .
caritatis . constantiæ . intvebatvr.

Decessit . v . id . Qvintiles . an . MD . CCC . LXXIIII . Bonis .
omnibvs . ingemisvntibvs . morienti . adsedit . Pontifex .
Maximvs . Qvi . Mortvvm . vti . Filivm . Insolabiliter .
lvxit.

(TRANSLATION.)

To the Memory of Xavier de Mérode.

Born of an illustrious family in Belgium, the day of the Ides of March, the twentieth year of this century, his father was Count Philip Felix, who showed himself in public affairs a consummate statesman. As soon as he was of age to bear arms he repaired to the camp, made two campaigns in Africa, and was named Knight of the Legion of Honour.

In the year 1847, having higher views, he gave up the army and came to Rome. There as Priest, Canon of the Vatican Basilica, and finally Archbishop of Mélitène, he attracted universal consideration from his rare and admirable qualities. Tenderly cherished by Pius IX., he was admitted among his secret Chamberlains, and appointed first War Minister and then Almoner to the Pope. Favoured by these striking proofs of Pontifical favour, he consecrated his whole person and all that he possessed to the service and care of him whom he considered a model of piety, constancy and charity. He died on the 5th day of the Ides of July, in the year MDCCCLXXIV., lamented by all honest men, and assisted in his last moments by the Sovereign Pontiff, who was as inconsolable at his death as a father to that of a well-beloved son.

NOTES.

GENEALOGY OF THE HOUSE OF DE MÉRODE, SHOWING THEIR DESCENT FROM ST. ELISABETH OF HUNGARY.

1. St. Elisabeth of Hungary marries Louis VI., the Saint, Duke of Thuringia ✠ 1227.
2. Sophia, the only child of the Saint who left posterity, marries Henry II. the Magnanimous, Duke of Brabant ✠ 1239.
3. Henri, the child, Landgrave of Hesse, ✠ marries Adelaide, Duchess of Brunswick, 1300.
4. Otho, Landgrave of Hesse ✠ 1328, marries Adelaide, Countess of Ravensberg.
5. Louis, Landgrave of Hesse ✠ 1343, marries Margaret, Countess of Spanheim.
6. Hermann the Wise ✠ 1414, marries Margaret, Viscountess of Nuremberg.
7. Louis I., the Pacific, ✠ 1458, marries Anne, Duchess of Saxony.
8. Louis II., the Courageous, ✠ 1471, marries Mathilda, Countess of Wurtemburg.
9. William II., who united the whole of Hesse, ✠ 1509, marries Anne, Duchess of Mecklenburg.
10. Philip, the Magnanimous, ✠ marries Christina, Duchess of Saxony.
11. William IV., the Wise, head of the branch of Hesse-Cassel, ✠ 1592, marries Sabina, Duchess of Wurtemburg.

z

12. Maurice ✠ 1632, marries Julia, Countess of Nassau-Siegen.
13. Ernest, chief of the Catholic branch of Hesse-Rheinfels ✠ 1693, marries Mary, Countess of Solms.
14. William, Landgrave of Hesse-Rheinfels ✠ 1725, marries Mary, Countess of Lowenstein-Wertheim.
15. Elisabeth, Princess of Hesse-Rheinfels, marries in 1695 Francis, Prince of Nassau-Hadamar.[1]
16. Charlotte, Princess of Nassau-Hadamar ✠ 1721, marries John, Count of Mérode and of the Holy Empire, called the Marshal of Westerloo, widow of Maria Pignatelli, niece of Pope Innocent XII.
17. Philip, Count of Mérode, a Grandee of Spain ✠ 1759, marries Mary de Mérode, Princess of Rubempré.
18. Charles, Count of Mérode, Prince of Rubempré and of Everberg, marries, in 1778, Mary d'Oignies de Mastaing, Princess of Grimberche.
19. Felix, Comte de Mérode, marries, in 1809, Rosalie de Grammont.
20. Frederick Francis Xavier de Mérode, Archbishop of Melitinensis, Minister and Almoner of Pius IX.

THE RESIDENCE OF XAVIER DE MÉRODE AT THE COLLEGE OF JUILLY.

An old Professor of Xavier de Mérode's at the College of Juilly sent the Author the following note:—

"I remarked in my pupil, Xavier de Mérode, a strong spirit of Faith. He was an intimate friend of young Paul la Chaumelle, my server at Mass, and one day showed him a letter from his sister, in which Madame de Montalembert reminded him of what had been the real glory of their family. 'Our ancestors have been greatly distinguished at all times, but less by the brilliancy of their talents and their illustrious actions, than by the qualities of their souls, the nobility of their feelings, and *their devoted love for the Church*,' &c., words which Xavier had underlined.

"A few months before he left Juilly, I asked him for his copybook of History. He was behindhand in his last lessons, but told me he was preparing to enter the Military College of Brussels . . . . When looking over his book I was very much edified at reading on several of the pages, in a large schoolboy hand, different passages from the 'Imitation,' among the rest the following : '*Ille vere magnus est qui magnam habet charitatem.*' . . . .

"At Rome I found my old pupil once more, and he had not forgotten me. He said 'he was quite ashamed of having profited so little by my lessons.' I saw him several times during my two journeys. He was then War Minister. One day I said to him that if I had listened to what he was saying to one of his officers I should have found out his whole policy. He laughed and answered : 'Here we have only one policy, so that we can speak out loud and say what we mean to everybody.' Another time he talked of his disagreement with Cardinal Antonelli : 'His Eminence thinks it is ridiculous, in the present state of things, to keep up an army which can be no real protection. I think just the reverse, and only the other day it made the Pope's excursion to Porto d'Anzio possible when he blessed the standards. Our little Army, which Antonelli would like to replace by a strong police force, is the safeguard of a principle, the independence of the Pope and of his temporal sovereignty, which it will cause to be respected to the end.' "

LETTER FROM M. FRANÇOIS DE CORCELLES TO THE AUTHOR.

"MONSEIGNEUR AND REVERED FRIEND,

"While acknowledging the safe receipt of your MS., I must hasten to tell you how it has touched, edified and instructed me; for I did not know all the evidence you have collected to make us appreciate, in such beautiful language, our heavenly friends Lamoricière and de Mérode. I am more than ever convinced that the heroic work undertaken by Mérode for the defence of the Holy See was necessary, although it has ended in our present trials. It was necessary that this fidelity should be shown alongside of the crime, and rouse in the hearts of all Catholic nations a stronger feeling for the authority of the Church, for the independence of its Head, and for the Divine Liberty of its teaching. Pius IX. was inspired with fresh courage when he felt he could rely on two such devoted and intelligent servants, who were armed, as St. Bernard says, with 'such faith within and such iron without.' Cardinal Antonelli was useful to him in another way; but he could not form or direct an army. Pius IX., therefore, employed each in the efforts which he thought indispensable for the protection of the Holy See.

"From 1849 to 1859 we defended, by diplomacy, not only the independence of the Church, but the general peace, which was often gravely compromised by the conditions Napoleon III. wished to impose upon the Pope, according to the imperious letter addressed to Edgar Ney. . . . . When M. Drouyn de Lhuys became Foreign Minister in France, there was a moment when Napoleon seemed inclined to moderate his policy towards the Holy See. I had amicable relations with his Ministers which the Pope strongly approved of, as well as Mérode, who took advantage of these improved relations to smooth many difficulties which had arisen. . . . . Each had his work and each his responsibility. The part taken by our friends was a very noble one. Lamoricière and Mérode brought to their work a regularity, a determined will and a perfection for which their education had prepared them; but in their ardour for reform they had much to bear from the trammels of routine and the apathy of less zealous souls.

"I conclude with a word of Pius IX. He quoted to me, in speaking of Mérode and Lamoricière, the verse in Holy Scripture: 'I have said to the wind and to the flame, be my Ministers.' He said it with truth, and this tempest of honour was a good preparation for the remorse of the present day and for the diplomatic reign of Leo XIII. I also wish to attest that during my long and frequent relations with Cardinal Antonelli he never said one word expressive of bitterness against Mgr. de Mérode, for whom, in spite of their differences of opinion, he had a very great admiration. The day Xavier died he wrote to me expressing all his sorrow at this irreparable loss to the Holy See. . . . . The restoration and maintenance of the temporal power lasted twenty years. Cardinal Antonelli, Mérode and Lamoricière all served this great cause, each according to his genius and his means. The clever diplomatic prudence of Antonelli had its use: the wonderful services of Lamoricière and Mérode their grandeur. Posterity will render them justice." . . . .

The following is an exact account of what took place with Mgr. de Mérode at the close of the Vatican Council, drawn from his own lips :—

"I am not a great theologian," he said. "I have never studied this science deeply enough to have a very distinct opinion upon this question of Papal Infallibility. As to the *opportuneness* of the decision at this moment, I had doubts which I could not succeed in dissipating. In this state of mind and conscience, I determined to abstain from giving a definitive vote : but being, by my functions, seated at the very feet of the Holy Father, and feeling that my abstention ought to be shown with a certain respect, and not by remaining motionless at the feet of the Pope at the moment when all the other Bishops got up to record their votes—in fact, not wishing in any degree to have the look of braving Papal opinion—I thought it would be more respectful to him to remain that day in my own apartment, and to say Mass in my chapel to invoke the light of the Holy Spirit upon my colleagues while they voted. Accordingly I did this and said my Mass with all my heart, with the firmest intention, naturally decided upon beforehand, to submit fully and entirely to whatever was decided by the Council. Hardly had the Fathers of the Council recorded their votes than a certain ecclesiastical personage dashed rather than walked into my room, and exclaimed :

"'But, Monseigneur! what have you done ? How ! you did not even go to the Council ? But . . . . in what a position you have placed yourself !'

"Stupefied at this agitation, and at his air of indignation, I answered him : 'What on earth do you mean ? I did what my conscience dictated. I had grave doubts on the *opportuneness* of the declaration of Infallibility, and so I made up my mind to say my Mass and invoke the lights of the Holy Spirit upon my colleagues whilst they settled the question.'

" ' But, Monseigneur, you can't have thought of what you have done ! . . . . But the Pope is very much displeased ! '

" ' Oh !' I answered, 'the Pope is very much displeased, is he ? But with whom ? and with what ? '

" ' But, Monseigneur, with you ! You don't seem to understand that you have done an unheard-of thing . . . . you have put yourself in a position——', And then, pulling out a great paper from under his arm, this personage lays it on the table, strikes the two fingers of his right hand on a certain part of it, and looking at me in the most imperious fashion, says : ' You are going to sign this declaration of Orthodoxy on the spot ! '

" ' A declaration of Orthodoxy !' I exclaim. 'But I am as orthodox as you or as any of my colleagues at the Council. I shall sign the declaration which the Council has just made when it is presented to me to sign. I submitted beforehand to the Council's decision, whatever that might be ; but I shall certainly not sign any of your papers ! '

" ' Well, Monseigneur, all I can say is, the Pope is very much displeased.'

" ' How do you know that, if you please ? Did the Pope say so to you ? '

" ' Well, no. But . . . . you understand that he must be very much annoyed ; and that you have placed yourself in a position——'

" ' I only know what my conscience tells me in such matters. I do not trouble myself in the least about what you call ' my position.' The Pope has never said a syllable to you on the subject. Be so good as to take back your papers.' . . . . And so thrusting them into his hands, I opened the door and made a sign to my servants to show this officious person out of the apartment.

" All day long my room was crowded with visitors :

some curious, watching my attitude, trying to catch me
out in some imprudent word ; others timid, anxious,
wondering what the Pope would think or say. As for
myself, I was perfectly tranquil and at my ease, with a
clear conscience. Towards the ' Ave Maria ' I went as
usual to the Pope for my customary duties. I remarked
that the Pope followed me now and then with his eyes,
as if his mind were pre-occupied ; and when the hour
came for me to retire, and that I knelt, as usual, to take
leave, Pius IX. said to me,—

" ' Monseigneur has nothing particular to say ? '

" I answered : ' Most Holy Father ! If I have been
wanting in my duty in anything, I beg your Holiness to
tell it to me and I will hasten to do whatever I may have
omitted.'

" ' But, no, no ! ' replied the Pope, smiling, ' I only
asked you if you had anything you wanted to say to me.
You may retire.'

" I went away full of admiration for the Holy Father,
saying to myself : ' The Holy Ghost is there and not
among the prophets of his supposed indignation against
me. I saw that he wished, from a motive of natural and
human curiosity, to know what I thought, and the
motives of my attitude ; but he would not go beyond
that first feeling. He has respected my inner faith, my
honest convictions, my position as a Bishop ; he understood that I had acted simply according to my conscience.
In consequence, not a word of blame or displeasure fell
from his lips. Only, foolish persons could not understand
him, and have judged the Pope's feelings by their own ! ' "

However imperfectly we may have rendered this conversation, we think our readers will feel the grandeur on
both sides in this true narrative of facts. First, the way
in which it proves the liberty enjoyed by the members of
the Council—a liberty which was respected by the Holy
Father ; and secondly, the purity of soul and conscience
shown by Mgr. de Mérode in this circumstance.

It seems to us that all this tells magnificently in favour of the Church and of its holy and venerable Head. Mgr. de Mérode only said, thought and acted in the same way as all the Bishops of the minority. He was, like them, entirely submissive beforehand to the decision of the Council, whatever that might be. But he thought, like them, that he could use his liberty of opinion to the end instead of dissimulating what was passing in his conscience, or voting contrary to it—until the time came when it was his duty to accept the decision, about which he never hesitated for a moment.

THE TRANSLATOR.